Survive your Li

Tips for teens

by Susan Viviers

ROEDURICO
t r u s t
Somerset West

This book is dedicated to Johan

Also available from
Roedurico Trust:

Survive your studies

and the

Study & *Master* series

Roedurico Trust
P.O. Box 810, Somerset West 7129
Tel: (021) 852-3104
Fax: (021) 851-6874
Set in 12 on 14pt Optima
Lithographed and bound by
NBD, Drukkery Street,
Goodwood 7460, Western Cape

ISBN 0-947465-69-3

Bible text: CEV © American Bible Society, 1995
Translation by Pat Heiberg and Annette de Witt

Index

SURVIVE YOUR LIFE

1 Why do you have to survive?

Welcome to SURVIVE YOUR LIFE.
This chapter will explain how and why you should use the book. Life will constantly demand more from you as you grow older. This chapter will enable you to determine whether you possess the specific skills which the business world will call for from you one day and how you may use this book to equip yourself for your future.

1. A letter from the author

Dear Reader

If someone should ask you "What would you like to know about life?", you would probably answer as follows:

1.   Teach me HOW to get to heaven without having to walk around with a sour face.
2.   Teach me HOW to accept and believe in myself.
3.   Teach me HOW to understand and handle my own and other people's feelings.
4.   Teach me HOW to make the correct choices in order not to make a mess of my life.
5.   Teach me HOW to set goals and how to reach them.
6.   Teach me HOW to get on with other people.
7.   Teach me HOW to handle difficult situations.
8.   Teach me HOW to use my time efficiently.
9.   Teach me HOW to learn.
10.   Give me the FACTS of life.

Instead, you often hear the following:

1.   Reform yourself, otherwise you'll go to hell!
2.   You are beautiful. You can get 100%. You can become a doctor if only you WILL …
3.   Behave yourself! Grow up! Forget him/her …there are plenty of fish in the sea.
4.   Don't this or that! That's sin! You were not raised that way!
5.   What would you like to become one day? What are you going to study? What plans do you have for your life?
6.   Say "please" and "thank you".
7.   Remember – you have only one name!
8.   Your room looks like a pigsty! That is what happens when you watch TV all day long!
9.   Go and study!
10.   Stay away from that, because I say so! You will die!

People are around all day long to offer you advice or to "preach" and you simply take it like someone being battered by hail. After a time you don't even hear them any longer and it becomes a matter of "in one ear and out the other". Why?

Perhaps it happens as a result of one or more of the following reasons:

1. Certain things are expected of you, but nobody bothers to explain HOW you should do it. People will tell you WHY and WHY NOT, but never HOW! You have to learn, but nobody teaches you HOW to learn!
2. You hear it at a time when you don't necessarily have the time or energy to listen to your father, mother and teachers preach about things, but you don't even know anybody who uses it. One day, when you are actually confronted by it, you can no longer remember why it is dangerous.
3. People do the selfsame things they warn you against. The minister who preaches each Sunday: "You may not commit adultery", divorces his wife.
4. Sermons usually end in a power struggle between you and the person preaching to you. "Do what I say, or else …"
5. The reasons given make no sense whatever! "You are not OLD enough to smoke or watch pornography!" You now begin to wonder: "When then, are you OLD enough to sin or use something which could be fatal?"

Six years ago a very dear friend walked into my messy office and proceeded to explain to me, step by step, how to attain order in my disorderly life and set out, in logical steps, how to set goals and keep a diary! The same dear friend later became the inspiration for the writing of this book – without preaching to me once in his life!

Two years ago I started researching for the first time in an effort to find the best and easiest methods of studying. I was busy with a post-graduate diploma course and for the first time received an A+ aggregate for all my subjects! Why didn't someone teach me HOW to learn while I was still at school? Imagine how many A pluses I could have had then!

A year ago a pastor explained to me – within the space of one hour – how to truly understand Jesus as a personal living God. I subsequently experienced healings and miracles I would never have thought possible! For the first time I could actually hear God speaking to me! I didn't only learn how to live, but how to SURVIVE my own life here on earth, so to speak! Today I know that the book of Revelations is as true as Genesis. I no longer experience the Bible as a story book, but as a daily requirement for advice, strength, promises, healing, miracles, love, peace and happiness.

Most of the lessons I learnt in life, I learnt the hard way, like many other people do. Believe me – I can confidently state: "BEEN THERE, DONE THAT!" I have followed the straight and narrow way and most of the byways – often with serious repercussions to myself and those I love.

Consider this – your life consists of 4 phases:

DEPENDENCY	–	0-7 YEARS
PREPARATORY PHASE	–	YOUR SCHOOL AND POST SCHOOL EDUCATION
INDEPENDENT PHASE	–	YOUR CAREER AND RETIREMENT
DEPENDENCY	–	WHEN YOU ARE ILL OR NEEDY

Your preparatory phase is the time you need to PREPARE yourself to become INDEPENDENT one day. The more you mess up this preparatory phase, the less your eventual independence becomes! Become pregnant at the age of sixteen because you are "old enough to do as I like!", and I guarantee that this will more or less be the last time that you won't have to consider others as well. Smoke at fourteen because it makes you feel independent and grown-up in front of your pals and you are sure to realise, at the age of forty, how it feels to crave a little stick shorter and thinner than your middle finger, exactly like a baby craving a dummy!

SURVIVE YOUR LIFE is an effort to give meaning to all the preaching and advice you may be subjected to. This book will teach you not only the WHY and WHY NOT, but especially the HOW. If I save you a few tears and grazed knees, this book will have served its purpose. SURVIVE YOUR LIFE is not a story book, but a guide on life skills. Use it as you would a manual. Read it whenever you need advice. Apply and practise the principles it contains until you master them. Believe me – it works! I have thoroughly researched all the facts mentioned in this book and have, as far as possible, quoted several sources to prove my views. By following the same advice, you will not only reach your goals and success in life, but will save yourself a great deal of heartache and pain.

SURVIVE YOUR LIFE is the first of two books which I have written to supply answers and to give advice on matters important to teenagers. SURVIVE YOUR LIFE focuses especially on study methods and offers you fast and easy ways to study. Pore over it and consider each point. Don't shoot it down in flames if I step on your toes or differ from you. As the pop group OFFSPRING puts it:

> *If this sounds dangerous –*
> *don't try this at home (or at all)*
> *If it sounds sarcastic –*
> *don't take it seriously.*
> *And if it offends you*
> *JUST DON'T LISTEN TO IT!*

May you enjoy this book and
experience great success in life!

The Author

2. *How should this book be used?*

a) Consider the aim of the book

This book, SURVIVE YOUR LIFE, is written as an INSTRUCTION MANUAL and WORKBOOK in order to assist you in organising your life and studies and to use suitable techniques and methods to succeed. The book was not compiled to skim through in a day or week, but to digest over a period of months.

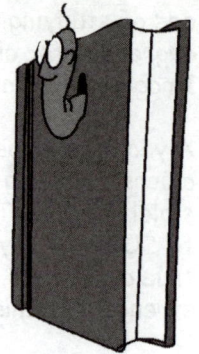

Each chapter is a follow-on of the previous chapter. Please don't jump about by skipping chapters to find instant solutions. You may not benefit much by simply paging through the book hoping to organise your life. However, when you have worked through the entire book, you may again study those sections important to your particular needs.

Ask yourself: What is better: a healthy life-style or a crash diet? This is no short cut to better living, but a programme designed to teach you a healthy lifestyle which you can apply successfully for the rest of your life!

Read carefully and feel free to offer better methods and views, should you differ from any of those stated.

b)   Are you willing?

The biggest part of your day and time is spent on schoolwork. To spend the largest part of your year sitting at a school desk for at least six hours per day, can be very exhausting! When you consider that the rest of each day is spent doing homework, attending extra-mural activities and paying attention to others, it is probably time to start managing your life like the manager of a very successful business. Managers of successful businesses usually possess two characteristics which determine the success of the business.

i)   The manager's willingness to explore and use new methods and techniques.

ii)   The manager's willingness to change.

Without these two characteristics, we would surely still have been stuck in the Middle Ages! You need the same skills if you plan on being successful in your studies and life!

i)   *Firstly you have to be willing to read every page, complete every task and practise every method until it becomes habit.*
     (Remember, it took me six years to rid myself of my bad habits.)

ii) *Secondly, you have to be willing to change your faulty study methods and habits!*

Over the years, several researchers have spent many hours to determine how the human brain functions. Businessmen are constantly attending courses to acquire the best management techniques to apply to their businesses.

SURVIVE YOUR LIFE is an effort to combine important management and life skills in such a way that you may confidently deal with your career and life.

> **ARE YOU WILLING TO LISTEN AND TO CHANGE?**

c) Decide why you want to read this book

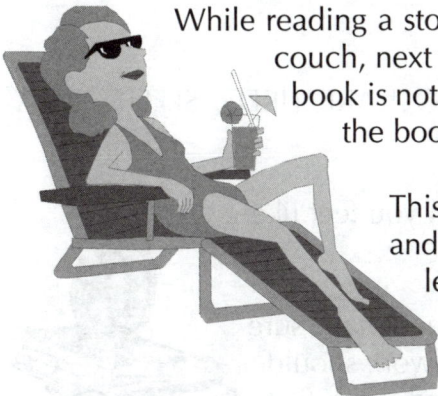

While reading a story book, you are probably lying peacefully on your bed, the couch, next to the swimming pool or at the beach. You read to relax! This book is not for relaxation, otherwise all suggestions made will be lost and the book will hold very little benefit for you.

This book was written to help you! It is brimming with suggestions and facts specially selected to assist you with your daily life, problems, decisions and crises. When you, therefore, start the next chapter, be sure that you are reading it BECAUSE YOU WOULD LIKE TO CHANGE YOUR LIFE!

SURVIVE YOUR LIFE is an INSTRUCTION MANUAL for your life and career. Practise the methods and techniques until you can achieve them with ease and confidence.

SURVIVE YOUR LIFE is a WORKBOOK. Several sections in this book are to be filled in by yourself. It is your personal property and the information you supply is for your eyes only! Don't be shy to state exactly how you feel. Various questionnaires give you the opportunity to get to know yourself and to measure your own progress at a later stage.

d) Find the right place

While you are reading a manual such as a recipe book to test a recipe, you will stand next to the stove! When you are reading the instructions to install a computer game, you would certainly not lie on the beach to read it, but sit in front of your computer!

Organise a spot in your bedroom where you can work undisturbed. Decide on a place where this book can be permanently kept at hand.

e) Stationery

i)   Fill in the necessary sections in the book using PENCILS and COLOURED PENCILS. Errors can then be erased and changed. Try to write neatly so that later you will want to read what you wrote!

f) Choose the right time

DON'T READ THIS BOOK IF YOU ARE TIRED, SLEEPY, IN A HURRY OR LAZY!

i)   Remember, this is a **workbook**. Choose a time when you feel like working on it!

ii)   Don't do too much at a time. Complete one chapter and make sure that you understand what it consists of and how the work should be done. Repeat the chapter if you didn't understand it the first time.

iii)   Try to complete at least **one chapter per week**.

iv)   By all means work through chapters which are important to you, more than once. The chapter covering drugs and sex may not be important to you at this stage, but may save your life later on! Rather go and make sure by reading those chapters again before you swallow a tablet which may cause you to end up in a coma or before you perhaps forfeit your freedom in an irresponsible way.

g) Read and learn critically.

If you are going to read the whole book in a monotonous voice while leaning on your elbow and wondering when your favourite soapie is going to start, you should rather stop and attempt it again when you really feel like it.

READ THE BOOK AS IF:

i)   you are having a serious conversation
ii)   you are trying to convince yourself or someone else
iii)   your future depends on it
iv)   you need to do a critical evaluation of it.

h) Apply what you have learnt

It is obviously senseless to study a recipe book if you are never going to prepare a meal. Try to actually apply what you have learnt. Nothing worthwhile is ever easily come by. **These methods take time and sacrifice to acquire** and will, initially, take *even longer* since you are not used to it. If you have never studied, you are definitely not going to study faster now. If your life has always been a mess, you will take longer to work according to a timetable to begin with.

Remember, however, that everything will become easier and easier with practice and dedication. The trained athlete can run much easier, faster and further than one who has never practiced. Still, that trained athlete also had to start somewhere and at the beginning he or she found it just as difficult and painful. The difference between mediocrity and success lies mainly in your ability to persevere. The saying goes;
    "The road to mediocrity is paved with good intentions."

Start today!

i) Enjoy it!

Tell yourself:
I want to learn and make a success of my life.
I am going to give my best.
I am going to try each method and technique personally until I master it.
I am going to fill every task in carefully.
I ENJOY IT EVERY TIME!
Before you know it, your life and studies
are – A FEAST!

3. What does the career world expect of you?

If you are not yet convinced that your old methods need changing, you should please read this section with concentration. The career world changes from day to day and you will never fit in unless you adapt to this ever changing world. Consider: If people never followed the example of the man who invented the wheel, we would all perhaps still be lugging around heavy loads!

HAS ANYBODY DISCOVERED A BETTER WAY YET??

Businesses across the world change constantly. Careers which did not exist years ago, have taken over today's market. Technological changes have caused the business world to be much faster and far more is expected of people. Time is an important factor and people no longer have time to wait for others or to correct other people's mistakes.

The days of Master and Slave are over. Successful businesses depend on the **participation, initiative and creativity** of all their employees. You will be relied upon to share in decision making, discussions, finding solutions and to work without supervision. You must be able to work on your own, think for yourself and assume responsibility yourself.

The business world calls for certain characteristics from you which may not necessarily be found amongst the pages of your history book, but are embodied in the **way** you deal with that book.

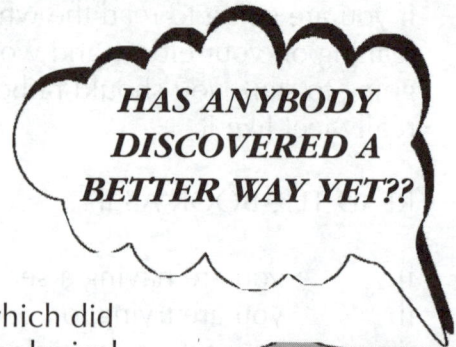

This is determined by

- ☞ Your **attitude**
- ☞ Your **willingness to learn**
- ☞ Your **ability to study on your own**
- ☞ The **ability to evaluate information critically**

    and

- ☞ The **ability to relate knowledge in an orderly fashion.**

No subject is therefore USELESS INFORMATION if you view it as such.

Perhaps your greatest ambition is to marry a rich man or woman so that you never have to work again. Even then you will have to master these skills to keep your fortune!

4. *Do you possess the necessary skills?*

Study the following table and mark those skills you possess definitely and with total confidence.

DO I POSSESS THE FOLLOWING SKILLS?		
Skills the career world will call for	✔	✗
1. I get on well with **all** people.		
2. I can get on with people of different races, cultures and religions.		
3. I can communicate well and listen to others.		
4. I can show my feelings in a positive and constructive way.		
5. I can positively cope with emotions such as stress, fear and anger.		
6. I can positively and confidently evaluate my own life and those of others.		
7. I can recognise my own potential and extract it.		
8. I can set goals for myself and achieve them.		
9. I can concentrate and complete tasks successfully and without supervision.		
10. I can plan and organise my own life and manage my time effectively.		
11. I can think and act pro-actively and creatively.		
12. I can handle and solve conflict and problems in a goal orientated manner.		
13. I can find and collect information.		
14. I can easily remember, evaluate, analyse and relate information.		
15. I can pinpoint the most important aspects of information, relationships and life without condescending to trivialities and pettiness.		
16. I can use the technology required for my profession without supervision.		
17. I can apply mathematical concepts to my daily life.		
18. I am creative.		
19. I don't feel threatened by the possessions and knowledge of others.		
20. I can do my best every day.		
21. I can endure and persist.		
22. I can forgive and forget.		
23. I like studying.		

These skills need to become a habit if you intend to be successful in your career! THAT IS WHAT **SURVIVE YOUR LIFE** DEALS WITH!

5. Success begins with yourself

Making a promise to yourself to achieve success, is already better than to simply speculate or dream about it. Read the following undertaking fill it in and sign it. THIS IS YOUR FIRST STEP TO SUCCESS.

Undertaking

Hereby, I,

_____

undertake to afford the suggestions and methods in this book a fair opportunity by doing the following:

1. I will be positive.
2. I will read through every chapter carefully and observantly.
3. I will complete each task truthfully.
4. I will do every exercise.
5. I will practise all the methods and techniques and apply them practically.
6. I will be honest with myself.
7. I will do my very best.
8. I will not reject the entirety if I don't agree with everything.
9. I will regard the book as a help and not as a hindrance.
10. I will live what I learn.
11. I will not lose courage if I struggle.
12. I will not deface, mess up, share, lend or allow the book to be copied.

Signed at _____ (Address)

on this _____ day of _____

_____
Signature

2   Why me?

Did you know that God knew you even before you were born and dedicated you to Him? If you have ever wondered what you are doing on this earth and where you are really heading if you were to die today, you should read this chapter very attentively ...

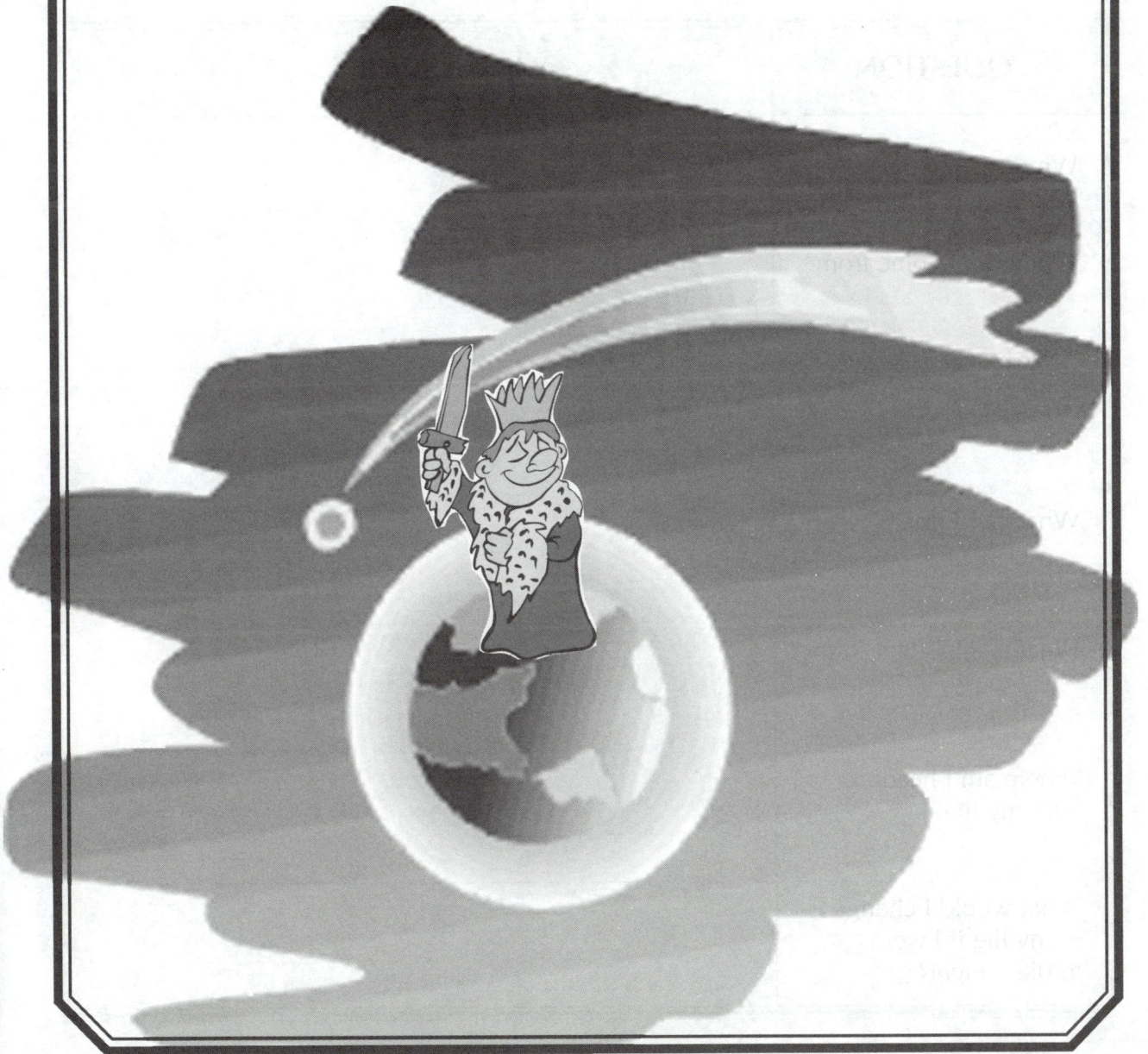

1. *Where do I come from?*

Take a few minutes to quietly think about the following questions and then answer them honestly in PENCIL.

To answer these questions will not be very easy and the more you consider every question, the more you will realize that your initial answer may differ consider- ably from the answer you may get later – after you have completed reading this chapter.

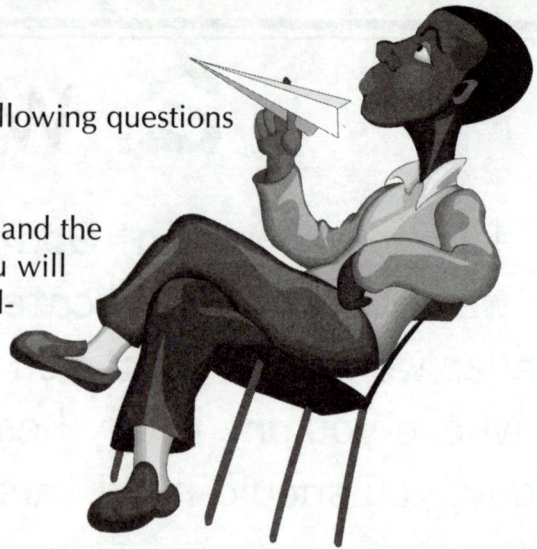

QUESTION	MY ANSWER
Why was I born?	
Where do I come from?	
Who and what am I?	
What can I do?	
What is important to me?	
Where am I heading with my life?	
What would I change in my life if I were to die tonight?	

Imagine that you are standing in front of a full length mirror, looking at yourself from head to toe. Now write down very truthfully how you view yourself in the mirror.

THIS IS HOW I LOOK

How do you feel about yourself when you look in the mirror or think about yourself?

HOW DO YOU FEEL?	CHOOSE ONE	X	WHY?
Very happy!	Always		
	Often		
	Sometimes		
	Never		
Satisfied	Always		
	Often		
	Sometimes		
	Never		
Feel nothing	Always		
	Often		
	Sometimes		
	Never		
Dissatisfied	Always		
	Often		
	Sometimes		
	Never		
Very unhappy!	Always		
	Often		
	Sometimes		
	Never		

Did you know that some famous models, actresses and actors' photos are doctored to camouflage crooked noses, floppy ears, protruding chins and zits?

Let us now find out exactly who and what you are.

a) You were created by God!

You were not just haphazardly put together in a laboratory. You were created by God! The ability to breathe, to move, to hear, to speak, to think and to feel were given to you by God when He created you. You were already perfectly formed by God when you were placed in the womb.

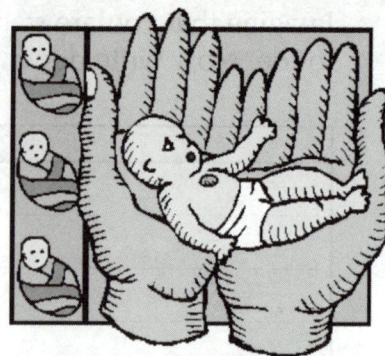

> "You are the one who put me together inside my mother's body"
>
> Psalm 139:13
>
> "Nothing about me is hidden from you! I was secretly woven together inside my mother's body."
>
> Psalm 139:15
>
> "I am your Creator. You were in my care even before you were born."
>
> Isaiah 44:2

b) You were created in the image of God

Do you become distressed over your bow legs, crooked toes, thin hair and freckles? Remember – God created you IN HIS IMAGE. Have you ever watched a sculptor working at a creation? It could take months or even years to chisel a lifeless image out of wood or stone. God does not create images of wood, wax, stone or clay, but living, growing, thinking, speaking, laughing, crying, moving, drip-dry people such as you!

You **carry** the **image** of God. When you look at a statue of a soldier, you know what a soldier looks like. God want others to see who He is when they look at you. Are you dissatisfied with the way you look? Think about this …

> So God created humans to be like himself: he made men and women.
>
> Genesis 1:27
>
> You let us rule everything your hands have made. And you put all of it under our power
>
> Psalm 8:6
>
> You surely know that your body is a temple where the Holy Spirit lives. The spirit is in you and is a gift from God. You are no longer your own. God paid a great price for you. So use your body to honour God.
>
> 1 Corinthians 6:19-20

Your body is the temple in which God wishes to live.
Do you nurture your temple or do you pollute and neglect it?

c) You are an heir

When you are an heir, it means that someone has left his or her money or possessions to you in a testament so that you can inherit it after their death. Wouldn't it be wonderful to inherit millions when your parents die? Your first reaction may well be – "YES, OF COURSE!" In your mind you can already see what you are going to do with all that money! But remember – they have to **die** first before you can inherit! Now the idea no longer sounds so great! Surely you don't want the people you love so dearly, to die!

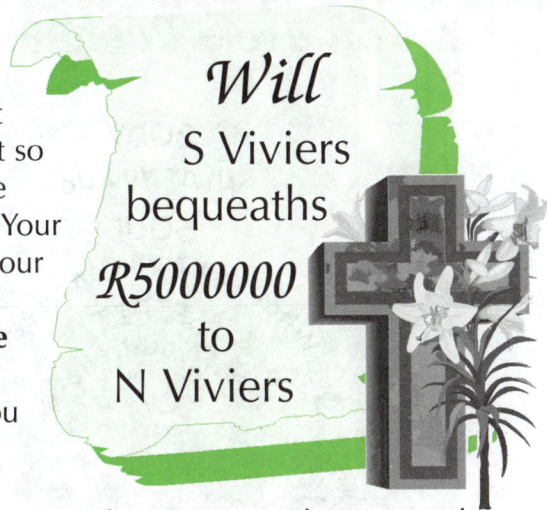

Will
S Viviers bequeaths
R5000000
to
N Viviers

Yet, God has **already** allowed His Son to die on a cross so that you can inherit eternal life! Think about this carefully. Would you allow the person you love most to be crucified so that someone else you love too, can inherit something? Would you be willing to be nailed to a cross and to hang there until you die – so that someone else can inherit something?

GOD AND HIS SON, JESUS CHRIST, HAVE ALREADY DONE THIS FOR YOU SO THAT YOUR SPIRIT WILL LIVE FOREVER – EVEN IF YOUR BODY DIES!

God loved the people of this world so much that He gave his only Son, so that everyone who has faith in Him will have eternal life and never really die. John 3:16

You are no longer slaves. You are God's children and you will be given what He has promised. Galatians 4:7

Do you need proof of your inheritance? **Then read the Testament!** The Bible is divided into the Old Testament and the New Testament. Both parts contain the proof and guidelines for the inheritance awaiting you! Testaments usually include certain conditions which have to be met in order to receive the inheritance. It gives guidelines about the age at which you will be allowed to inherit, who will control the money, how it is to be paid out and how it will be divided.

In the Bible, God gives us clear guidelines on exactly what your inheritance comprises, how you can obtain it and what you have to do to ensure that you do not forfeit it. It should now be clear that the Bible is not, simply, a storybook about old people, but a Testament that God granted to be written so that you will know exactly what it means to be a child and heir of God!

Keep reading your Bible until you find answers to the following questions:

Seek God's promises and ask Him to fulfil them in your life.

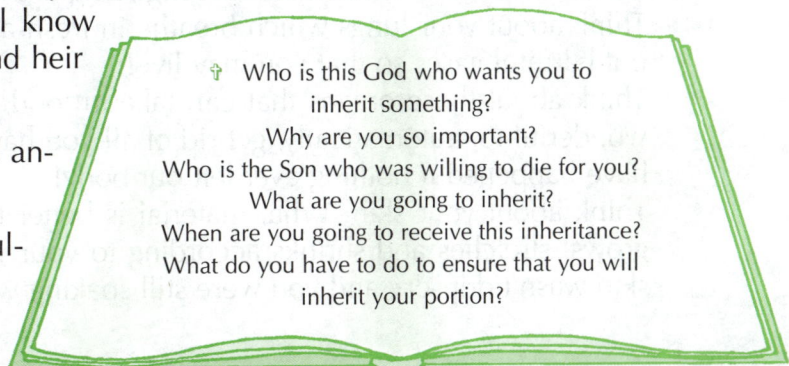

✝ Who is this God who wants you to inherit something?
Why are you so important?
Who is the Son who was willing to die for you?
What are you going to inherit?
When are you going to receive this inheritance?
What do you have to do to ensure that you will inherit your portion?

2. You are a living being!

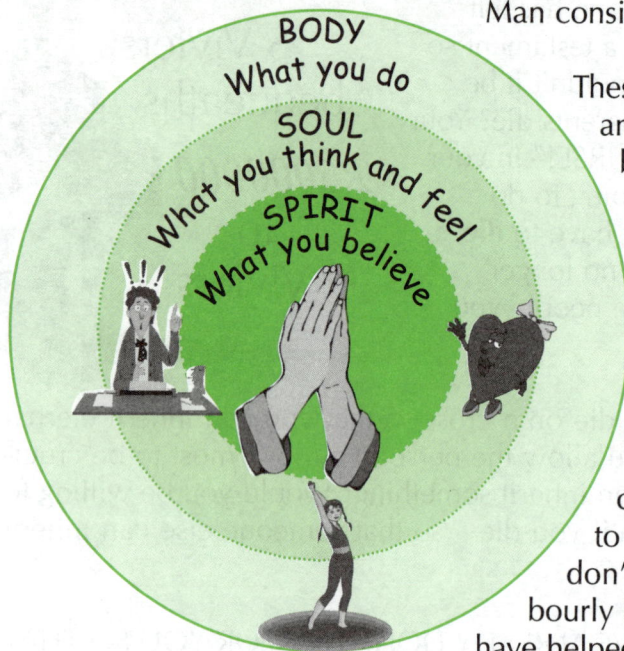

BODY
What you do
SOUL
What you think and feel
SPIRIT
What you believe

Man consists of a body, soul and spirit:

These parts cannot be separated from one another and nobody can say with certainty where one begins and the other ends. The facts are that your spirit has an influence on your soul and that your soul and your spirit determine the reactions of your body.

For example:

You believe in neighbourly love (**spirit**). This creates feelings of love (**emotions – soul**) which make your mind (**intellect – soul**) decide to smile at an old lady (**deeds – body**) and to help her across the street (**deeds – body**). If you don't believe in neighbourly love, you wouldn't have helped her.

a   You have a wonderful body

God is perfect and therefore He cannot create something which is not perfect. Even if you have a disability, it is there for a reason and a purpose!

REMEMBER:
GOD DOES NOT CREATE RUBBISH – DON'T SLANDER WHAT HE HAS MADE!

☞   Think about your eyes: No technological device can see that well, look in love and cry!
☞   Think about your voice which can produce sounds and make music!
☞   Think about your ears which can differentiate between 500 different sounds per second.
☞   Think about your brain which can absorb millions of messages at a time; process, store and relate them.
☞   Think about your hands. Do you know of any tool which can firmly pick up and put something down, create and mend something and over and above that, softly stroke and make music?
☞   Think about your heart which pumps 1.6 gallons of blood through arteries of 12000 miles! That is the distance from Hong Kong to New York via the Panama Canal.
☞   Think about your lungs which breathe in fresh air every second of the day and breathe out harmful gases so that you may live!
☞   Think about those organs that can take in food, process it and excrete it again. Isn't it wonderful to, automatically, get rid of all you have consumed? Just think of what would have happened if nothing ever left our body!
☞   Think about your skin. What material is better that your skin? It heals itself, breathes, grows, stretches and shrinks according to your weight! How would it have felt if your skin wasn't drip-dry and you were still soaking wet hours after your bath?

Man can make many things, but only God can give life. The air you breathe was given to you by God. The ability you have to draw it into your lungs and blow it out again proves that God loves you and wants you to live!

What do you do with the temple God gave you? Do you abuse, neglect or pollute this temple? Remember that the Holy Spirit wants to live in you! Do you moan all day long about your "thunder thighs" or Dumbo ears? God loves you as you are! It is wrong to ridicule something He has made. Just think of how wonderful it is to be alive!
USE YOUR BODY AND DANCE WITH JOY – EVEN IF YOU ONLY WIGGLE YOUR EARS!

b) You have a soul!

Your soul is your personality which consists of **emotions and intellect**. These include the feelings you experience, the thoughts you have and the way in which you think.

INTELLECT	EMOTIONS
What you know and think	How you feel and act

Example:
Your *intellect* tells you, you are seeing a "chick" and not a "chicken". Your *emotions* make you like the girl. Your intellect enables you to do arithmetic while your emotions determine whether you like it or not.

Your personality is formed in various ways:

1. Heredity:
   Proof exist that you can inherit certain characteristics, such as a flair for sport, from your parents. Nevertheless, a large part of your behaviour is copied when you notice people acting in a certain manner and achieving results …!

2. Culture:
   Spaniards have habits which differ from those of the French. You normally adopt the habits and values of the people in your environment and cultural group (e.g. curried food or watching soccer).

3. Social class, status and rank.
   The way you view yourself, those around you, your possessions and the world around you, is determined by the group of people which you and your family regard as friends. If you grow up in an environment where race, possessions, clothing or money are very important, you will probably think it important as well.

4. Personal environment:
   This is the environment you create for yourself. You meet people of different cultures, classes, races and sexes. You also meet people with similar or differing values to yours. To survive amongst these people, you adapt your values, habits and personality so that you can get along better with them.

5. Personal qualities:

Your personal qualities are those characteristics, talents and intelligence with which you are born. It develops as you use opportunities, the training or education you receive and the experience you accumulate.

Your personality determines your actions!

Your personality determines your actions. If you are an aggressive person, you will easily lose your temper. If your intellect is well developed, you have the ability to exceed. If you are friendly, loving and helpful, you will act that way!

Write down your 10 best characteristics (friendly, clever, lighthearted, etc.), as well as 10 worst characteristics (temperamental, touchy, grumpy, etc.)

MY 10 BEST CHARACTERISTICS	MY 10 WORST CHARACTERISTICS

Can you change your personality (Soul)?
YES, YOU CAN!

● You can eliminate your bad characteristics and improve your good qualities. You can decide to be neater, friendlier, to study harder, have more patience and even get rid of a few layers of fat!

● You can alter your principles and values.

● You can learn how to adapt to your environment, your responsibilities and the people around you.

● You can allow opportunities to slip through your fingers, neglect your education and learn nothing from your experience, or you can decide to grasp every opportunity, improve your education and use your experience as a springboard instead of a hammock!

Unfortunately it is not always that simple;! You try to lead a good life, to be friendly, neat and hardworking, but before you know it, you have already done something wrong, shouted at someone, fought, messed up your room or did not study at all!

Even the Apostle Paul had similar problems!

> In fact, I don't understand why I act the way I do. I don't do what I know is right. I do the things I hate. Although I don't do what I know to be right, I agree that the law is good. So I am not the one doing these evil things. The sin that lives in me is what does them. I know that my selfish desires won't let me do anything that is good. Even when I want to do right, I cannot. Instead of doing what I know is right, I do wrong.   Romans 7:15-19

When your soul is in control of your body, you will always act according to how you feel at that moment. If you feel friendly, you will be friendly and when you are in a foul mood, all those around you will suffer from your screaming!

If you really want to change, you not only have to change your actions, but your attitude as well: How do you manage that?

BY ALTERING YOUR SPIRIT.

c) You have a spirit!

To understand how your **spirit** works, it is necessary to look at the way in which God created man.

> The Lord God took a handful of soil and made a man. God breathed life into the man and the man started breathing.   Genesis 2:7

Do you still remember that, as God's image and representative, your were created to rule? When you act as representative to rule on behalf of someone else, it is surely important that you remain in **constant contact** with that person so that you will know what he expects of you! This connection keeps the communication and the relationship between you and the other person going! That's why there are cellphones, faxes, e-mail and hundreds of other ways by which to be in daily contact with each other.

God gave you a spirit to communicate with Him. Through your spirit you can constantly be in contact with Him, talk to Him and receive commands from Him as to how you should act and rule. This spirit of yours is your connection to God. It is your way of chatting to God by way of virtual reality!

With the first sin, Satan made the spirit of man die. Virtual reality became a terrible nightmare. The cable linking God and man was thereby severed and man now had only his body and soul to rely on! By the mercy of God the nation of Israel was chosen from which Christ would later be born.

Adam and Eve did not obey Gods' command, but listened to Satan instead. In this way, the link between man and God was broken and man became susceptible to sin. This original sin resulted in all people losing this bond with God.

Instead of Adam and Eve being able to receive direct commands from God, as to how they should act, there now was doubt. Satan changed God's exclamation marks into question marks. Once Eve began to doubt, she believed Satan's lie!

God says: "You may eat fruit from any tree in the garden except the one that has the power to let you know the difference between right and wrong. If you eat any fruit from that tree, you will die before the day is over!" Genesis 2: 16-17

Satan asks: "Did God tell you not to eat from any tree in the garden?"

Don't you do this too?

God says: "I made you – slightly less than a heavenly being and crowned you with glory and honour."

Satan asks: "How could you possibly resemble an angel with those huge thighs and crooked teeth?"

And you believe the lie – You are worthless – you are ugly! And then you cannot possibly rule!

God says: "Don't sin! I see everything you do."

Satan says: "Do it, man! Just make sure nobody sees you!"

And you believe the lie – you do the wrong thing and all you have managed is to add to your sins!

Think carefully about what happened next in the garden of Eden … Adam and Eve did not drop dead.

✝ **Their bodies were still so alive** that they realised they were naked.
✝ **Their souls were still in place**, because they felt shy and guilty (emotions) and so they made plans to hide from God (intellect).
✝ **But Adam and Eve's spirit had died.** Their connection to God had been broken. Now they could no longer rule. They could no longer represent him.

Would a ruler and representative hide in a bush, ashamed and guilty?

This is what happens to you when you try to live according to your own will by not believing in God. This is exactly what the devil wants!

✧ He wants you to control your soul – then your emotions rule your actions.
✧ He wants you to doubt everything – then you can believe his lies.
✧ He wants you to break off communication with God – then you listen to him!
✧ He wants your spirit to die – then you will become dumb and numb.

Their minds are in the dark and they are stubborn and ignorant and have missed out on the life that comes from God. They no longer have any feelings about what is right. Ephesians 4:18

(This sounds very much like someone writing exams, but without having studied.)

Have you become numb? Do you still listen to God's Spirit warning you when you are busy with dangerous or wrong deeds? Do you have excuses such as:

"But everybody does it!"   "Nothing will happen to me."
"Don't preach to me!"   "I will do it myself."
"It's my life."   "Keep your nose out of my business!"
"There's nothing wrong with it!"   "Nobody knows about it!"
"I won't get addicted to it!"   "I know what I'm doing!"
"But they are my friends!"   "But we love each other!"

3. God is merciful!

Yet God was merciful. He decided to send His Son, Jesus Christ, to earth, to awaken this spirit in man again. Jesus died for your sins when he died on the cross. He was humiliated, beaten and impaled with nails for your sins. Your sins are all those wrongs you have done and are still going to do! He descended into hell to conquer eternal death for you. When Jesus rose from the dead, he restored your spiritual link to God! That link is the Holy Spirit!

When Jesus was taken to Heaven after He had risen from the grave,
He sent the Holy Spirit to live in the hearts of man.

> **"Then I will ask the Father to send you the Holy Spirit who will help you and always be with you. The Spirit will show you what is true."**
> John 14:16-17

In the book of Acts you can read how the Holy Spirit then descended on Jesus' disciples, like tongues of flame. When this happened they were filled with the Holy Spirit and received various talents so that they could act in the image of God. Simple fishermen could how speak in foreign tongues, heal people and spread the Word of God.

> **Suddenly there was a noise from Heaven like the sound of a mighty wind! It filled the house where they were meeting. Then they saw what looked like fiery tongues moving in all directions and a tongue came and settled on each person there. The Holy Spirit took control of everyone and they began speaking whatever languages the spirit let them speak.**
> Acts 2:2-4

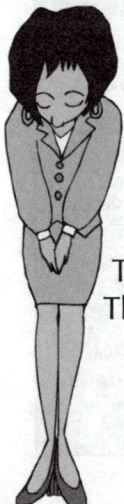

However, God did not just let His Holy Spirit descend on His disciples, but still does it today in many ways for those who believe in Him!

> **Later, I will give My Spirit to everyone. Your sons and daughters will prophesy. Your old men will have dreams and your young men will see visions.**
> **Then the Lord will save everyone who worships Him.**
> Joel 2:28, 32

The possibility to speak to God in virtual reality is here again!
This time, however, God has given you the choice of asking for a "connection" first!

IT IS YOUR CHOICE WHETHER YOU WANT TO BE
CONNECTED TO GOD OR NOT!

4. Connect with God!

Once you have truly connected with God, He will never break that connection with you again! Do you want your spirit to revive by linking your life to God again?

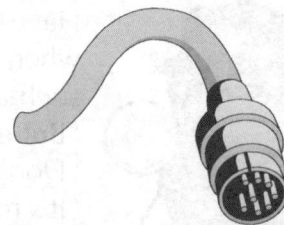

CONNECT WITH GOD AND REVIVE YOUR SPIRIT!

Say the following on your own, aloud, in your own words and believe every word you say!

✝ **Admit that God lives and is almighty.**
Eternal life is to know You, the only true God and to know Jesus Christ, the One you sent.

John 17:3

✝ **Admit that Jesus Christ is the Son of God.**
God stays one with everyone who openly says that Jesus is the Son of God.

1 John 4:15

✝ **Admit that God loves you.**
I pray that you and all of God's people will understand what is called wide or long or high or deep. I want you to know all about Christ's love, although it is too wonderful to be measured. Then your lives will be filled with all that God is.

Ephesians 3:18-19

✝ **Admit that Jesus died on the cross for your sins so that you may be forgiven.**
Christ carried the burden of our sins. By His cuts and bruises you are healed.

1 Peter 2:24

✝ **Admit that Jesus died on the cross and rose to heaven so that your spirit may live forever.**
But God let Christ make you alive, when He forgave all our sins. He took them away and nailed them to the cross.

Colossians 2:13-14

✝ **Admit that you have wronged and that you regret it.**
But if we confess our sins to God, He can always be trusted to forgive us and take our sins away.

1 John 1:9

✝ **Ask God to revive your spirit by filling you with His Holy Spirit.**
God sent Jesus Christ our Saviour to give us His Spirit.

Titus 3:6

✝ **Ask God to reveal His plan for your life.**
Don't let me follow evil ways, but lead me in the way that time has proven true.

Psalm 139:24

✝ **Ask God to change your thoughts and to rid your life of all those things not part of His plan for you.**
Don't be like the people of this world, but let God change the way you think. Then you will know how to do everything that is good and pleasing to Him.

Romans 12:2

✝ **Ask God for the gifts that the Holy Spirit gives you, according to 1 Corinthians 12, so that you can live the plan He has for you.**
Christ has generously divided out His gifts to us.

Ephesians 4:7

✝ **Ask God to enable you to live every day in His image.**
So we must get rid of everything that slows us down, especially the sin that just won't let go. And we must be determined to run the race that is ahead of us. We must keep our eyes on Jesus, who leads us and makes our faith complete.

Hebrews 12:1-2

Let us consider the advantages this huge step holds for your life.

What happens when the Holy Spirit lives within you?	
Text	**What does the Holy Spirit do?**
Romans 8:6	… if our lives are ruled by the Spirit, we will have **life and peace**.
Romans 8:11	God's spirit now lives in you and he will **raise you to life** by his spirit.
Romans 8:14, 17	Only those people who are led by God's spirit are **his children. We will also share** in the glory of Christ, because we have suffered with him.
Romans 8:26-27	In certain ways **we are weak**, but **the Spirit is there to help us** … when we don't know what to pray for, the **Spirit prays for us** in ways that cannot be put into words. God can understand what is in the mind of the spirit.
Acts 1:8	But the Holy Spirit will come upon you and **give you power**. Then you will tell everyone about Me.
Luke 12:12	At that time the Holy Spirit will tell you **what to say**.
1 Corinthians 2:15	People who are guided by the Spirit, **can make all kinds of judgements.**
Romans 8:9	You are no longer ruled by your desires (soul and body), but by **God's Spirit, who lives in you**.
Romans 14:17	God's Kingdom isn't about eating and drinking. It is about **pleasing God**, about living in **peace** and about **true happiness**.
Galatians 5:22-23	God's Spirit makes us loving, happy, peaceful, patient, kind , good, faithful, gentle and self-controlled. There is no law against behaving in any of these ways.
1 Corinthians 12	There are different kinds of spiritual gifts, but they all come from the same spirit. – the **works of the Spirit**. – the gift to speak words of **wisdom.** – the gift of **knowledge.** – **faith.** – the gift of **healing.** – the power to perform **miracles.** – the gift to **prophesy** (tell what will happen). – the gift to **recognise** different Spirits. – the gift to speak **different kinds of languages.** – the gift to tell **what these languages mean.** Find out what other talents and gifts the Holy Spirit wants to give you by – reading the Bible. – praying and listening to God. – keeping your channel to God open and clear.

5. God has a plan with your life

Even if it sometimes feels as if nobody cares for you, be assured that God has a plan with your life. He knew you before you were born and had already, then, worked out a very specific plan for your life.

But even before I was born, God had chosen me.	*Galatians 1:15*
I am your Creator and before you were born, I chose you to speak for me.	*Jeremiah 1:5*
The Lord chose me and gave me a name before I was born.	*Isaiah 49:1*
I have called you by name; now you belong to Me.	*Isaiah 43:1*
Even before I was born, you had written in your book everything I would do.	*Psalm 139:16*
You notice everything I do and everywhere I go.	*Psalm 139:3*

Even before you were born, God had a plan for your life. Your way in life is already mapped out for you. God has already mapped out your road to a happy and wonderful **final destination in His Kingdom**.

✝   To help you, God has given you a map – His Word – to help you get to Him.

✝   To further ensure that you don't get lost, He gives you His Spirit as navigator on the journey. If you ask God, the Holy Spirit will clearly tell you whenever you start taking the wrong track. The moment you start to feel guilty, you must know that you are messing up.

✝   To make even more sure, He appoints other believers as beacons along your way, where you can ask for advice or rest. Speak to others about God. They will give you advice and answers. Find a congregation where you feel happy and at ease.

✝   Seek God and get to know Him! God's message is to be found in nature, on the radio and even on the internet.

Even when you have totally lost your way, He waits – without condemning – for you to again reach the right way to your destination!

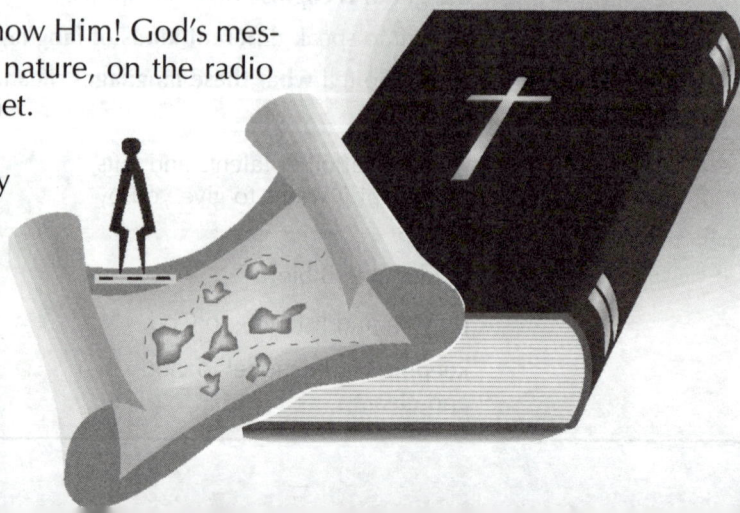

6. *Your purpose here on earth*

Were you created simply to die and then go to and live with God? Absolutely not! You have a special purpose here on earth. Let us see what God expects of you:

a) Commandments from God

Apart from really ENJOYING LIFE, the Bible lists many other commands which God gave man. Read through a few of these commands and see how many of them you can perform!

COMMANDMENTS FROM GOD

Represent God and rule
God said: "Now we will make humans and they will **be like us.** We will let them **rule** the fish; the birds and all other living creatures."
Genesis 1:26

Live, learn and work
Fill the earth **with people** and bring it under your **control. Rule** over the fish in the ocean, the birds in the sky and every animal on the earth.
Genesis 1:28

Love
Love the Lord your God with all your heart, soul and mind. This is the first and most important commandment. The second most important commandment is like this one. And it is: **Love others as much as you love yourself.**
Matthew 22:37-39

Testify, worship and praise
Go and **preach the good news** to everyone in the world. Then you will tell everyone about me in Jerusalem, in all Judea, Samaria and everywhere else in the world.
Acts 1:8

Believe
Have faith in God and **have faith in Me**. There are many rooms in My Father's House.
… After I have done this, I will come back to take you with me. Then we will be together. I am the way, the truth and the life!
John 14: 1-3, 6
Their **faith helped them** conquer kingdoms and because they did right, God made promises to them.
Hebrews 11:33

Confess
So you will be saved, if you honestly say: Jesus is Lord and if you believe with all your heart that **God raised Him from death.**
Romans 10:9
But if we **confess our sins** to God, He can always be trusted to forgive us and take our sins away.
John 1:9

Fight against evil powers
Be ready! Let the **truth** be like a belt around your waist and let **God's justice** protect you like armour. Your **desire to tell the good news about peace** should be like shoes on your feet. Let your **faith** be like a shield and you will be able to stop all the flaming arrows of the evil one.
Ephesians 16:14-16

---

b) Listen to God

God speaks to you through the Bible, your conscience and through other people.

Hints on how to recognise God's voice	
God speaks	**Satan speaks**
God speaks clearly	Satan confuses
God is patient, soft and won't force you	Satan forces and exerts pressure
God brings peace, hope and joy	Satan brings fear, hopelessness and depression
God corrects, teaches and improves	Satan condemns, dooms and spoils
God gives life	Satan destroys
God builds you up	Satan wants us to abuse our bodies with destructive behaviour and addiction.

Speak to people who know God and look for Him in places where God's teenagers get together. The whole coffee shop, CSA and CYA can't be full of nerds only! They need you!

Be "in" and start your own thing!
God is present where two or more people gather in His name.

c)   God's rules

Rules and regulations are part of life. Even in your own circle of friends there are certain rules you have to adhere to, otherwise you cannot remain part of that circle. You may not, for instance, blab your friend's secrets, go out with your friend's boyfriend, gossip behind their backs or borrow things you don't return. By doing this, you damage the friendship and the relationship!

God wants to ensure that we don't damage our relationship with Him. He created you as carrier of His image to represent Him. To manage this, you have to be in constant contact with Him so that you can receive advice, perform instructions and even moan and groan if things become too much! If this relationship between you and God is damaged, you can no longer do all this!

When the relationship between you and your boyfriend, girlfriend or parents has been damaged, you will no longer be on speaking terms and the relationship dies. In order to prevent the relationship between you and God from dying, He has given you certain rules to obey.

God's rules will also protect you from the evil powers of Satan. Satan is described as someone who walks around like a roaring lion, looking for someone to devour. The shepherd leads his sheep into an enclosure to prevent them from straying too far. At times he will even take a stick to them to keep them away from cliffs and keep them safe. God does exactly that! His rules and regulations are the safe enclosure in which the devil cannot devour you.

> **God says: I am the Alpha and the Omega, the First and the Last, the Beginning and the End.**   Revelations 21:13

God knows in advance what is good or bad, safe or dangerous for you. He is a practical God who gives rules to make sure that you don't hurt yourself.

He already knows the dangers of sin. He can foresee what will happen is you overstep the rules! He wants to protect you against yourself and the devil.
- ☛ He knows what will happen if you experiment with drugs.
- ☛ He knows what will happen between you and your boyfriend or girlfriend if you go ``too far".
- ☛ He knows what will happen if you don't study hard enough.
- ☛ He knows what the results of your bad choices will be!

Make sure you know and understand God's rules. Read Exodus 20 in the Old Testament and the Books of the New Testament. The rule: "Be faithful in marriage", does not only mean that you may not divorce, but also that you may not be sexually active before marriage!

When you break the house rules, school rules, hostel rules or the rules of your country, you are punished. God also punishes. He punishes all sin. He sees no difference between big and small sins. God's punishment for your sins is your spiritual death! He warned Adam and Eve: "You will surely die!" He warns you too! Your spirit will die and you won't be able to enter His Kingdom.

However, if you confess your sins and STOP doing them, He is merciful, loyal and fair and He will forgive you!

REMEMBER:
You may not break God's rules! That is "cast in stone"! They were there long before you and will be there long after you have died.
You can only break yourself against God's rules!

7. *What if you die?*

How many people have you known who have died? All people die. Your body is like a clay pot which will break at one time or another. Our bodies are not built to last forever.

In the book *Tuesdays with Morrie* of Mitch Alborn, the dying Morrie Swartz says:

"Everybody knows they're going to die, but nobody believes it!
If we did, we would do things differently!'

You need to believe that you will die one day and that you have no idea when that moment will arrive! What is important, is not the clay pot of your body, but the treasure (your spirit) you carry within. If you have this treasure within you and your spirit is alive to God, you never have to fear death! Then it simply becomes the door through which you have to step to have everlasting peace and happiness!

> We are like clay jars, in which this treasure is stored. The real power comes from God and not from us.
> 2 Corinthians 4:7
>
> We never give up. Our bodies are gradually dying, but we ourselves are being made stronger each day.
> 2 Corinthians 4:16
>
> But whether we are at home with the Lord or away from Him, we still try our best to please Him. After all, Christ will Judge each of us for the good or bad that we do while living in these bodies.   2 Corinthians 5: 9-10
>
> I am the one who raises the dead to life! Everyone who has faith in Me will live, even if they die! And everyone who lives because of faith in Me, will never really die.   John 11:25-26

In Revelations God describes exactly what will happen to your Spirit after you have died and after He has come again to judge everyone who has ever lived.

> ... and then the book of life was opened. The dead were judged by what those books said they had done.
> Revelations 20:12
>
> God's home is now with His people. He will live with them, and they will be His own. He will wipe all tears from their eyes and there will be no more death, suffering, crying or pain.   Revelations 21:3-4
>
> ... They will be thrown into that lake of fire and burning sulphur. This is the second death.   Revelations 21:8

8. Are Satan and hell simply scary stories?

Satan is a reality and is far cleverer and slyer than you would ever believe. Remember he has already been judged and is doomed to the lake of fire and sulphur forever. Unlike Jesus Christ, he is afraid to go alone. He is so arrogant that he tried to seduce Jesus – who is without sin – with food, riches and power. Remember, Satan is after your blood!

He fights day and night to break your spiritual connection to God. He uses films, videos and computer games about vampires, violence, witches and spirits to contaminate your spirit ! He uses media, your friends, drugs, money, sex, horoscopes, your personality and even your own body to force you off course.

Satan won't easily appear to you in his true form. He comes like a wolf in sheep's clothing or a "thief in the night". Disobedience to God usually starts with small things and before you know it, these things have taken over your life and spirit. You begin to doubt your own worth and start depending on other people and things in your life to prove that you are important. Soon you are a slave to others, your possessions or habits. As you no longer have a spirit, you act the way you want to, your conscience becomes insensitive and you do more and more things you know to be bad and harmful. You even begin to justify it and encourage others to do it as well.

That is what Satan wants. He pesters people with illnesses, seduces believers, prevents you from praying and stops you from experiencing God's love or the opportunity to testify about it.

☞ Can you really talk to God after you and your girlfriend have "gone too far"?
☞ Can you speak to God while marijuana fumes bubble from your nose?
☞ Can you kneel before God with a clear conscience if you copied your homework, lied to your parents, gossiped about your friend or humiliated someone?
☞ Can you truly believe God's advice if you have already read what the stars foretell about what you should do and what is about to happen to you?

That is how Satan breaks your spiritual cable!

Have you read how horrific hell will be? Have you ever been so lonely that it scared you? Has it ever felt as if no one on earth loves or understands you? Have you ever burnt your hand? Have you had so much pain that it doesn't even help to grit your teeth? Have you ever been stuck for hours in a pitch dark hole? Has anyone ever tied you so that you cannot move at all? Imagine yourself being bound and thrown into the pitch black heart of a crater. You burn and burn. Nobody helps you. Nobody gets you out.

THAT IS HELL – THE ONLY DIFFERENCE IS THAT IT WILL NEVER END!

Let us see how the Bible describes Heaven and Hell:

WHAT DOES HELL LOOK LIKE?

God's peace and love and everything beautiful, is gone forever.
There you are separated from God forever.
Their punishment will be eternal destruction and they will be kept from the presence of our Lord and His glorious strength.

2 Thessalonians 1:9

You are bound with unbreakable chains.
God chained them with everlasting chains and is now keeping them in dark pits until the great day of judgement.

Jude, verse 6

It is deep and dark.
We should also be worried by what happened to the cities of Sodom and Gommorah. God made an example of them and punished them with eternal fire. They are like wandering stars, forever doomed to the darkest pits of hell.

Jude, verses 7,13

You burn, day and night, suffering in a pool of fire and sulphur.
If your hand or foot causes you to sin, chop it off and throw it away! You would be better off to go into life crippled or lame than to have two hands or two feet and be thrown into the fire that never goes out. If your eye causes you to sin, poke it out and get rid of it. You would be better off to go into life with only one eye than to have two eyes and be thrown into the fires of hell.

Matthew: 18: 8-9

The pain and grief will last forever.
Then the devil who fooled them will be thrown into the lake of fire and burning sulphur. He will be there with the Beast and the false prophet and they will be in pain day and night forever and ever.

Revelations 20:10

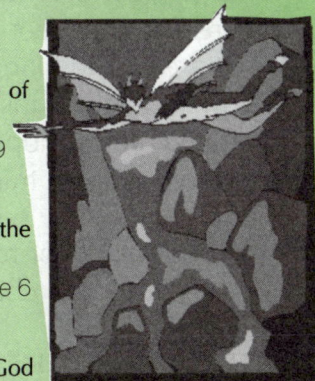

WHAT DOES YOUR HOME IN HEAVEN LOOK LIKE?

The glory of God made the city bright. It was dazzling and crystal clear like a precious jasper stone.

Revelations 21:11

The city has a high wall with twelve gates, guarded by twelve angels.

The gates are never locked.

The city is square.

The wall is built of jasper and the city is made of pure gold, clear as crystal.

The foundations of the city wall are decorated with precious stones.

The gates are made of solid pearl and the streets of pure gold.

There is no night or day as God is the light.

There is a river of life giving water and a tree of life that bears fruit all year.

Nothing unworthy, dirty or false will be allowed to enter.

There will be no death, grief or pain.

There is peace, love and security.

Read Revelations 21

Just think – No crime! No heartache! No pain! No death! No fear!

Only Safety, Peace, Love and Happiness!
Would you like to live there forever?
GET YOUR "PASSPORT" FROM JESUS AND LET US EMIGRATE!

9. *Make your choice today!*

☞ What do your eyes look at? What do you do with your hands? Where do your feet walk to? What does your tongue say? What are you thinking about? What are you busy with?

☞ Are there feelings inside you which make you ashamed, sad, frustrated, angry, hopeless or dissatisfied?

☞ Would you like to trade in your life for a new one?

☞ Would you like to feel happy, satisfied and safe again?

☞ Are you looking for meaning to your life?

☞ Would you like to change your life?

THEN START FROM THE *TOP*!

DON'T FIRST LOOK FOR FRIENDS, EDUCATION, MONEY, HAPPINESS AND LOVE AND THEN – IF ENOUGH TIME IS LEFT – TRY TO FIT GOD IN AS WELL!

Jesus Christ gives you the recipe for everything you need!

> **But more than anything else, put God's work first and do what He wants. Then other things will be yours as well.**
> Matthew 6:33

SEEK GOD BEFORE ALL ELSE!
THEN HE GIVES YOU WHAT YOU NEED – IN YOUR SLEEP!
God knows what you "*need*". If you ask Him, He will give it to you. Remember – HE IS GOD!
God, who can make an axe float, a donkey speak, a city wall fall, the sea to open up, the sun to stop, heals the sick, makes the lame walk again, gives sight to the blind, hearing to the deaf and can revive a corpse after four days in the grave – HE CAN HELP YOU TOO!

> **Ask and you will receive. Search and you will find. Knock and the door will be opened for you.**
> Matthew 7:7
>
> **Everything you ask for in prayer will be yours if you only have faith.**
> Mark 11:24

Does this mean that you will get EVERYTHING you ask for?
God gives you everything you NEED. He gives you what you need according to His will. If it is not according to His will, does not fit into His plan for you, or will break the connection between you and Him, He will not give it to you.

REMEMBER:
GOD SEES THE FULL PICTURE, WHILE YOU SEE ONLY ONE PART OF THE PUZZLE AT A TIME.

10. Heaven is not for sissies!

Have your ever seen a good sales representative who is shy to sell his company or product? If that were so, he wouldn't have been able to sell anything and wouldn't receive a salary! The poor guy has a door slammed in his face about ten times before someone is prepared to, at least, listen past his: "Good morning!" Yet he perseveres each day! He wears shirts, ties and caps with his company's logo. Even the bumper sticker on his car tells you exactly what you should buy and where you will find it!

What do you do when you represent God? Do you tell people of the wonderful peace and joy they will experience if they believe in Jesus, or do you shake your head like Peter and say: "Miss, I don't know Him!"

Do you behave like a chameleon when it comes to your religion?
Is it another "personal matter" you don't wish to discuss?

Jesus warns: **"Don't be ashamed of Me and My message among these unfaithful and sinful people! If you are, the Son of Man will be ashamed of you when He comes in the glory of His Father with the holy angels ."**

Mark 8:38

Jesus warned that those who believed in Him, would be persecuted. So Christians have, through the ages, been insulted, mocked, locked up, tortured, crucified, stoned, burnt, gassed and murdered. John the Baptist was even beheaded as a result of the wiles of a teenage girl and her mother!

WHAT WILL YOU SACRIFICE FOR JESUS? WILL YOU DIE FOR HIM?

To believe in God, means to work on it every moment of every day! You must make time for God every day!

The more you are in touch with God, the more the devil will try to entice you. The Holy Spirit living inside you is, however, much stronger than the devil. God gives you the Holy Spirit and all the gifts of the Holy Spirit, His love and His power to change your life completely and to live according to His will.

All you have to do, is ASK!

BELIEVE IT AND CHANGE YOUR LIFE TODAY – TOMORROW MAY BE TOO LATE – LIVE AS IF TODAY IS YOUR FIRST AND LAST DAY ON EARTH!

REMEMBER: WITHOUT GOD'S CONNECTING CABLE YOU WILL PLUNGE TO DEATH...!

(My thanks to Pastor James Grout who assisted with this chapter)

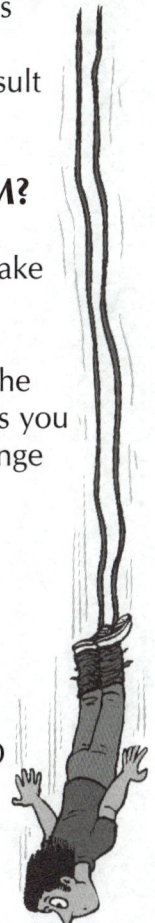

JESUS SAYS

I am the way, the truth and the life! Without me,
no one can go to the Father.

John 14:6

I know what you are doing.
I know that you are neither cold nor warm.
If only you were cold or warm!
But now, because you are lukewarm,
not warm, nor cold,
I will spit you out.

You say: "We are rich, very rich,
And we need nothing more"
and you don't realise that you are pitiful
and miserable,
poor, blind and naked.
I therefore advise you
to buy gold from Me,
gold cleansed by fire,
so that you may be rich.

Be in earnest and become reborn.
Look, I stand at the door and I knock.
If someone hears my voice, open,
so that I may enter
and enjoy the feast with him
and he with Me.
Everyone who obtains the victory
will sit with Me on the throne,
as I obtained the victory
to sit with my Father on his throne.

Revelations 3:15-17; 20-21

3 Who am I?

How well do you know yourself? Is your life happy and balanced or merely a wild goose chase? If you wish to use this book to improve yourself, it is important that you first determine exactly who and what you are. Interesting questionnaires will assist you to discover aspects about yourself which you have possibly never thought about!
Go ahead – fill it in and re-discover yourself!

1. Who am I?

- Have you ever wondered what kind of person you really are?
- When you listen to your best friend, you are very "cool". However, when you listen to the school bully, you are stupid, slow-witted and ugly!
- When you listen to your father, you are the naughtiest child in the world. Yet, when he tells his friends about your achievements, it sounds as if you are straight from heaven!
- If you listen to your mother, you are probably completely confused. One moment you're the baby she wants to kiss and cuddle and the next you are "grown enough" to study, clean house and do your own washing!
- Because you still often "do what you don't want to do" and "do things which you hate", it is very easy to become extremely confused about yourself.

It is, however, very important that you know exactly who and what you are so that others also know where they stand with you. If your body, soul and spirit are constantly at war and you continuously have to act the way others expect you to do, you may encounter serious psychological problems later in life. Stress can make you very ill and if there's battle raging in your head all day long, you may soon find yourself in hospital!

The way in which you let your body, soul and spirit co-operate will determine how mature you are and how successfully you can manage your life. If these three parts work against each other, you won't only battle to handle your own life, but also to study.

Do you feel like a cat in a tumble-drier when thinking of yourself? In that case, this chapter is especially for you!

In this chapter, you will have the opportunity to study your weak and strong points, how you really feel about yourself and what aspects need attention.

This chapter contains several questionnaires which you should fill in slowly and carefully. The purpose of these questionnaires is to help you understand yourself better. Think carefully about each statement and then mark your choice. Don't try to fill in all the questionnaires in one go! Read the questions in each section, think about them for a while and then answer.

Read all the instructions through thoroughly and fill in only that which is required from you.

2. How do I and others see me?

There are five ways by which others and you think of yourself:

Five ways by which others and you think of yourself	
Self image	The person as you see yourself. (You may think you're cool and in control of yourself and others)
Self expectation	The person you would like to be. (You would like to be the hero whom everyone likes)
Self revelation	The person you are by what you do and say. (You actually behave like a bully, insult others and gossip about everybody)
Social self	The person as others see you. (Many think you are cruel, selfish and a real devil)
Social expectation	The person others expect you to be. (Your parents want to be proud of you and think you are an angel)

Processed from: Cilliers, Coetzee and De Klerk: *EK EN EK*

Is your SELF five different people?

That would make you very confused about yourself! Many people never really know themselves, because they keep acting the way they think others expect them to. The irony is that others won't expect anything of you which you haven't shown them in the first place!

Your friends probably expect you to know a few swear words, since you often use them. Your minister, however, believes you don't know a single swear word, as he has never heard you swear.

If you are serious about getting to know yourself, it is important that you are honest with yourself and with others on who and what you really are. Let your words and deeds agree and allow people to get to know you as you really are. The advantage in this is that others will then stop expecting you to be what you are not prepared to be or incapable of being.

We all have good and bad points. Some can be changed, others not. Would it really help you to walk around with a sour face all day long, simply because you are too short or too tall? Observe yourself in the mirror again. Look for the good things and concentrate on those. You look much better with a smile than without!

Decide who and what you would really like to be and act accordingly. You cannot continuously tell little white lies and be honest at the same time. If you want to be friendly, you cannot constantly offend others.

Remember that people cannot see how you feel, but they can see how you act. If you scream at your friends because you feel hurt, they merely see someone who is screaming and not someone who is hurting. Be honest with others about your feelings.

IMPORTANT:

- **BE THE SAME TO EVERYBODY!**
- **SHOW OTHERS WHO YOU REALLY ARE.**
- **SHOW PEOPLE HOW YOU REALLY FEEL.**
- **WITH HYPOCRISY AND COWARDICE YOU ARE BLUFFING NOBODY BUT YOURSELF.**
- **ADMIT YOUR WEAK POINTS AND FAULTS AND DO SOMETHING ABOUT THEM.**
- **"DO UNTO OTHERS AS YOU WOULD HAVE THEM DO UNTO YOU."**

REMEMBER:
☞ **YOU ARE SPECIAL BECAUSE GOD DOES NOT CREATE RUBBISH!**

3. Are you lost?

What would happen if you got lost in a city? You would have to ask the way or look at a map to find out how to reach your destination.

However, if you don't know where you are **at that moment**, you won't know which route to follow on the map to reach your destination.

If you don't know who you are, you won't know what to do, either, to become the person you would like to be.
If you know what is wrong, you will know what to change!

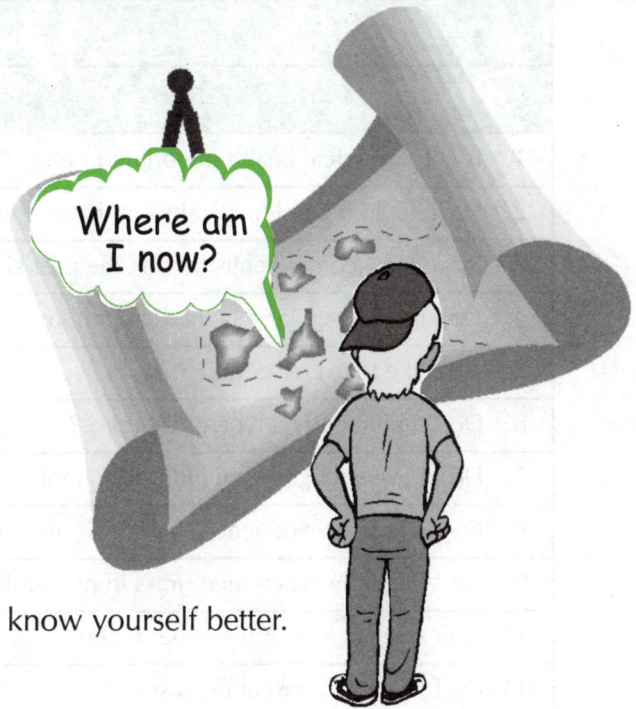

The following questionnaire will help you to get to know yourself better.

Where am I now?

INSTRUCTIONS:

1. *ANSWER YOUR QUESTIONS IN PENCIL.*

2. *Read each question carefully.*

3. *Decide how you feel about it.*

4. *Be completely honest with your answer.*

5. *Mark YES or NO with a cross.*

6. *Don't fill the third column in yet. You are going to do that with the chapter on goals.*

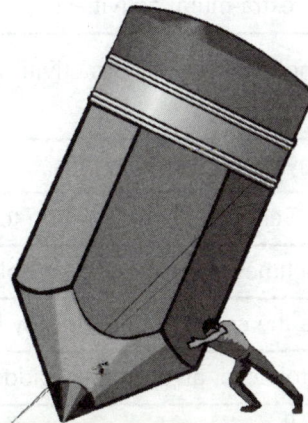

Important: *This questionnaire deals with what you think.*

Don't ask your parents or friends, but rather write down how you feel about the question.

1. MY HEALTH			
QUESTION	YES	NO	+ or −
1. Is good physical health important to me?			
2. Have I had a good medical examination during the past year?			
3. Have I visited my dentist during the past six months?			
4. Do I have a regular, planned programme for exercise and sport?			
5. Do I like to exercise?			
6. Do I do the correct type of exercises?			
7. Do I have enough energy for my school work and other activities?			
8. Do I regularly experience stress with my school work?			
9. Do I regularly experience stress in my family?			
10. Do I sleep at least 8 hours per night?			
11. Do I skip meals or eat too fast ?			
12. Have I been absent for more than three days during the past year?			
13. Am I usually the spectator while relaxing?			
14. Do I plan extra-mural activities?			
15. Are my holidays so full of activities that I am tired when school starts again?			
16. Do I always eat balanced meals?			
17. Do I know enough about nutrition to make healthy choices about food?			
18. Do I sometimes overeat or do I nibble between meals?			
19. Do I have the correct weight for my height, age and bone structure?			
20. Do I use tobacco, alcohol or forbidden substances?			
21. Am I usually calm and in control of my emotions?			
22. Do I often lose my temper?			
23. Am I often depressive for more than a few hours at a time?			
24. Do I worry too much?			

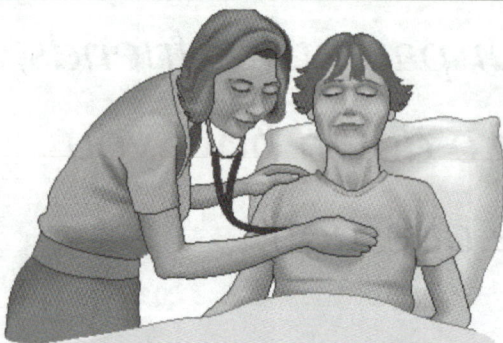

2. MY SOCIAL LIFE			
QUESTION	YES	NO	+ or –
1 Do I like people?			
2 Am I a friendly person?			
3 Am I friendly with certain people only?			
4 Am I a good listener?			
5 Do I have a good sense of humour?			
6 Do I often laugh at people instead of with them?			
7 Can I laugh at myself?			
8 Are rules and good manners important to me?			
9 Do I consider other people's feelings?			
10 Do I always keep appointments I have made?			
11 Am I always on time for appointments I have made?			
12 Do I take the initiative to introduce myself to strangers?			
13 Do I greet everybody when walking into a room?			
14 Am I good company?			
15 Do I like entertaining my friends?			
16 Do I have many friends?			
17 Do I have different types of friends for the different areas in my life?			
18 Am I basically the same person with each group of friends?			
19 Do I learn from my friends?			
20 Do I contribute in any way to enrich the lives of my friends?			
21 Do I have a special group of friends with whom I can share my personal thoughts or problems with, in confidence?			
22 Do I often feel uneasy or am I unsure as to how to behave myself in social situations?			
23 Do I remember people's names when I meet them?			
24 Do I easily communicate with people regardless of whether I know them or not?			
25 Do I give more attention to popular and important people than the others?			
26 Do I like to gossip?			
27 Do I have a regular schedule for social activities?			

MY SOCIAL LIFE (continued)			
28. Do I take part in any activity offered by the community in which I live?			
29. Am I normally positive about my own choices?			
30. Am I normally positive about the community in which I live?			
31. Am I usually positive about the country in which I live?			
32. Do I judge people according to their colour, sex, background or appearance?			
33. Do I consciously attempt to make a contribution to the lives of others?			
34. Am I selfish?			
35. Do I like to boast?			

3. MY INTELLECT

QUESTION	YES	NO	+ or −
1. Is my intelligence level above average?			
2. Is my intelligence level average?			
3. Is my intelligence below average?			
4. Am I a fast learner?			
5. Do I learn at an average speed?			
6. Am I a slow learner?			
7. Do I read fast?			
8. Do I read at average speed?			
9. Do I read slowly?			
10. Is it important to me to complete my school education?			
11. Is it important to me to study further after finishing school?			
12. Do I do well at school?			
13. Do I really do my best in my school work?			
14. Do I know which career or direction I want to follow one day?			
15. Do I regularly read newspapers and magazines?			
16. Should I know more about life than I do now?			
17. Would I like to know more?			
18. Am I shy because I know so little?			
19. Am I inquisitive enough to find out more about life?			
20. Do I like hobbies, culture or handwork?			
21. Can I use my imagination to determine what the relationship is between the things now happening in my life and the consequences thereof?			
22. Can I use my imagination to reach my goals?			
23. Can I use my imagination to help others?			
24. Are my thoughts normally positive and uplifting?			
25. Are my deeds normally positive and uplifting?			

4. MY SPIRITUAL LIFE

QUESTION	YES	NO	+ or −
1. Do I have a responsibility towards the welfare of other people?			
2. Do I like to help people less fortunate than I am?			
3. Am I, in any way, responsible for the actions of others?			
4. Do I consciously attempt to make a difference in my community?			
5. Do I regard honesty and integrity as true standards for my behaviour?			
6. Is it possible to, always, be honest?			
7. Do I have any values according to which I live?			
8. Do I have any rules according to which I live?			
9. Do I have values on issues such as alcohol, gambling, sexual behaviour, drug abuse, smoking, etc?			
10. Do I feel compelled to use my talents and skills?			
11. Do I use my talents and skills to the best of my ability?			
12. Would I be happier and more successful were I to use more of my talents?			
13. Is there a purpose to my life?			
14. Do I believe in a personal God?			
15. Do I regard myself as a religious person?			
16. Does my faith influence the decisions I make on a daily basis?			
17. Does my faith influence the things I do every day?			
18. Do I believe in prayer?			
19. Do I pray as often as I should?			
20. Would my life be better if I gave more attention to the spiritual part of my life?			
21. Am I a member of a church or congregation?			
22. Do I live according to the religious convictions and standard of this group?			
23. Do I support this group with my time and money?			
24. Am I able to discuss my religion and standards without becoming aggressive and defensive?			
25. Do my words and deeds match my religious convictions?			

5. MY MONEY MATTERS

QUESTION	YES	NO	+ or –
1. Do I give enough attention to the development of my knowledge of financial matters?			
2. Do I regularly receive pocket money?			
3. Do I regard myself as "adult" in handling financial matters?			
4. Do I buy something only because my friends have it?			
5. Am I jealous of others who have more money and possessions than I have?			
6. Do I often buy on the spur of the moment?			
7. Do I spend my money on important things?			
8. Do I spend more money than I receive?			
9. Is my pocket money spent long before the end of the month?			
10. Do I regularly have to borrow or ask for extra money after having spent my pocket money?			
11. Do I work according to a budget which I compile on a monthly basis?			
12. Do my parents and I often fight over money?			
13. Do I save some money each month?			
14. Has the amount of pocket money I receive increased over the last two years?			
15. Am I willing to do extra work for extra pocket money?			
16. Do I really know how bank statements, interest, inflation and debt work?			
17. Do I regard money as the most important indication that somebody's life is successful?			
18. Do I regard money as a way in which important goals can be achieved?			
19. Do I really deserve the amount of pocket money or money I receive?			
20. Can I earn extra money on my own?			
21. Would I like to take care of myself one day?			
22. Has provision been made for my studies in case I would like to study further after school?			
23. Do I know of anyone who can help me to handle and understand money matters better?			

6. MY FAMILY			
QUESTION	**YES**	**NO**	**+ or –**
1. Is my family very important to me?			
2. Do my actions show how important this family is to me?			
3. Do I spend as much time with my family as I would like to?			
4. Do I plan the time I am going to spend with my family, in advance?			
5. Do I regularly spend time with each member of my family?			
6. Do I have a good relationship with each member of my family?			
7. Am I interested in the personal problems and decisions of each member of my family?			
8. Are every member of the family's problems and decisions discussed?			
9. Do I listen to my father or mother's advice?			
10. Do I discuss my emotions with my parents?			
11. Do I act nastily on purpose to hurt members of my family?			
12. Do I stick to "house rules"?			
13. Do I give my parents time to be alone?			
14. Am I often disobedient?			
15. Do I help with chores and responsibilities if requested to do so?			
16. Do I help with chores and responsibilities even when not asked to?			
17. Do I apologise when I am wrong?			
18. Do others respect my privacy?			
19. Do I make time for myself?			

7. MY BELOVED			
QUESTION	YES	NO	+ or −
1. Do I have any idea as to what kind of husband or wife I would like one day?			
2. Do I spend time with people from whom I will be able to choose that person?			
3. Do I have to change or enlarge my circle of friends to meet the right sort of person?			
4. Can I change my habits and behaviour to consider others?			
5. Do I care about my beloved's needs and emotions?			
6. Can I communicate well with my beloved?			
7. Do I like being with him or her?			
8. Can I sometimes change my own plans to accommodate his or her plans?			
9. Can I receive and give love?			
10. Can I have a conversation with him or her?			
11. Do I have enough respect for myself that others will respect me as well?			
12. Do I like myself enough for others to like me as well?			
13. Do I have enough interests for others to be interested in me?			
14. Do I have other friends and interests other than those I share with my beloved?			
15. Do I feel neglected and sorry for myself when I am alone?			
16. Do I often have to do something I don't like or don't want to do?			
17. Does the relationship make me happy?			
18. Do I really relax when I'm with this person?			
19. Can I lead a full, happy life without being seriously involved with someone?			
20. Do I know enough about drugs, alcohol, transmittable diseases and pregnancies to make responsible choices?			
21. Can I forgive and forget?			

Processed from: *The Dynamics of Personal Motivation*

NOW USE THE FOLLOWING QUESTIONNAIRE TO FIND OUT HOW YOU REALLY FEEL ABOUT YOUR SCHOOLWORK AND HOMEWORK …

8. MY SCHOOLWORK			
QUESTION	YES	NO	+ or −
1. Do you like school?			
2. Do you like all your subjects?			
3. Do you normally understand the work being dealt with?			
4. Do you normally understand the work you have to learn?			
5. Do you easily master mathematical subjects?			
6. Do you easily master factual subjects such as History?			
7. Do you usually ask a teacher for help when you don't understand the work?			
8. Do you easily concentrate in class or do your thoughts wander?			
9. Are your thoughts easily distracted by children who pester you?			
10. Do you pester other children while they are trying to concentrate?			
11. Do you take special notes in class while the teacher explains the work?			
12. Are you constantly writing little notes or drawing pictures while the teacher is explaining the work?			
13. Is your satchel packed before you leave for school?			
14. Do you do homework every day?			
15. Do you do only the homework expected of you?			
16. Do you do extra work to ensure that you will keep up with work being handled in class?			
17. Do you make summaries of the work handled in class that day?			
18. Do you sometimes lie about the amount of homework you have?			
19. Do you start revising for exams in time?			
20. Do you revise according to a set timetable?			
21. Do you start revising for tests in time?			
22. Do you read faster than most of your friends?			
23. Do you read slower than most of your friends?			
24. Do you spell better than most of your friends?			
25. Do you spell worse than most of your friends?			
26. Do you go to any trouble to improve your spelling?			
27. Do you battle to remember work you have learnt?			
28. Are you scared to write tests?			

8. MY SCHOOLWORK (continued)			
29. Are you scared to write exams?			
30. Do oral tests make you nervous?			
31. Does anyone help you with your homework?			
32. Does anyone sometimes do your homework or tasks on your behalf?			
33. Do you have other problems which prevent you from giving attention to your schoolwork?			
34. Is there anyone you can discuss your personal problems with?			
35. Are you brave enough to seek help when you experience problems?			
36. Are you doing better or worse than you are capable of?			
37. Do you always do your best?			
38. Is your work neat enough to proudly show it to others?			

Fill in the last questionnaire now and find out how many positive things you can write down…

4. *Positive things about myself*

Fill in the following questionnaire very honestly.

5 Things I can do very well	
Answer	Reason
1	
2	
3	
4	
5	

5 Things which make me happy	
Answer	Reason
1	
2	
3	
4	
5	

5 People I admire	
Answer	Reason
1	
2	
3	
4	
5	

5 Wonderful friends	
Answer	Reason
1	
2	
3	
4	
5	

5 Things life has taught me	
Answer	Reason
1	
2	
3	
4	
5	

5 Problems in my life I would like to solve	
Answer	Reason
1	
2	
3	
4	
5	

5 Goals I would like to achieve	
Answer	Reason
1	
2	
3	
4	
5	

5 Good characteristics I possess	
Answer	Reason
1	
2	
3	
4	
5	

You will never really get to know yourself completely. This questionnaire is merely a start to help you to get to know yourself better …

5. Why is it important to know myself?

- ✓ It helps you to make decisions
- ✓ It helps you to accept yourself
- ✓ It gives you more self-confidence
- ✓ It helps you to deal with criticism
- ✓ It helps you to take responsibility for your own life
- ✓ It helps you to grow and develop as a person

6. How can I improve my self image?

SELF ACCEPTANCE

ENTHUSIASM

LIVE FULLY

FORGIVE AND FORGET

IMPROVE YOUR GOOD POINTS

MORE HONESTY

ADMIT YOUR MISTAKES

GIGGLE AT YOURSELF

EMPOWER YOURSELF

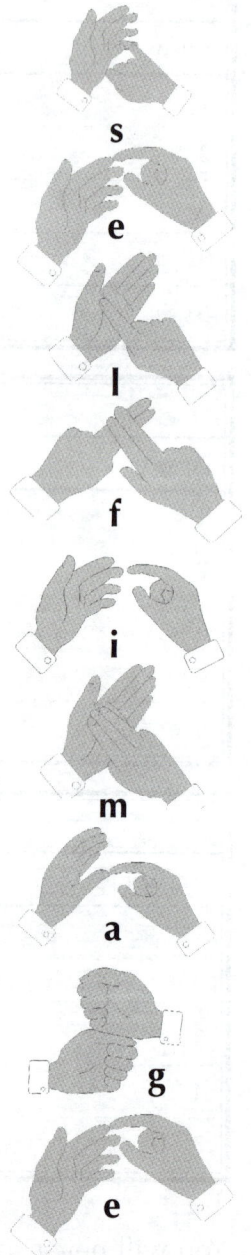

From: *Leierskap*: A. Nortjé

7. *Your life cycle*

Your life consists of various parts:

✳ Yourself (what you believe, what you do and how you feel)

✳ Your family

✳ Your friends

✳ Your health and leisure

✳ Your pocket money and possessions

✳ Your school

✳ Your homework

✳ Your sport

✳ Your religion

Certain things you give attention to because you like it.

Certain things you give less attention to because you don't have enough time.

Other things receive no attention because you don't like it or are not interested in it.

After you have completed the various questionnaires, you should have a good idea as to how important or unimportant certain areas of your life are to you.

The following page contains a wheel. This wheel consists of different parts illustrating the different parts of your life.

Let us look at your **"Life Cycle"**.

Keep in mind: there are no correct or wrong answers.
There is only honesty.
There is only how things really are.

See how many marks each part of your life deserves and then colour it in from the central point to the correct number.

Give each part of your life a different colour.

Colour in how you feel about each of these sections of your life.

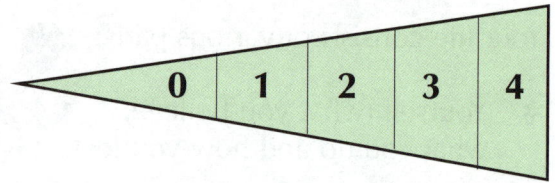

| | 0 | 1 | 2 | 3 | 4 |

4	=	**I give a lot of attention to it**
3	=	**I give attention to it**
2	=	**I give little attention to it**
1	=	**I give no attention to it, but I would like to**
0	=	**I am not interested in this**

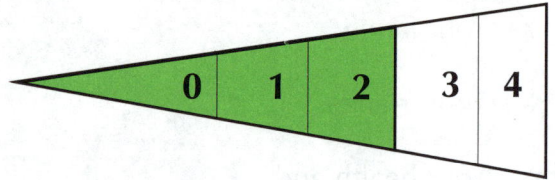

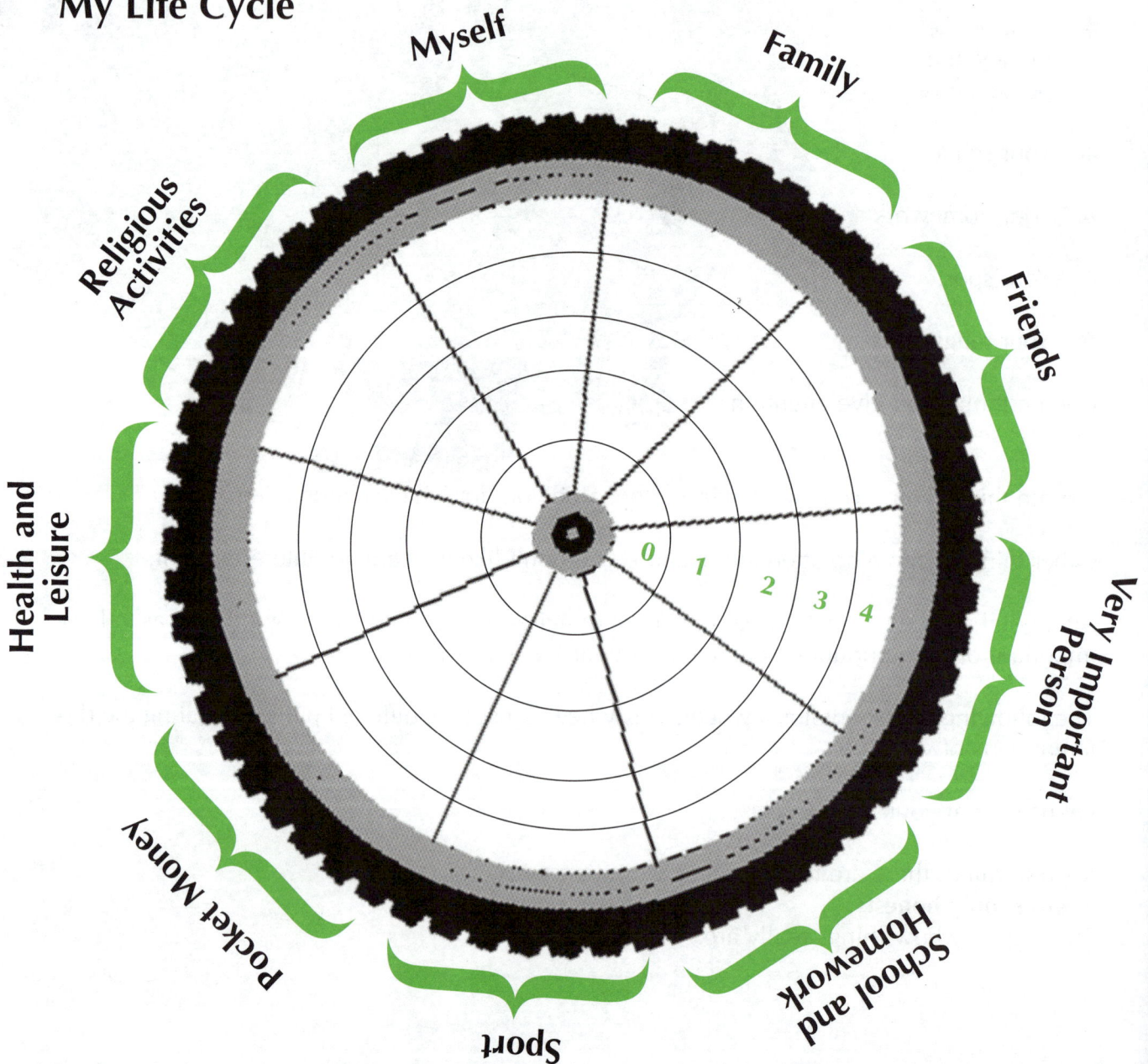

| | 0 | 1 | 2 | 3 | 4 |

My Life Cycle

8. *Is your life balanced?*

What does your coloured wheel resemble?

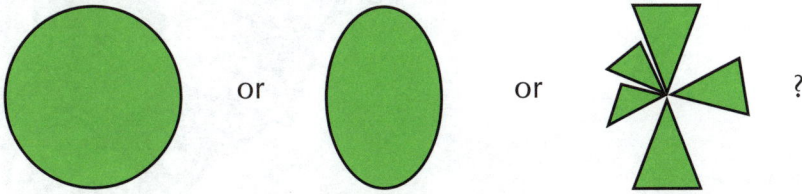

   or   or   ?

_____

Which sort of wheel would be best to make a bike ride?

In the same way in which a bike cannot ride with skew, uneven or flat tyres, you can never really be happy if your life contains no **balance**. It is important to have balance in your life and to give all aspects of your life the same amount of attention.

If you hang out with your friends all day and don't study, chances are that you will not make a success of your studies. If, however, you spend all day behind your books and have no friends, you will be very lonely and find it impossible to enjoy life!

Perhaps all the parts of the wheel are not important to you at this stage, but by all means keep this "Life Cycle" in mind for future reference.

If your life cycle is skew and unbalanced, you will easily encounter problems which could derail your Life Cycle…

REMEMBER:

✴ **Just as a balanced diet is important to keep your body healthy, a balanced lifestyle is important to keep your soul healthy!**

OBTAIN BALANCE!

What is Life?

Life is a challenge
Accept it
Life is a gift
Take it

Life is an adventure
Risk it
Life is sorrow
Overcome it

Life is a tragedy
Face it
Life is a duty
Execute it

Life is an opportunity
Grasp it
Life is a journey
Complete it

Life is a promise
Fulfil it
Life is love
Enjoy it

Life is a struggle
Attempt it
Life is a puzzle
Solve it!

From: Gedagtes oor Sukses

4 Get to know your brain

It is extremely important to know how your brain is formed and how it functions, if you wish to absorb information, process it, store it and relate it. This chapter gives important information which will make you understand how your brain absorbs information, processes it and stores it. The way in which you think, does not only determine your self image, but also your ability to strive toward goals and to study.

1. Facts about your brain

DID YOU KNOW?

➡ The human brain, which weighs approximately 1,450 gram and is the size of your two fists with the thumbs placed together, is regarded as the most complex machine in the world.

➡ The brain is organised in almost the same way as a well organised army or government. Each level of the brain receives instructions from a higher level and each unit on each level executes its own functions. When a crisis arises, the higher level takes over control.

➡ The latest research calculates that the average person uses only 0,1% to 5% of his brain, as his higher intelligence is often applied incorrectly. The brain can attain wonderful results if our teaching methods are in line with the natural way in which our brain operates.

➡ By the time a *baby* is 6 months old, he has 10 to 100 trillion neurons – as many as the stars in the Milky Way.

➡ The *adult brain* contains 10 to 15 billion neurons which have thousands of connections with other brain cells. There are approximately 60 000 km of nerve fibres in the brain. All the complicated telephonic systems in the world are equal to a part of your brain the size of a pea.

➡ Each neuron can handle 5000 messages per minute more than the average secretary in five years!

➡ Eight active brains can generate enough electricity to operate a large television set!

(Processed from: *Ontgin jou brein* by Dawie Fourie

This information won't make much sense if you don't know how your brain is formed and how it works, but once you understand how the brain functions, these facts will make you think twice about what it is possible for you to achieve …!

2. How is your brain formed?

All babies are born with a certain number of brain cells or neurons.

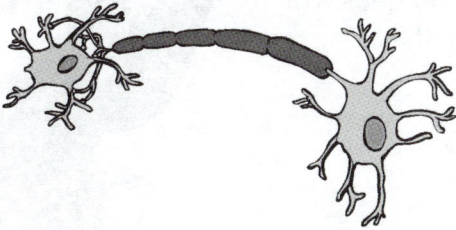

At birth, these brain cells or neurons are reasonably loose of each other.
After birth, each of these neurons forms tentacles or dendrites which connect the neurons to each other.

The more the brain functions, the more of these tentacles or dendrites are formed.

It can be compared to a muscle in your body. The more you exercise this muscle, the stronger it becomes. The stronger this muscle becomes through exercising, the more you can do with that muscle.

The more you can give your brain to think about, the better it is able to think.

The sturdier these connections between the neurons form, the more the brain is capable of and the more the brain can do, the more connections form between the neurons. The more connections there are between the neurons, the cleverer you become. Unfortunately this process does not last forever. Just as your body stops growing at a certain stage, so will these connections between neurons also stop forming at some stage.

However, if you stop eating and doing exercises simply because you have stopped growing, you will soon become ill and die. Just like your body needs continued exercise and healthy food, your brain also needs constant exercise to maintain itself and continue to think fast and well.

Schoolwork and homework are ways in which to develop your brain. Yet, many of us battle with our schoolwork because we use incorrect study methods as well as wrong ways in which to memorise huge amounts of work. It is, therefore, extremely important that you should acquire the correct study methods to give your brain the best opportunity.

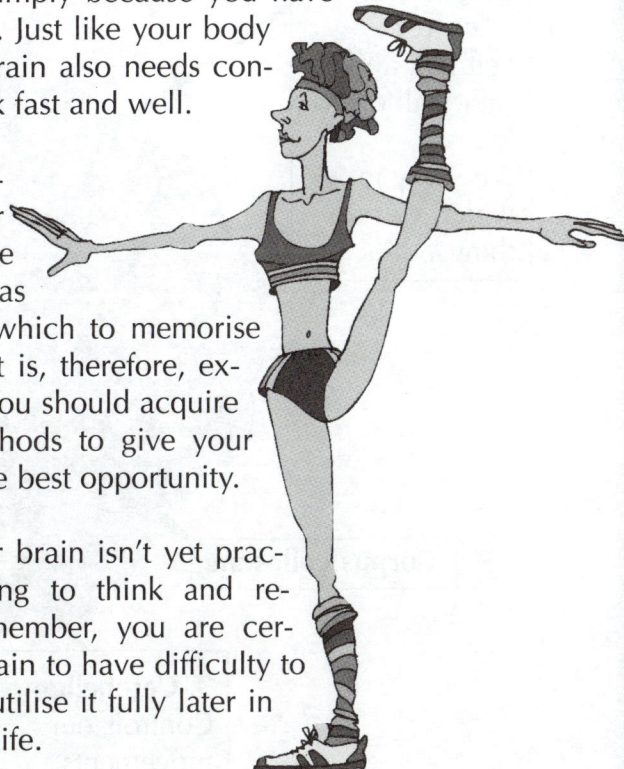

If your brain isn't yet practicing to think and remember, you are certain to have difficulty to utilise it fully later in life.

If you adopt the correct study methods and apply them, you won't only find learning easier, but will also enable your brain to assimilate information in the right manner, to process, store and relate correctly.

These study methods are based on specific techniques which are described in full in SURVIVE YOUR STUDIES.

3. How does your brain function?

Your brain consists of several parts:

1.	Cerebral cortex	–	Left brain half and right brain half.
2.	Limbic system	–	Automatic system.
3.	Cerebellum	–	Controls movement.
4.	Brain stem	–	Reticular activating system

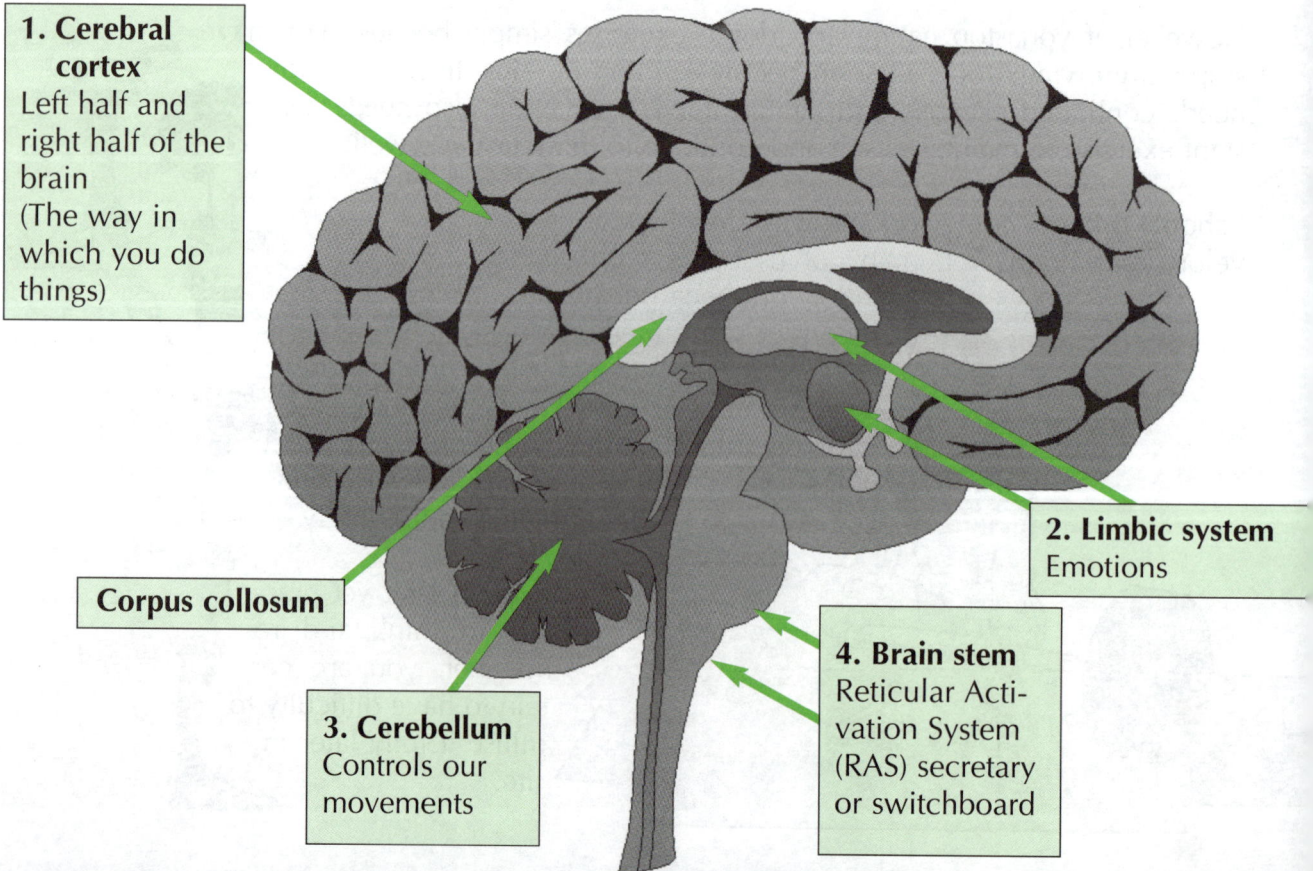

1. Cerebral cortex
Left half and right half of the brain
(The way in which you do things)

2. Limbic system
Emotions

Corpus collosum

4. Brain stem
Reticular Activation System (RAS) secretary or switchboard

3. Cerebellum
Controls our movements

a) How does information reach the brain?

All information going to the brain, comes from your senses.
Example
- You see an apple
- You touch the apple
- You smell the apple
- You bite and taste the apple
- You hear the apple crunching between your teeth

When your senses see, feel, smell, taste and hear the apple crunch,
the nerve cells in your body take this information to the brain.

The brain receives the information and now has to process it.

When information such as: **"I see a round, red object that looks edible"** is sent to the brain,
it first goes to the rear of one of the brain halves.

This information now becomes an electro-chemical impulse.
At this stage, however, your brain cannot do much with the information.

APPLE!

b) How does your brain process the information?

The electro-chemical impulse (information about the apple you saw) is now sent to the front
half of the brain, where all the knowledge you have already accumulated, is stored. (like in a
computer) This part is called the Association area.

This is where the information which your brain has just received, is compared to any suitable
information, as well as words which can describe it.
You saw an apple and you know the word apple = "It fits! I am seeing an APPLE!"
The left side of your brain processes information, changes experiences into words and helps
you to understand information.

After your have recognised the red, round, edible, healthy thing as an apple, the information goes to the opposite rear brain where it is stored as an anagram or pattern.
Now that the information has been recognised and stored, messages are sent to other parts of the brain to react to it.

You bring the apple to your mouth, close your mouth and bite the apple. Hear how the apple crunches between your teeth!

As you see more and more apples in your life, touch them, smell them, hear them crunch between your teeth and taste them, your brain will find it easier and easier to recognise them as "apples"!

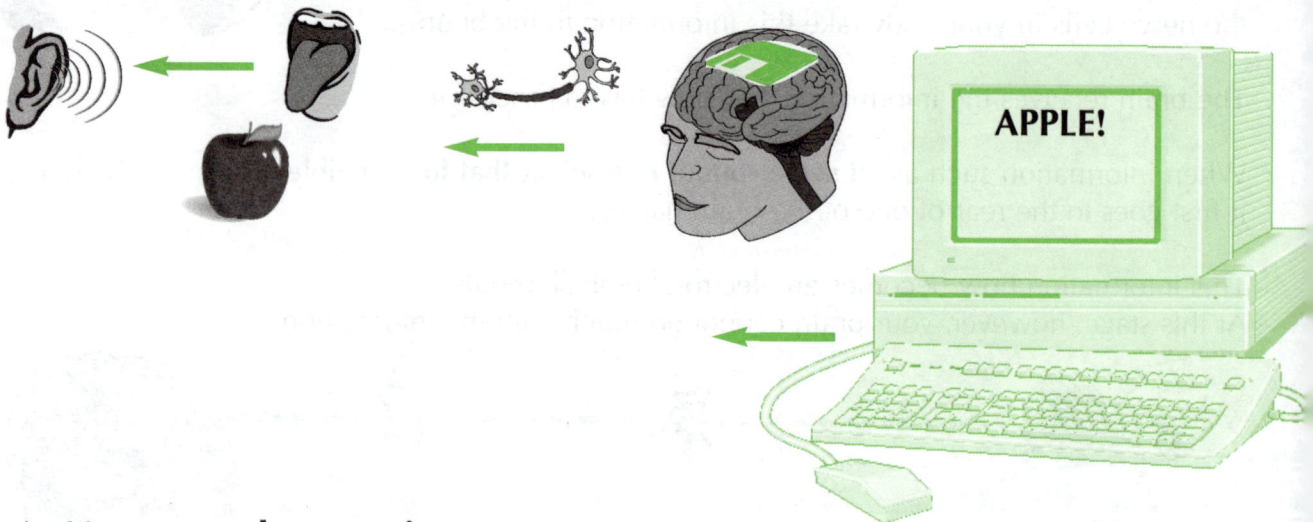

c)   Neurons and connections

Neurons play an important role in conducting information, because the information from one point of one neuron is conducted to the next neuron's point, by way of chemical substances that your brain discharges and sprays from one neuron to the other. If your brain does not discharge these substances, the information is blocked instead of being conducted.

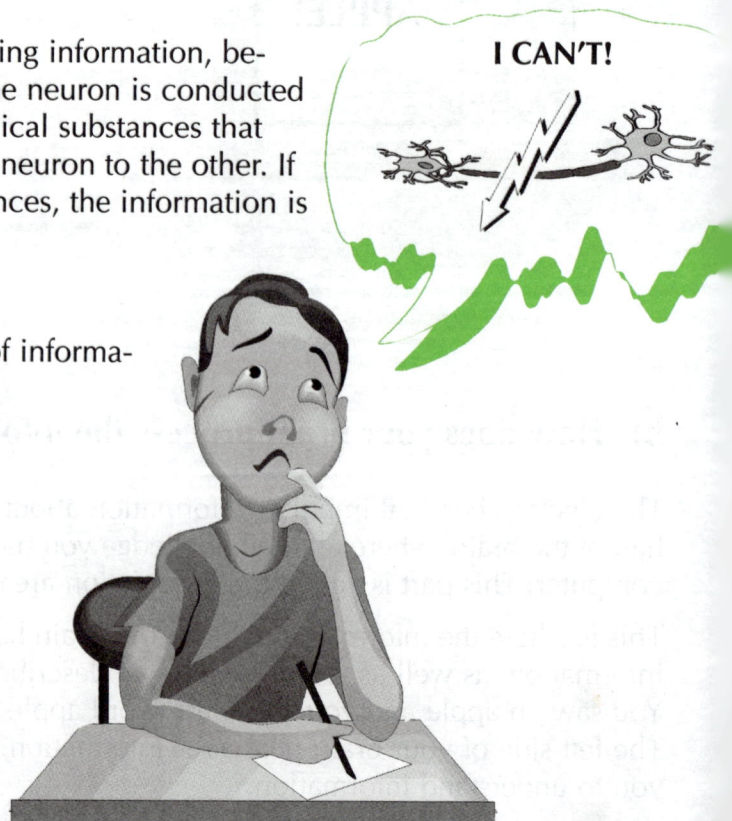

Several factors may block the conducting of information by neurons, e.g.

● stress

● lack of certain nutritional substances.

● illnesses

● drugs and addictive substances

● negative thoughts

● lack of concentration.

If you, therefore:

- are stressed or worried
- eat the wrong food
- are sick
- use drugs or addictive substances
- have negative thoughts (e.g. I can't do it!)
- concentrate on something else,

your brain will not be able to conduct the chemical substances to make those connections required to transmit the information.

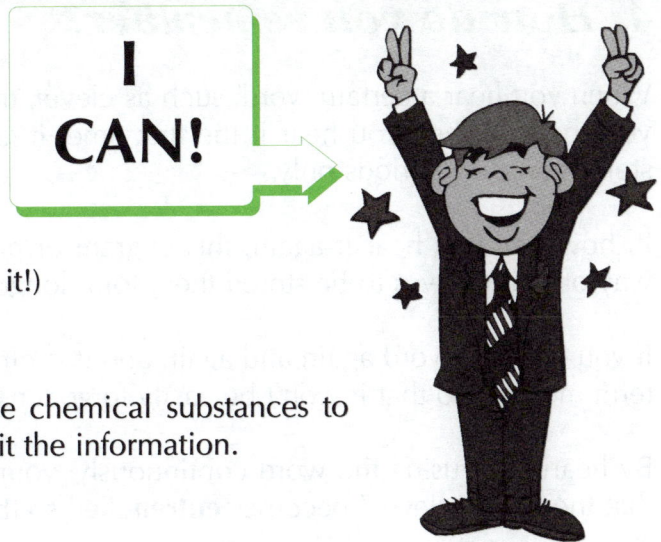

d) Millions of messages at a time!

A good manager of a company usually has a good secretary! If the secretary does her work, she will see to it that the manager has enough time to give all his attention to important matters.
She will see to it that he receives the most important information and visitors.
She will keep away those people hampering him when he is busy. In the corporate world she is often referred to as the "GATEKEEPER".

If the secretary does not do her work properly the manager won't be able to do his work properly either.
If the manager is hampered by petty matters when he should be doing important work, his business will suffer and deteriorate.

Your brain also needs a "secretary or a "gatekeeper". It is a part which is situated at the rear of the brain.
We call it the **RETICULAR ACTIVATION SYSTEM** or **RAS**.

Every day and every second your brain receives thousands and thousands of messages via your senses. You see, hear, smell, and taste all day long. If your brain had to process all this information you would soon lose your mind and not know what to do!
To prevent this , the Reticular Activation System sees to it that only those matters which are important to you are let through. We then speak of

- information which is necessary
- information which is not necessary.

**IMPORTANT:
YOU ARE THE MANAGER OF YOUR BRAIN. YOU HAVE TO TELL YOUR SECRETARY WHAT IS IMPORTANT. HE OR SHE WILL THEN SELECT THIS INFORMATION AND OPPORTUNITIES FOR YOU!**

4. How do you remember?

When you hear a certain word, such as clever, this word form forms an engram or pattern in your brain. When you hear it the first time, it goes to your **short term memory** where it is stored for short periods only.

If, however, you hear it again, this engram or pattern is sent to your **long term memory** by way of brain waves to be stored there for a longer period of time.

If you hear the word again and again and it is often repeated, it becomes rooted in your long term memory so that it won't be easily forgotten.

By hearing or using the word continuously, your brain forms a **protein residue** that ensures that the word "clever" becomes **entrenched** so that you won't forget it.

Your sub-conscious mind also helps you to further **strengthen** this word by making you believe that the word is important to remember.

Let us see how it works ...

1)   YOU SEE OR HEAR SOMETHING.
2)   IT GOES TO YOUR MIND WHERE IT IS PROCESSED.
3)   BY WAY OF REPETITION IT GOES TO YOUR SUB-CONSCIOUS MIND WHERE IT IS ENTRENCHED.
4)   YOUR CREATIVE SUB-CONSCIOUS MIND STRENGTHENS THAT WHICH YOU HEAR OR SEE AND ENTRENCHES IT EVEN FURTHER IN YOUR SUB-CONSCIOUS.

EXAMPLE:

If you hear you are clever from the time that you are small, you will feel good about yourself. Soon you will believe that you are clever and you will do things which will make you even cleverer.

But:

If you hear you are naughty from the time that you are small, you will feel naughty. Soon you will believe that you are naughty and will do things that will make you even naughtier.

5. Repetition and revision

In the same way your brain stores and remembers words, images and concepts by repetition, your schoolwork is also remembered and stored by repetition. Researchers maintain that you have to repeat something at least **SIX TO TEN TIMES WITHIN 72 HOURS** before it is stored and entrenched in your long term memory. This repetition must, however, be done the right way so that your brain gets the opportunity to form the protein residue which will entrench the information.

When it comes to learning, there is, unfortunately, no other way out.

If you want to learn and remember something,
you should repeat it regularly and over a long period of time!

You should repeat it so many times that it can be moved from your short term memory to your long term memory where it can be established.

If you don't do this,

- you will learn your work and forget it the next day.
- you will become confused with information.
- you will hit a blank.
- you will become tense and remember even less.
- you can remember certain parts of your work, but not every-thing.

That is why you cannot study for a test or exam the previous day only and think that you will remember your work. If you don't re-peat your work regularly, it will not be entrenched in your long term memory and then you will forget it! You can use many clever ways in which to help your brain to remember things more easily.

REMEMBER:
YOU HAVE A BRAIN.
YOU HAVE A VERY CLEVER BRAIN.
YOU HAVEN'T EVEN USED 20% OF IT!
YOU ARE WHAT YOU BELIEVE YOURSELF TO BE ...

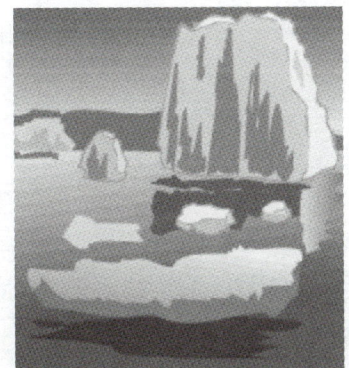

YOU SEE ONLY THE TIP OF THE ICEBERG!

Celebrate Being Alive

Celebrate being alive every day.
Live your highest aspirations;
Learn what you always wanted to learn.
Don't wait until you get hit by a truck
or acquire a terminal illness
to change the things that prevent you
from living your life to the full.
Whatever your habits,
whatever your age,
you can change …
you can learn.

Michael Gelb and Tony Buzan
Lessons from the Art of Juggling;
How to Achieve Your Full Potential in Business, Learning and Life.

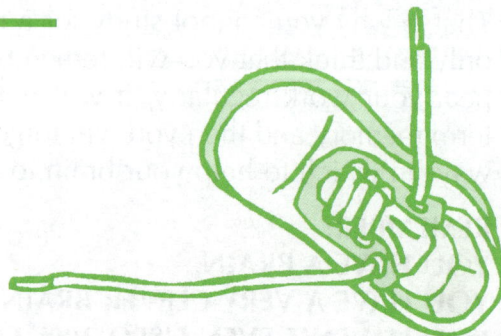

5 A whole brain!

Your brain consists of two parts which each perform specific functions. In this chapter you can find out which part of your brain is dominant. It will help you to understand why you reason and act in a specific manner. Use the information in this chapter to strengthen the other part of your brain!

1. Different parts of your brain

You have two hands – a left hand and a right hand. Which hand do you write with?

That hand is your dominant hand.
Yet, you use both hands. What would happen if one hand is bound behind your back all day long? You would battle!

Look at the picture on this page. That is what your brain looks like from above. Can you see that your brain consists of two parts?

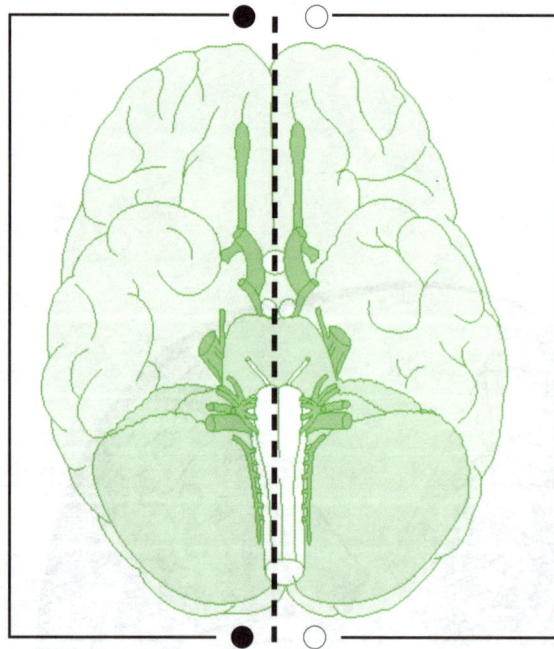

LEFT BRAIN   **RIGHT BRAIN**

Each of these parts has specific tasks to perform, yet most people use one part of their brain more than the other. In this chapter we are going to look at which part of your brain you are going to use more often and how you can learn to use the other half more often. The following questionnaire will show you which part of your brain is dominant when you learn or think.

Please answer the following questionnaire VERY HONESTLY!
REMEMBER – THERE ARE NO RIGHTS OR WRONGS!

INSTRUCTION:
Read every statement through carefully and decide which answer, A, B or C is **most** like you. Write down your answer in the last **answer column.**

2. Questionnaire: Am I "Left Brain" or "Right Brain"?

Statement	A	B	C	Answer A, B or C
1. I best remember …	names.	faces.	both names and faces.	
2. I prefer things to be explained to me …	with words.	by showing me.	in both ways.	
3. I like classes …	where I am given one task at a time.	where I can work with different tasks at the same time.	where these methods are alternated.	
4. I prefer …	multiple questions in tests.	short and long question tests.	both types of tests.	
5. I am …	not good at reading body language. I'd rather listen to what people say.	good at understanding body language.	sometimes good and sometimes not so good at understanding body language.	
6. I am …	not good at thinking of funny things to do or say.	good at thinking of funny things to say or do.	sometimes good at saying funny things.	
7. I prefer classes …	where I can listen to "experts".	where I can walk about and try various things.	where I listen but also try out things.	
8. I decide what I think about things …	by looking for facts.	in relation to my own experiences.	by considering facts and my own experiences.	
9. I solve problems …	in a serious manner.	in a playful manner.	playfully and seriously.	
10. I like …	to use the right material to do a job.	to use anything available to finish the work.	to use the right material but also try something else.	
11. I like it if my classes …	are well planned so that I know exactly what I am doing.	include possible changes as the work progresses.	are planned but also like changes.	
12. I am …	never creative.	very creative.	creative sometimes.	
13. I prefer classes where I am expected …	to learn things I'll be able to use in future.	to learn things I can use now.	to learn things for the future but also what I can use now.	

Statement	A	B	C	Answer A, B or C
14. I …	would rather **not guess** or do things by instinct.	like to **guess** and do things according to instinct.	sometimes don't guess and sometimes do things by instinct.	
15. I like to express my ideas and feelings …	in **ordinary** language.	in **poetic form, songs, dance or art.**	in ordinary language, poetic form, songs and dance.	
16. I get insight from poetry, songs, art and symbols …	very **seldom** (rarely).	**usually.**	sometimes.	
17. I prefer …	to solve **one problem at a time.**	to solve **more than one problem at a time.**	to solve one or more problems at a time.	
18. I react better toward people when …	they talk about **logical and intellectual** things.	they talk about **emotions and feelings.**	they talk about logical, intellectual and emotional things.	
19. I prefer to learn from …	those parts of the topic which have already been **well-established and researched.**	the **unclear** parts of the topic and the **hidden possibilities** not yet explored.	researched facts and unclear and hidden things not yet explored.	
20. I prefer …	**analytical** reading matter to take ideas apart and think about them separately.	**creative reading matter,** to compile a lot of ideas and group them.	both types of reading matter.	
21. I prefer to …	use **logic** to solve problems.	use my **instinct** to solve my problems.	use both logic and instinct to solve my problems.	
22. I prefer …	to analyse problems by reading **works by experts** or by listening to them.	to see things **in my imagination** when I solve problems.	to study the work of experts and use my imagination.	
23. I am very good at …	explaining things in **words.**	explaining things by **gestures, actions and movements.**	I have no preference.	
24. I learn best from teachers who …	explain with **words.**	explain with **actions and gestures.**	I understand both equally well.	
25. When I remember things or think about them, I do it best with …	**lists of words.**	**images and pictures.**	lists of words, images and pictures.	

Statement	A	B	C	Answer A, B or C
26. I prefer to …	examine things that are **complete and concluded.**	organize or complete examining things that are **not completed.**	examine complete and incomplete information.	
27. I enjoy …	**speaking and writing.**	**drawing** and the **handling** of things.	speaking, writing, drawing and handling of things.	
28. I …	easily **get lost.**	**don't** easily **get lost.**	don't easily get lost, but isn't very good either at finding my way.	
29. I am …	mainly **intellectual** (act as I think).	mainly **intuitive** (act as I feel).	both intellectual and intuitive.	
30. I prefer to …	learn **detail** and specific **facts.**	learn from **general overview** by viewing the full picture.	learn detail, facts and a general overview.	
31. I read …	to note specific **detail and facts.**	to note the **main ideas.**	to note detail, facts and main ideas.	
32. I learn and remember …	only things I **specifically** learnt.	detail and facts in the area which I have **not specifically** learnt.	I have not discovered the difference.	
33. I like to read about …	**realistic stories.**	**fiction or fantasy.**	non-fiction, fiction and fantasy.	
34. I think it's more fun to …	**plan realistically.**	**dream.**	Realistic planning, dreams and fantasy are equally enjoyable.	
35. I prefer to …	read or study when it's **dead quiet.**	listen to **music** while I study.	let music play while I read for enjoyment, but not for studying.	
36. I'd like to …	write **non-fictional** stories (factual).	write **fictional** stories.	I like writing fiction and non fiction equally.	
37. If I need counseling or advice for my spiritual health I prefer …	the **confidential conversations** of personal counseling.	**group therapy** and to share my feelings with others.	confidential counseling and group therapy help me equally.	
38. I enjoy …	the **transcription and filling in** of detail.	drawing my **own images, pictures and ideas.**	both equally.	

Statement	A	B	C	Answer A, B or C
39. It is more exciting to …	**improve** something.	**find out** something.	Both are equally exciting.	
40. I enjoy it more to …	**examine** things.	**explore** things.	I enjoy both equally.	
41. I prefer …	**algebra.**	**trigonometry.**	I enjoy both equally.	
42. I am good at …	arranging **ideas in order.**	showing the **connection between ideas.**	I enjoy both equally.	
43. I prefer …	**dogs.**	**cats.**	I like dogs and cats.	
44. I …	take time to **organize** myself and my personal activities.	**battle to organize** my personal activities within specific times.	easily plan personal activities according to planned times.	
45. I have …	practically **no mood changes.**	**frequent** changes of mood.	My moods change sometimes.	
46. I am …	almost **never bewildered.**	**often** somewhat **bewildered.**	bewildered only sometimes.	
47. I am good at …	**remembering verbal (oral) information.**	**remembering general information.**	I remember verbal and general information equally well.	
48. I am good at …	**statistical and scientific forecasts** of outcomes.	**instinctive forecasts** of outcomes.	I can forecast outcomes equally well in all manners.	
49. I prefer …	**outlines** to summaries.	**summaries** to outlines.	I use both out lines and summaries.	
50. I prefer …	**oral instructions.**	**demonstrations.**	I like oral instructions and demonstrations.	

PROCESSED FROM: McCarthy: The 4mat System: Teaching to learning Styles with Right/Left Mode Techniques

HOW DO YOU CALCULATE YOUR SCORE?

1. Count the number of A's, B's and C's and write down the totals in the following column.

A	B	C

2. Now deduct your number of **A's** from the number of **B's** and write down the answer in the following column.
The answer could be a minus or plus in number.

B MINUS A SCORE	
No. of B's	
Minus No of A's	
= Total	

3. Should your **C** score be **15 or more points**, **divide** your **B minus A score** by **3**. Round off your score to the nearest figure. The answer will be your final score.

B MINUS A ÷ 3	
B – A score	
÷ 3	
= Total	

4. Should your C score be from **9 to 14 points**, **divide** your **B minus A score** by **2**.

Round off your answer to the nearest figure to arrive at your final score.

B MINUS A ÷ 2	
B – A score	
÷ 2	
= Total	

5. Should your C score be **less than 9**, don't divide at all.
    Your **B minus A score** is then your final score.
*

6. **TAKE YOUR FINAL SCORE AND WRITE IT ON THE NUMBER LINE ON THE FOLLOWING PAGE.**
    This will give you an indication of how you think and learn.

7. **Afterwards read how people in this group think and learn and see whether you can recognise yourself.**

8.   MARK YOUR SCORE ON THE NUMBER LINE.

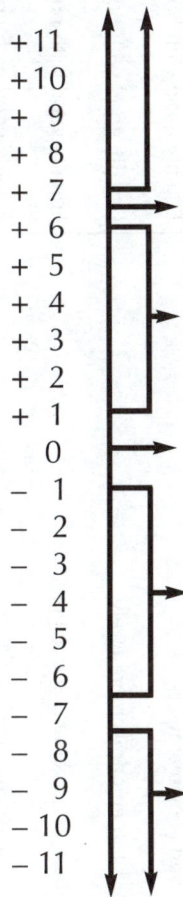

+11
+10
+ 9   RIGHT brain dominant
+ 8
+ 7
+ 6   WHOLE brain dominant,
+ 5   but right brain is stronger
+ 4
+ 3
+ 2
+ 1
  0   WHOLE brain dominant
− 1
− 2
− 3
− 4   WHOLE brain dominant,
− 5   but left brain is stronger
− 6
− 7
− 8
− 9   LEFT brain dominant
−10
−11

MY SCORE IS _____

THE GROUP INTO WHICH I FALL IS

_____

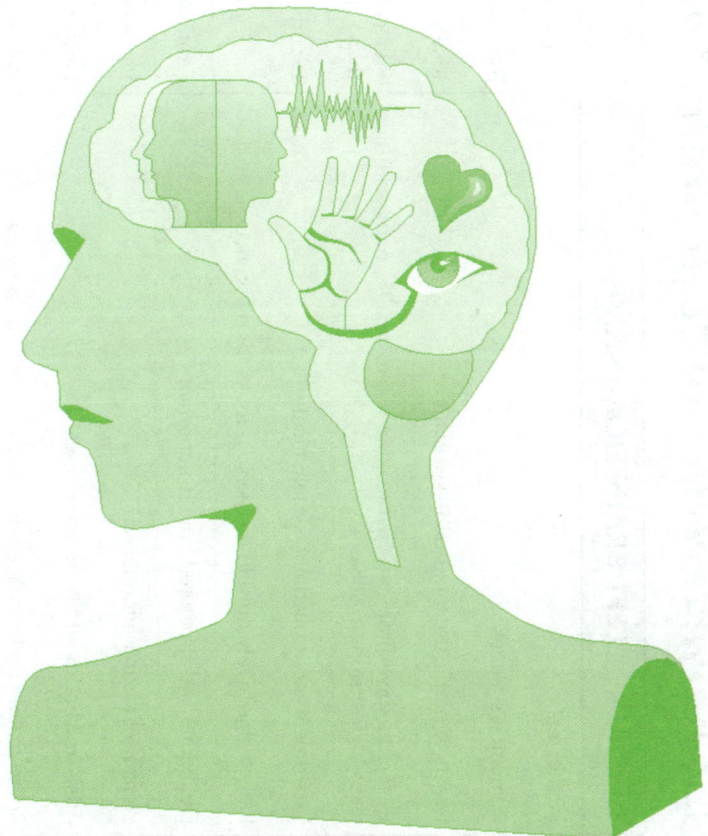

3. *Characteristics of "Left Brains" and "Right Brains"*

LEFT BRAIN DOMINANT	RIGHT BRAIN DOMINANT	WHOLE BRAIN
Intellectual	Instinctive (intuitive)	Equally good with both
Remembers names	Remembers faces	Equally good with both
Reacts to oral instructions and explanations	Reacts to demonstrated, illustrated or symbolic instructions	Equally good with both
Prefers to solve problems by breaking it into smaller parts and then takes logical steps to solve it	Prefers to solve problems by looking at the total external or form and then solves by way of patterns using instinct	Equally good with both
Experiments controlled and systematically	Experiments without calculation and less controlled	Equally good with both
Judges objectively outside the person, looks for differences	Judges subjectively from inside the person, looks for similarities	Equally good with both
Deliberate and structured time is important	Erratic and spontaneous. Time is of no importance	Equally good with both
Prefers set factual information	Prefers general, uncertain information	Equally good with both
Analyse what should be done or read	Groups or bands together that which should be done or read	Equally good with both
Relies mainly on language when thinking or remembering	Relies mainly on images when thinking or remembering	Equally good with both
Prefers speaking and writing	Prefers drawing and handling objects	Equally good with both
Prefers multiple choice questions	Prefers open questions	Equally good with both
Prefers that studies and work be thoroughly planned	Prefers not to plan studies and work thoroughly	Equally good with both
Prefers merit order of authority	Prefers partaking teamwork	Equally good with both
Controls emotions	Gives vent to emotions more freely	Equally good with both
Reacts best to what you see and hear	Reacts best to movement and actions	Equally good with both
Not good at interpreting body language	Good at interpreting body language	Equally good with both
Adapts to the neighbourhood	Lets the neighbourhood adapt to you	Equally good with both
Doesn't often use metaphors or comparisons	Often uses metaphors or comparisons	Equally good with both

LEFT BRAIN DOMINANT	RIGHT BRAIN DOMINANT	WHOLE BRAIN
Prefers logical problem solving	Prefers to solve problems instinctively	Equally good at both
Good at dealing with daily duties, but sometimes battles to see the full picture	Creative in solving problems, to plan and make decisions, but does not always complete tasks or detail	Equally good with both
Sees to it that plans, tasks and programmes are executed, but is not creative enough	Is creative, can plan fast, but is not always logical	Equally good with both
Good at seeing that things get done, but is sometimes too strict and unfeeling	Good at interpersonal relationships, but is sometimes not strict enough	Equally good with both
Is logical and rational in times of crisis, but battles to accept changes	Can motivate others, but easily changes the original programme to suit you	Equally good with both
Usually prompt and punctual	Tends to be tardy (late)	Sometimes late but usually on time

PROCESSED FROM: Mc Carthy: The 4 mat System Teaching to Learning Styles with Right/Left Mode Techniques

As you will notice, the left brain and right brain are practically opposites to each other! It's almost as if two different persons are living in your head!

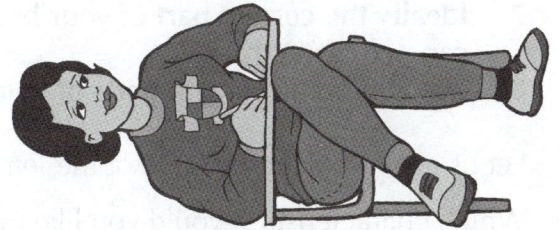

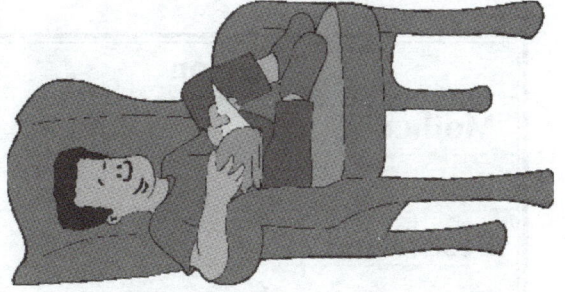

Think awhile about people you know. Which part of their brain do you think is the stronger?

Person	Which part do you think is stronger?
Mother	
Father	
Best friend	
Favourite teacher	

IMPORTANT!!

1. *We often like people who do things the way we do or would like to do.*
2. *People are often attracted to others with characteristics which they don't have themselves.*
3. *People also don't often get on with others, because their views differ!*
4. *The way in which your brain thinks will greatly determine how easily you absorb information, process it and remember it.*
5. *Once you realise people think differently, you could become more tolerant.*
6. *Keep in mind that you have another brain part, but only use it less often. By practising and concentrating on the other part, you can develop and strengthen your brain.*
7. **Ideally the correct part of your brain should take over in the right situation so that you can act correctly.**
8. **The ability to use both parts of your brain is not a talent but a skill which can be learnt.**

Let us again look at the table of the left brain and the right brain's characteristics.

Which characteristics would you like to have which don't occur in the dominant part of your brain?

Characteristics I would like to have	

4. Use both parts of your brain!

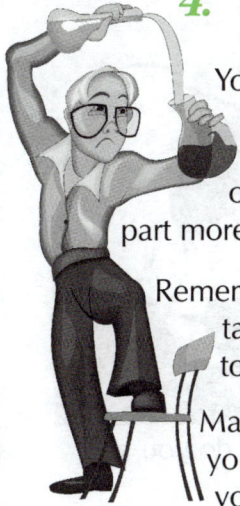

You already possess all the good characteristics you would like to have. All you have to do is exercise both parts of your brain so that you can use the good characteristics from both parts when you need them. One part of your brain is stronger because you use it more often. You use this part more easily because your brain has become used to doing things this way.

Remember that both sides of your brain contain advantages and disadvantages. Concentrate on the positive aspects of each brain half and try to cut the negative aspects!

Make a conscious effort to develop the other side of your brain. If you are completely disorganized, learn to plan and organise. Use your imagination if you're not very creative!

5. Why must I use both parts of my brain?

☺ Each part of your brain looks at the world around you in different ways. This gives balance to your life.

– Your right brain can show you the bigger picture while your left brain again notices all the finer detail.

– Your right brain helps you to plan, while the left brain sees to it that those plans are executed.

– It is your right brain which enables you to recognize a face in a crowd or identify a song after you have heard only two bars of it.

– Your left brain can break up information into smaller parts so that you can learn new things, one at a time. It also helps you to organize your life and communicate with others.

– Your right brain helps you to think of good ideas for essays, art and projects.

– Your left brain, on the other hand, helps you with the steps of a mathematical problem.

☺ Every part of your brain also controls certain functions and tasks which your body has to execute.

☺ Managers and leaders usually have the ability to use both parts of their brain.
BOTH PARTS ARE IMPORTANT!

Study the pictures on this page.

1. What do you see?

2. What do you see?

3. What do you see?

4. What do you see?

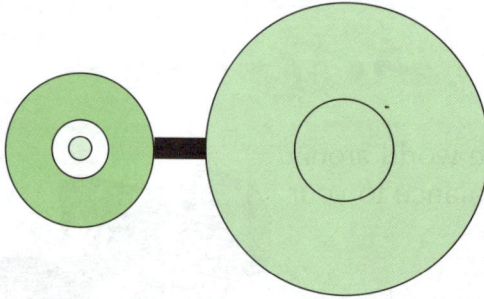

5. What do you see?

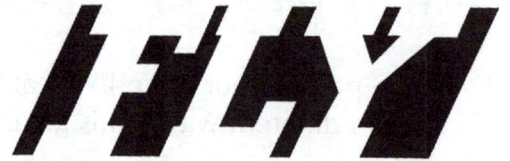

6. What do you see?

Think of all the other things you would be able to do if you could apply the other part of your brain to
- ❖ notice things you don't notice now and
- ❖ do things which you can't do now!
- ❖ understand people better.

Allow the different parts of your brain to WORK TOGETHER and not AGAINST EACH OTHER!

ANSWERS:

1. Two men – one frowning and one smiling
2. Two people and a vase
3. Two women – one young and one old
4. A man and a mouse
5. A Mexican frying an egg in a pan
6. The word "FLY"

6 The choice is yours!

One of the most important characteristics distinguishing man from animal, is the ability to make choices. The older you become the more and bigger the choices which you have to make in your life become. In this chapter you will learn which choices to make in order to survive your life!

It is my choice!

1. A world full of abundance

People who achieve success in this life, are those who notice the abundance of the world in which they live and use it! These people have realised that the world with everything in it was created to their advantage to make the most of and to use!

Have you ever come to a standstill to admire the creation around you?
- The millions of stars in the sky
- The sea, the rivers and streams
- The mountains, landscapes and deserts
- The trees, grass, shrubs and flowers
- The animals, birds and fish

By all means fill a cup with sand and try to count the grains inside. Lie on your back and try to count the stars in the sky. Look at the leaves on a tree and try to count all of them. You will soon realise the impossibility of such a venture as soon as you first start counting … We certainly live in a world of abundance!

Although it is easy to notice the abundance of sand, leaves and stars, it is almost impossible for most people to recognise their own potential and abundance.

☹   These people don't believe in their own potential, skills or talents.
☹   They don't use their endless source of power, imagination, vision, creativity or memory.
☹   They create opportunities with teaspoons instead of shovels.
☹   They expect nothing of life and therefore receive nothing in return.

NOTICE THE OPPORTUNITIES AROUND YOU!

Successful people notice their own abundance and use it! They believe that they owe the world something, not that the world owes them something!

Scientists suggest that man does not even utilise 10% of his potential in general. The rest lies like layers of gold underground, It is only once that gold is refined that it becomes of true value to us. Your talents, skills and capabilities mean nothing while they are buried deep down inside of you.

Man is the crown and ruler of creation. This abundance has been given to us! We were created to rule over it. We were created to manage and control creation. If we are, then, the rulers of this creation, it surely means that we have the **ability** to rule over it! In order to rule, you need to have the knowledge, talents and skills or have the ability to acquire it. This ability is your **potential**.

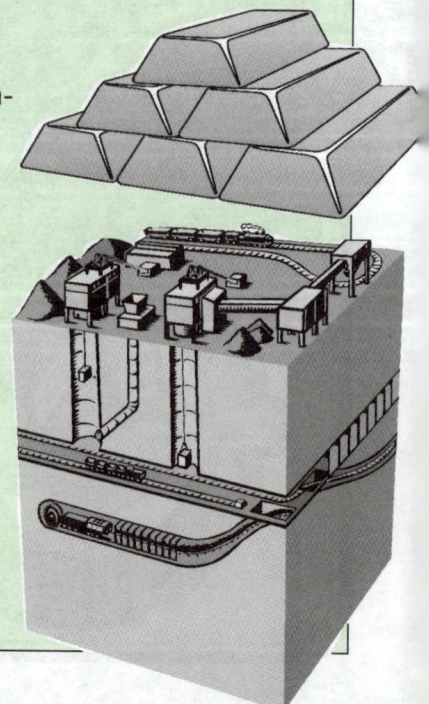

God said, "Now we will make humans and they will be like us. We will let them rule the fish, the birds and the other living creatures." So God created humans to be like Himself. He made men and women.   *Genesis 1: 26-27*

Perhaps you feel your are not clever, attractive, cute, tall, sporty or rich enough to truly achieve success. Even if you don't possess any of the above mentioned, you can still achieve success in life if only you want to.

☞ Ludwig von Beethoven composed nine symphonies by using different combinations and pitch, using eight notes only.

☞ William Shakespeare used only the 26 letters of the alphabet to write 35 dramas and several poems!

☞ Vincent Van Gogh used the three primary colours red, blue and yellow to produce some of the best paintings of all time.

☞ Lonnie Johnson designed the Super Soaker from an idea he got while in the bath one night and went on to sell 250 million of these toys!

☞ Jeff Bezos, founder of Amazon.com, started his business in his garage in 1996. Today he has 4 000 employees and 6 warehouses from which books, videos and music are being sold!

☺ These people managed it because they believe in their own potential and notice the potential and abundance around them.

☺ They manage it because they have high expectations of themselves and are not satisfied until they have given their very best.

☺ They manage it because they made the choice to use their potential.

You will never know your true potential until you have used it. How would you know whether you can swim if you never get into the water? How would you know if you can climb mountains if you never try? How would you know if you can excel at your studies if you don't really try?

REMEMBER

☞ *Believe in the abundance of life*

☞ *Believe in the abundance of your own potential*

☞ *Choose to use that potential*

☞ *Notice the opportunities around you*

☞ *Become ruler of your life*

☞ *Use the abundance which has been given to you*

☞ *You have been created in the image of God.*

2. You have a choice!

One of the most wonderful characteristics you have, is your power to choose! To exercise choices means that you have the power to decide and to choose. You have the right to choose. This is one of the most important **characteristics** which distinguishes you from an animal.

From the time of your birth until you die, you have to make choices and decisions. This ability to choose is, however, something you acquire with practice over a period of time. If you wish to play musical instruments really well, you have to practice very hard. In order to make good choices, you also have to practice to make choices. Why not start today to make your **own choices**?

BIRTH   **DEATH**

It is a **privilege** to make choices!

It is also a big **responsibility** because **every choice** you make, has **certain consequences**.

Try to fill the following in yourself: Peter has to study for the test that he has to write in a week's time.

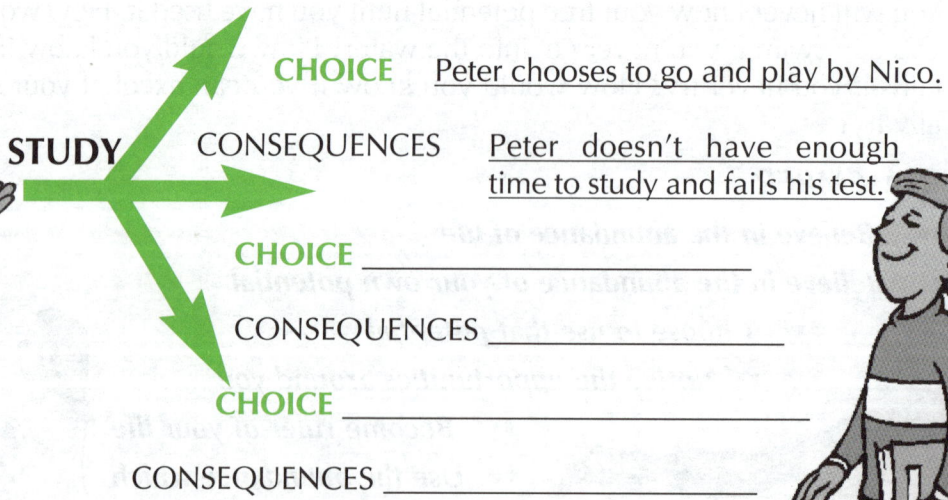

CHOICE   Peter chooses to go and play by Nico.

STUDY   CONSEQUENCES   Peter doesn't have enough time to study and fails his test.

CHOICE _____

CONSEQUENCES _____

CHOICE _____

CONSEQUENCES _____

Which choice do you normally make? _____

What is usually the consequence of your choice?

_____

3. Choices and consequences

While you are very small, other people decide on your behalf, as you can't yet carry the responsibility for your choices. Your parents or others have to carry the responsibility during the time they make choices for you. As you grow older, you have to make your **own** choices. Now you also have to accept the responsibility for the **consequences** of your **choices**. Look at the choices the following two people made:

I'M A GOOD GIRL

I'M A GOOD BOY

The older you become the bigger the choices you have to make and the more choices you are able to make.

EVERY ACTION HAS A REACTION

The larger and more the choices become, the bigger the consequences become

The bigger the consequences of your choices become the bigger your responsibility becomes when you make those choices

WHAT DO YOU CHOOSE FOR YOUR LIFE?

What would have happened if the girl became pregnant while at school? What would have happened if the guy stopped drinking and started studying?

4. Choose with all your heart

One of the greatest gifts you receive, is your freedom to do what you want to and to be who you would like to be. This freedom of choice is your birthright! Don't make a choice unless you make it with all your heart. Half hearted choices usually fail and make you unhappy.

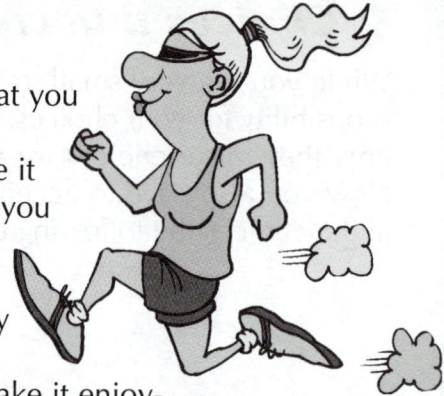

♡ You will never become fit if you jog only once a week. Get up, jog with all your heart, see the beauty around you and make it enjoyable for yourself. Soon you will look forward to jogging every morning.

♡ If you have chosen to go shopping with your family, enjoy it! Do it with all your heart and don't sulk and make it an unpleasant day for everybody.

♡ If you have chosen to study, do it with all your heart. Enjoy it, concentrate and give it all your attention. Do your homework regularly and on time.

♡ If you choose a career one day do it with all your heart. Become the best employee in that career. No-one forced you to choose that career or company. The choice was yours! Do it with all your heart!

♡ If you choose a life partner one day, do that with all your heart too. Don't make a half-hearted attempt to make someone happy while keeping several back doors open in case it doesn't work. No one forces you to marry a certain person. The choice is yours.
Do it then, with all your heart.

Do your work willingly, as though you were serving the Lord Himself and not just your earthly master.
Colossians 3:23

5. The freedom to choose

Since you have this freedom of choice, you can determine your own future. However, remember that:

☛ All actions have reactions. You don't have to eat, but you will become hungry. You don't have to learn, but you'll fail if you don't. You don't have to get up in the morning, but if you don't you have to take the consequences …

☛ No one can really make choices on your behalf. If somebody else chooses for you, it is **their** choice and not yours. Learn to make your **own** choices early in life and take the consequences yourself. **Show others that you are responsible enough to make responsible choices yourself.**

☛ The ability to make choices is something you have to **practice**.
You will make mistakes, but at the same time you'll learn to make **better choices**. The more choices you make, the better those choices will become. The more you practice this ability you have, the more possibilities you will see to choose from!

☛ You can choose your own characteristics, emotions and actions. You don't "inherit" your temper, you "copy" it. You can choose to change this characteristic to patience. You can choose to be happy or unhappy. You can choose to be successful or unsuccessful.

☛ The inability to decide is a sign that you don't know how to make choices. Keep in mind that you also have the choice to **make no choices**. On the other hand, that will result in others making choices and deciding for you. Your inability to decide hampers relationships and will only lead to people not knowing where they stand with you.

6. How does your Life Cycle turn?

Do you remember your Life Cycle?
Name the parts of the cycle wheel in this picture.
Which part makes the wheel turn? _____
When you look at your Life Cycle, you will notice
that it also has a focal point which keeps all the
facets of your life together and makes your
"wheel turn".

That focal point of your life is:

● That which is so important to you that you cannot live without it.
● That which makes you feel so good about yourself that you are happy and satisfied.
● That which makes you believe that everything will be all right.
● That which makes you endure and persevere.
● That which makes you so happy that you want to make others happy too.
● **That which you live for.**

Who or What is the focal point of your life?

_____

What could happen if one of the following is your focal point and something happens to it?

Focal point	What could happen?	What will happen to you then?
Your sport		
Your family		
Your beloved*		
Your friends		
Your enemies		
Your schoolwork		
Your possessions		
Your music		
Television		
Computer		
Going out		
Yourself		
Your body		

* Your beloved is your guy, chick, boyfriend or girlfriend.

From the beginning of time and through all the ages, people have come to the realisation, over and over, that there is only **one focal point** which never lets you down.

- Adam and Eve realised it in Paradise
- Moses realised in Egypt
- The Israelites realised it in the desert
- Job realised it with his illness and misery
- David realised it as king
- The disciples realised it at the cross
- The whole world realised it at an open grave

Man unfortunately has always tried other focal points first, before realising how wonderful it is to make **GOD** the focal point of your life.

ETERNAL LIFE GUARANTEED

REMEMBER: GOD GIVES AN EVERLASTING GUARANTEE THAT HE WILL ALWAYS BE WITH YOU AND WILL NEVER LET YOU DOWN.

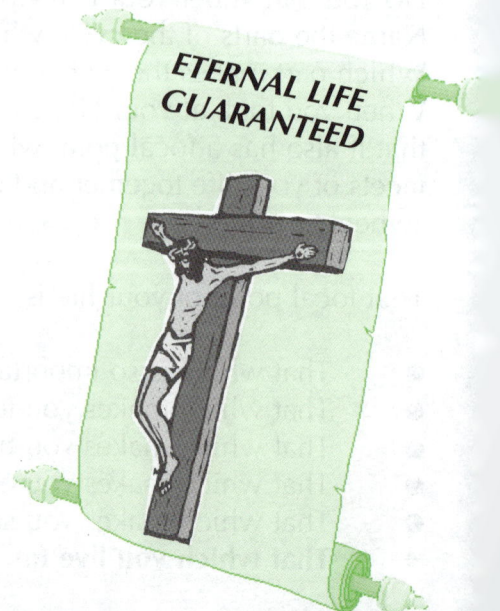

7. *What do I expect from my Focal Point?*

What do I expect from my Focal Point?	What does God's Word say?
My Focal Point must **love me unconditionally**	1 John 4:9 **God showed His love for us when He sent His only son into the world to give us life.** 1 John 4:13 **God has given us His Spirit** 1 John 4:16 **God is love** 1 John 4:19 **We love because God loved us first**
My Focal Point must **always be there** for me	Psalm 90:2 **You have always been God – long before the birth of the mountains, even before you created the earth and the world** Psalm 23:6 **Your kindness and love will always be with me, each day of my life and I will live forever in your house, Lord.** Revelation 22:13 **I am Alpha and Omega, the first and the last, the beginning and the end.**
My Focal Point must **understand** me	Psalm 139:1 **You have looked deep into my heart, Lord and you know all about me.** Psalm 139:2 **And from heaven you discover my thoughts** Psalm 139:16 **But with your own eyes you saw my body being formed. Even before I was born You had written in your Book everything I would do**
My Focal Point must take **care** of me.	Mathew 6:30 **God gives such beauty to everything that grows in the fields, even though it is here today and thrown into a fire tomorrow. He will surely do even more for you!** Mathew 6:23 **Your Father in heaven knows that you need all of these.**
My Focal Point must **help** me	Mathew 7:7 **Ask and you will receive. Search and you will find. Knock and the door will be opened for you.** Mathew 11:28 **If you are tired from carrying a heavy burden, come to Me and I will give you rest.** Hebrews 13:6 **That should make you feel like saying: "The Lord helps us." Why should I be afraid of what people can do to me?** Psalm 32:8 **I will be your teacher and watch over you.**

What do I expect of my Focal Point?	What does God's word say?
My Focal Point must **protect** me	Psalm 145: **You take care of everyone who loves You** Psalm 46 **God is always a haven and protection. He has always been willing to help us in need.** Psalm 121:3 **The Lord is your Protector and He won't go to sleep.**
My Focal Point must **forgive** me	Romans 5:8 **But God showed us how much He loved us by having Christ die for us, even though we were sinful.** Titus 3:7 **Jesus treated us much better than we deserve. He made us acceptable to God and gave us the hope of eternal life …** Isaiah 38:17 **You turned your eyes away from my sins.**
My Focal Point must make me **happy**	Psalm 112:1 **The Lord blesses everyone who worships Him.** Philippians 4:7 **God will bless you with peace that no one can completely understand and this peace will control the way you think and feel.**
My Focal Point must **never let me down**	Hebrews 13:5 **The Lord has promised that He will not leave us or desert us.** Hebrews 13;8 **Jesus Christ never changes! He is the same yesterday, today and forever!**
My Focal Point must **protect** me against all evil	2 Thessalonians 3:3 **But the Lord can be trusted to make you strong and protect you from harm.**

IF YOU HAVE A DIFFERENT FOCAL POINT, THEN BY ALL MEANS COMPARE IT TO THIS AND SEE WHETHER IT CAN COMPETE AT ALL!

ONLY YOU CAN MAKE THIS CHOICE!

8. *You have to choose!*

a) Choose your Focal Point

You have to choose who or what will be the Focal point of your life.
You also need to know that this choice will have certain consequences for you.
You must also take responsibility for your choices.

REMEMBER!
YOUR FOCAL POINT WILL DETERMINE YOUR FINAL GOAL IN LIFE!

b) Choose your attitude

Every day you have choices. You can get up or stay in bed. You can learn or not. You can play netball or hockey. You can be friends with Peter or Linda. You can have a serious relationship with Nicky or have a lot of friends. You can listen to your mother or be disobedient.

You can make God the Focal Point of your life or choose someone else.

The choice is yours. You are the one who must take the consequences and responsibility for your choices.

However, once you have made your choice, do it with all your heart and fully.

What does it help if you make your choices and then walk around with a sour face about the choices you have made? It was your choice!

c) Choose positive or negative

Sometimes we feel very good about ourselves and with life (positive).
Sometimes, however, we don't feel good about ourselves and about life (negative).
That is completely normal. Our emotions and feelings have this way of playing seesaw with us!

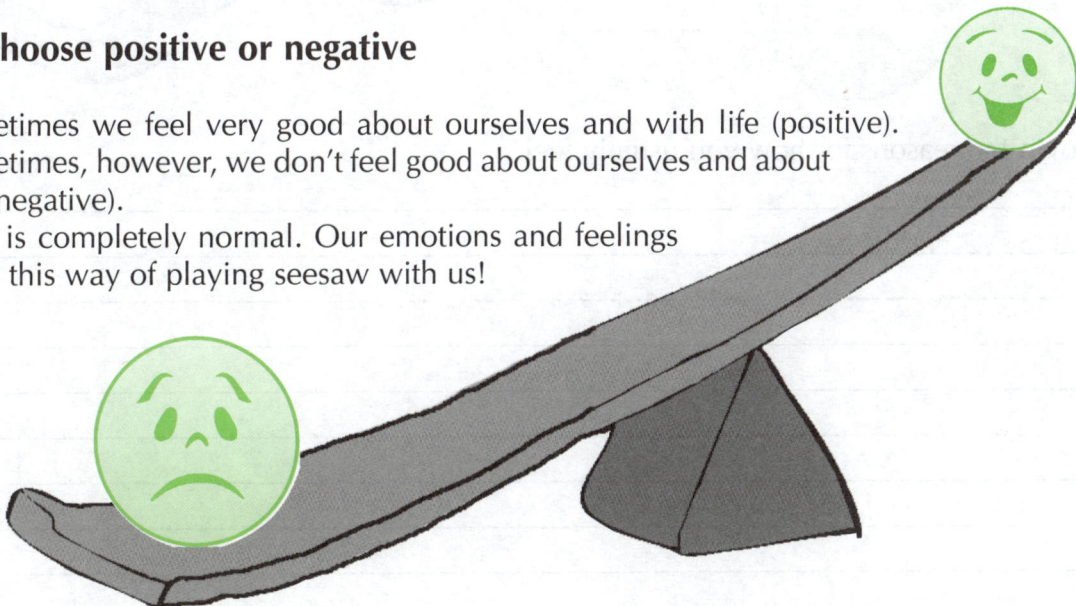

There are two ways which a person usually feels about oneself and about life.

POSITIVE   OR   NEGATIVE

ARE YOU USUALLY ...

POSITIVE

OR

NEGATIVE ?

Why?
Write down the reasons for how you usually feel.

_____
_____
_____
_____
_____
_____
_____
_____
_____

9. *The strengthening of positive and negative thoughts*

How does your brain process and strengthen positive and negative thoughts?

a) Reticular Activation System (RAS)

The brain stem is situated at the bottom and rear of your brain. This brain stem houses your Reticular Activation System (RAS). The Reticular Activation System acts like a secretary or switchboard of a large undertaking.

The "RAS Secretary" determines what information will be noted by your brain, and what should be processed and stored. In the same way a secretary controls and monitors her manager's telephone calls, visits and appointments, so the RAS helps to filter through important information and keeps other information out so that you can concentrate on that which is important.

When you concentrate on positive thoughts, the Reticular Activation System will look for positive information and send it to your brain. It is sifted from what you see, hear, what others tell you and also say about you. All negative thoughts are then eliminated or changed into positive criticism.

If you, however, focus on negative thoughts, your Reticular Activation System looks for all the negative things you can notice, hear, what is said to you or about you. It sends it through to your brain, while positive thoughts are lost.

b) Creative subconscious

Your creative subconscious is that part of your thought process where thoughts are processed. Problems are solved here and goals achieved. If your brain receives positive information, it becomes enlarged by your imagination and turned into images. Unfortunately the opposite is also true, so that negative information becomes enlarged by your imagination and turned into images.

When someone tells you that you are **attractive,** your creative subconscious will enlarge this positive thought and in your imagination you now experience yourself as a **very attractive** person.

Yet when someone tells you that you are ugly, your creative subconscious will also enlarge this negative thought so that in your imagination you regard yourself as **very ugly**.

c) Subconscious

All your attitudes, habits and previous experiences are stored in the thought process of your subconscious. Here, THE TRUTH, AS YOU SEE IT, is stored. This TRUTH may possibly differ a great deal from reality **because your brain believes what you tell it.** It can, therefore, not distinguish between reality and the "TRUTH AS YOU SEE IT".

When the positive thought of **very attractive** goes through your subconscious, it compares your experience to
– your emotions
– your attitude
– the truth as you see it.

If you recognise and believe this, this thought is strengthened and entrenched in your subconscious as reference point for further statements about your appearance. **"Very attractive"** now perhaps becomes **"Beautiful"**.

The same happens with negative statements. Negative statements are also compared to your emotions, your attitude and the truth as you see it. If you recognise and believe it, that negative thought is also strengthened and entrenched in your brain.
"Very ugly" now becomes **"Horrible"**.

d) Conscious mind

Even though your conscious mind absorbs the information and sends it through to the Reticular Activation System, your brain reacts to the information after it has been processed by your creative subconscious and your subconscious.

This is how it works:

Jack says: **You look pretty**
Your creative subconscious sees: **You look very pretty**
Your subconscious strengthens it and hears: **You are beautiful**
Your conscious mind reacts to that as a personal compliment and decides to compliment Jack as well.

Peter says: **You look ugly**
Your creative subconscious sees: **You look very ugly**
Your subconscious strengthens it and hears: **You are horrible**
Your conscious mind reacts to that as a personal insult and decides to insult Peter as well.

e) Your self-image

Your self-image is like the walls of a fort which protect you against negative criticism, remarks and events.

If you, in your subconscious, believe that you are pretty and feel good about yourself, it rejects the negative thoughts because it's not the TRUTH AS YOU SEE IT.

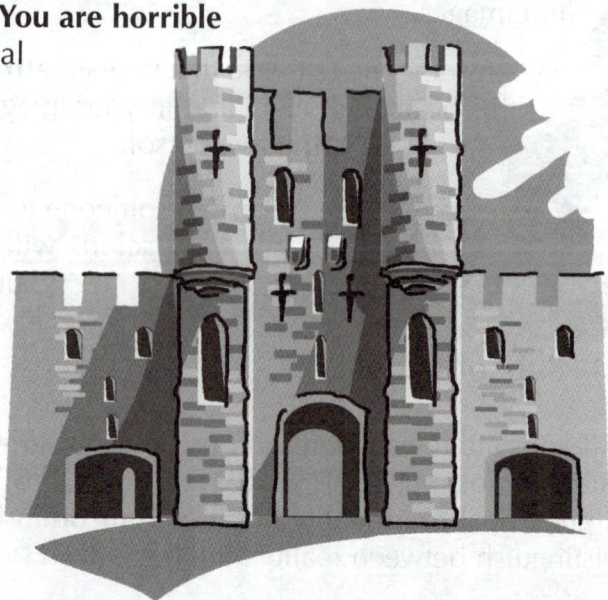

10. How are your thoughts strengthened?

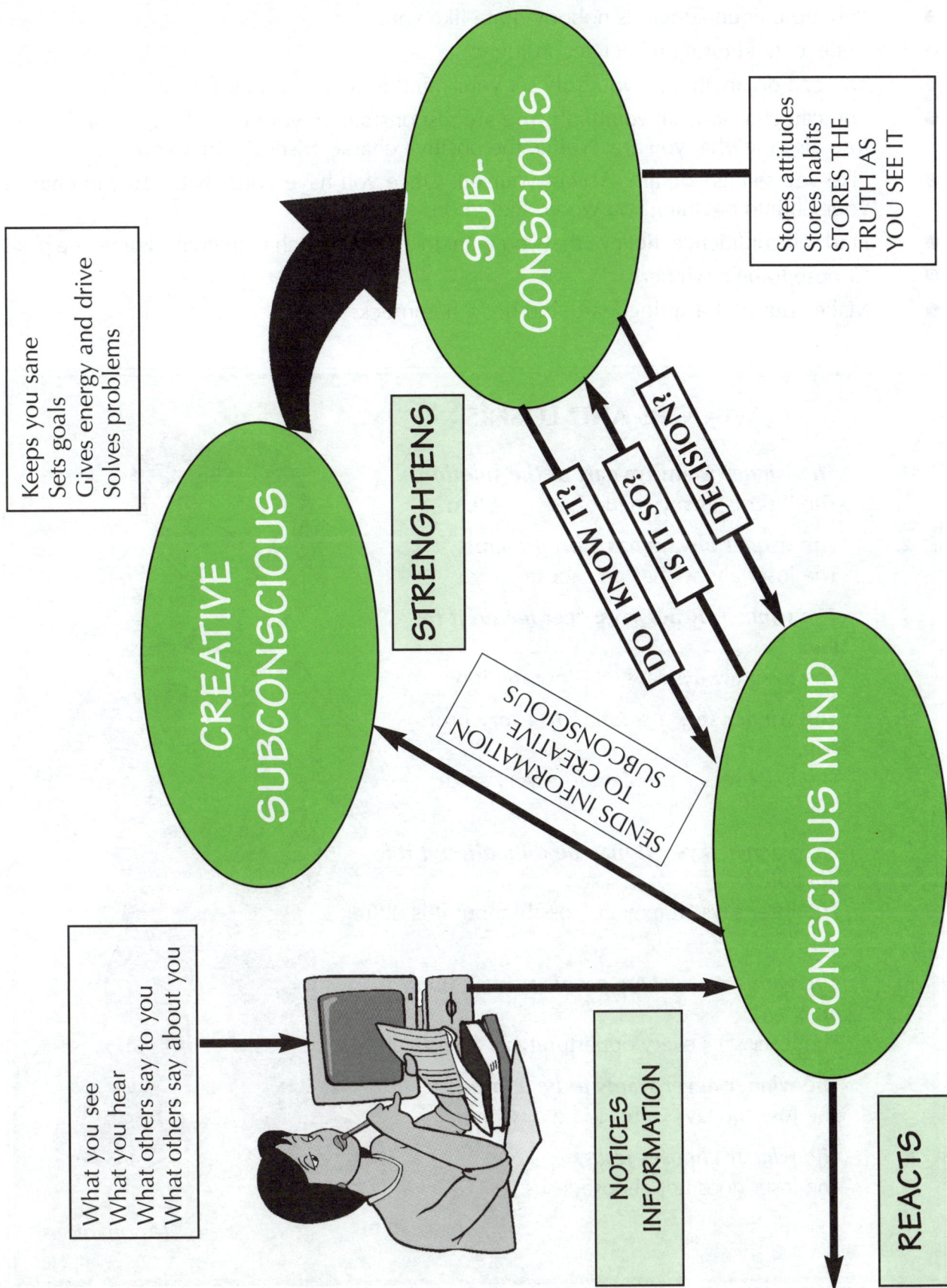

SUB-CONSCIOUS

Stores attitudes
Stores habits
STORES THE
TRUTH AS
YOU SEE IT

Keeps you sane
Sets goals
Gives energy and drive
Solves problems

STRENGHTENS

DO I KNOW IT?

IS IT SO?

DECISION?

CREATIVE SUBCONSCIOUS

SENDS INFORMATION
TO CREATIVE
SUBCONSCIOUS

CONSCIOUS MIND

What you see
What you hear
What others say to you
What others say about you

NOTICES INFORMATION

REACTS

REMEMBER:

- You are unique – there is nobody quite like you.
- Believe it, admit it and act accordingly.
- You can do anything if you truly set your mind to it and work on it.
- You can choose what you think. You are responsible for your own thoughts and therefore also for what you are. Notice the positive characteristics within yourself.
- Like yourself as you are. Accept yourself. Once you have done that, you can change yourself into anything you would like to be.
- Find self confidence. Believe that you want to and can reach your goals. Forget the past!
- Choose to be a winner!
- Make your past a springboard and not a hammock.

WINNERS AND LOSERS

1. **The winner is always part of the solution.**
   The loser is always part of the problem.

2. **The winner always has a programme.**
   The loser always has an excuse.

3. **The winner always says: "Let me do it for you."**
   The loser always says; "It's not my job."

4. **The winner sees a solution to every problem.**
   The loser sees a problem for every solution.

5. **The winner says: "It may be difficult, but it is possible."**
   The loser says:"It may be possible, but it is difficult."

6. **The winner sees every problem as an opportunity.**
   The loser sees every opportunity as a problem.

7. **The winner never wants to be a loser.**
   The loser always wants to be a winner.

8. **The winner chooses Jesus.**
   The loser does not choose Jesus.

(Anonymous)

11. *How do I remain positive?*

1) If your "RAS secretary" lets through only negative information, you will remain negative. You will also see only the negative in everything.

Fire that secretary immediately and appoint one who lets through only positive information.
Say to yourself:

"I SEE THE POSITIVE IN LIFE! I REFUSE TO BE NEGATIVE!"

2) Perhaps the cable between your "RAS secretary" and your creative subconscious has broken or perhaps you are not using your creative subconscious!

Become creative and think differently about life, yourself and what happens around you.

ARE YOU PART OF THE PROBLEM, OR PART OF THE SOLUTION?

3) Write your own POSITIVE BOOK.

This differs from your diary, because it may only contain positive things you have read, heard or which have happened to you. Keep it for your "off-days" when you don't feel good about yourself.

4) See everything in life as an opportunity to learn something. Even hardship and heartache can become positive experiences when you learn from it.

5) Speak to yourself and encourage yourself. This is quite normal and is done even by the greatest sports stars on earth.

6) Connect to God! Negative deeds and thoughts are signs that your spirit is suffering damage. Heal your connection – it works every time!

Here are two recipes you can follow to be positive or negative.

Believe me, both work excellently! The choice is yours!

RECIPE TO BE POSITIVE	RECIPE TO BE NEGATIVE
Believe in God	Don't believe in God
Believe in yourself	Don't believe in yourself
Keep promises to yourself and others	Break promises to yourself and others
Be honest – especially with yourself	Be dishonest – especially with yourself
Forgive yourself and others	Don't forgive anybody
Build and repair yourself	Break yourself down
Use your talents	Bury your talents
Do something good to another	Do something bad to another
Obtain a goal to live for	Live aimlessly
Live according to principles	Live without principles
Be grateful for what you have	Be ungrateful and complain about what you don't have
Take responsibility	Blame others
Do it now	Postpone it
Laugh	Cry
Say good things about others	Gossip about others
Ask advice	Ask nobody for advice
Rest and sleep enough	Don't rest and don't sleep enough
Eat healthily	Eat junk food
Surround yourself with positive people	Surround yourself with negative people
Bombard your senses with positive thoughts, words, music and images	Bombard your senses with negative thoughts, words, music and images.

Processed from: **Seven Habits for Highly Effective Teens: Steven Covey.**

WHAT RECIPE DO YOU CHOOSE? _____

12. *What do I do when negative things happen to me?*

a) Events

- You can control certain events in your life.
- You cannot, however, control or chose everything that happens.
- See how you can change your circumstances and learn from it.

Many people have survived dreadful circumstances by simply concentrating on the positive and eliminating the negative.

Use your imagination to improve your circumstances.

Eat your bread crusts as if they are chocolates! Change your jail to a castle! If life gives you lemons, make lemonade!

b) People

- People often disappoint us.
- People often let us down.
- People become old, get sick and die. That is part of life! Accept it!
- Remember that each person has to make his/her own choices and carry the responsibility for the consequences thereof himself/herself.
- You can, however, do a great deal to help a person by
  - forgiving
  - praying
  - supporting

IMPORTANT!

GOD, GIVE ME THE STRENGTH TO CHANGE THE THINGS I CAN, TO ACCEPT THE THINGS I CANNOT AND THE WISDOM TO KNOW THE DIFFERENCE
Work on that which you can change!!!
Look for help if things become too much for you!

Choices are easy when you have strong principles!

Maturity does not depend on your age, but, in fact, on your ability to accept responsibility for the choices you make!

Happy people don't necessarily have the best of everything, but they do make the best of what they've got.

The most important choice you will ever make, is to choose Jesus. The second most important choice which you will make, is who you will marry …

Learn from experience – preferably that of somebody else …

7 Success!

We would all like to be successful and yet few people know what success really means. What is success and when are you successful? In this chapter you will learn what success really means and how you can experience it on a daily basis. To set goals and achieve them, is a skill that can be acquired. Everybody can live successfully and purposefully – you too!

1. What do you want to achieve?

INSTRUCTION:
Read the following passage very thoroughly and decide what this person forgot to do and what the consequences were:

To build a house ...

A young man who had never possessed much in life, one day won 5 million Rand and he immediately decided to build himself a beautiful house against the slope of a mountain. He took a piece of paper and made a quick sketch of how his dream home should look.

He bought the best piece of ground against the mountain slope and immediately phoned a builder in town to come and build a house "exactly like that". The builder took the sketch from the man and was so excited that he was going to make so much money in these difficult times, that he dug foundations the very next day. Orders for bricks, cement, iron sheets, windows and doors, paint and wooden beams and roofing were placed at different firms and within a week, the house was window height.

As the young man didn't know much about building, he trusted the builder – who should surely know something – to build the house to his taste. Imagine his distress when the house was eventually completed. IT WAS A MESS!!

What did the young man do wrong? _____

Would you have your dream home built from a quick pencil sketch? _____

Your life can be compared to the building of a house. You cannot build a house without a clear building plan. Without a clear picture of what you hope to achieve in life, your life will have no direction or meaning and you will easily do the wrong thing at the wrong times in your life.

Without goals, there is no reason why you do certain things and not others. Then you act the way you feel.

If you have a clear picture in your mind of how you are going to be playing for the Proteas one day, you will not regard an Ecstasy tablet as something to try for fun to see how it feels, but as something that could land you in a coma and destroy your life!

If you have a **clear picture** of what you want to do with yourself and your **life,** then **every event** will form a part of the dream you are realising like the **bricks** of a house!

All of us have wishes and dreams. A very well known architect once said; **"Even a brick would like to become something!"** For that brick to become something there first needs to be a **building plan** so that a building can be constructed from it. For that reason you first have to form a **life plan** in your head!

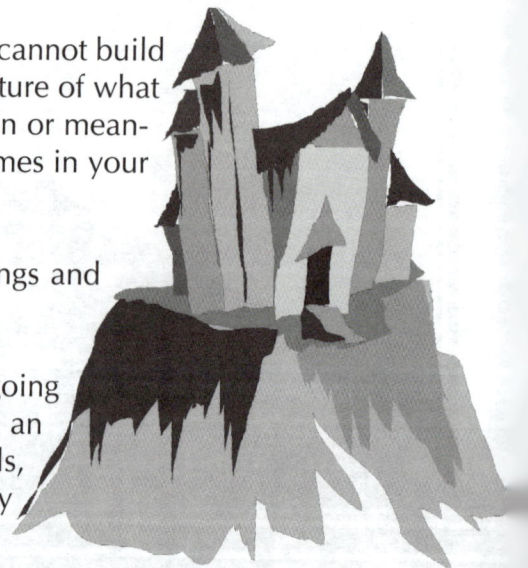

**If you really want to achieve success in
your life and studies you have to:**

a) **Know what you really want.**
   - Which goals do you want to achieve?
   - Which career do you want to follow?
   - What sort of salary do you want to earn?
   - What mark do you want to obtain?
   - What kind of friends do you want?
   - What kind of person would you like to marry some day?

b) **Form a clear picture of it in your mind.**
   - See it as if it has already happened
   - See the detail of each goal

c) **Execute the steps required to reach it.**
   - What do you have to put in?
   - What do you have to sacrifice?
   - What will it cost?
   - What steps do you have to follow?
   - Where can you get help?

REMEMBER:

*The man who moved the mountain,
started by carrying away rocks ...*

No plan is worth
the paper it was written on
unless it is executed.

*Unless you try something
you have never tried before,
you will never really grow!!*

**Without the help of the Lord it is useless to build a home or to guard a city. It is useless
to get up early and stay up late in order to earn a living.
God takes care of His own, even while they sleep.**   *Psalm 127:1-2*

2. What is success?

The difference between successful and unsuccessful people is that successful people continuously set goals for themselves and achieve them. Unsuccessful people have no goals or enjoy telling how much they would like to achieve but do nothing about it.

SUCCESSFUL	UNSUCCESSFUL

Before you, therefore, set goals for yourself you have to decide whether you really want to be successful or not!
 What does it mean if a person wants to succeed?

Paul Meyer wrote in his course "The Dynamics of Personal Motivation":

Success is the continuous achievement of goals which you set for yourself beforehand and which are worth achieving for yourself.

Success is not something you want to reach someday, but today and every day of your life. It starts with the choices you make today and the goals you set for yourself today and then achieve!

Success is a journey and not a destination!

3. Types of goals

In order to set goals you first have to divide your life into different phases.

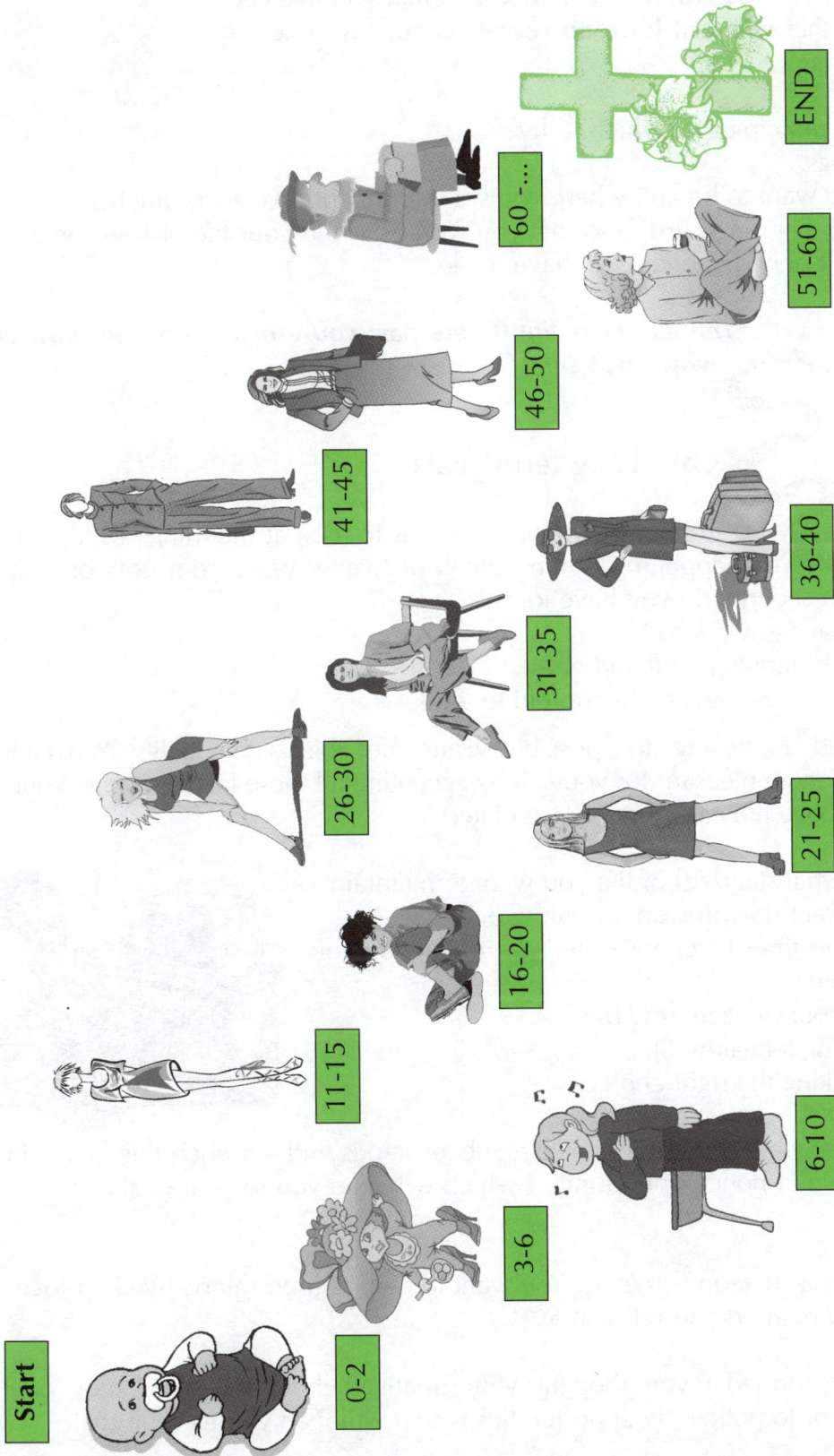

Start

0-2

3-6

6-10

11-15

16-20

21-25

26-30

31-35

36-40

41-45

46-50

51-60

60 - ....

END

Final goal	=	The final destination you want to reach **after you die**.
Long term goals	=	Those things you want to do 15 to 20 years from now.
Medium term goals	=	Those things you want to do 3 to 10 years from now.
Short term goals	=	Those things you want to do now and within the next month to 3 years.

a) Final goal

The only true certainty you have with regard to your final goal is that you will die someday.

Since you don't know when you will die, it is important that you live each day in such a manner that **you will have no regrets about the time you spend here on earth!**

Example:

☞ Choose values and principles by which to live.

☞ Right all your wrongs.

☞ Make sure who you want to be and where you want to go and live accordingly.

☞ Make the correct choices in your life so that you won't shorten your life or lose some of its quality as a result of bad choices you have made.

"The day your life flashes past you – make sure the show is worth watching."

b) Long term goals

To set long term goals one has to look at the things which will be happening in ten, fifteen or twenty years from now or even longer. What security do you have for this?

✔ You will certainly have to work to live.

✔ You will have friends, family and loved ones

✔ You will become older and eventually too old to work.

These things may sound depressing and possibly vague, but this is the reality. You can, though, make life much more pleasant for yourself by accepting all these facts now. Set yourself long term goals to make life easier for yourself later!

Example:

☞ Think of what standard of life you want to maintain.

☞ Which career do you want to follow one day?

☞ Now is the time to choose the type of friends you want one day.

☞ Invest in your old age now by:
  – living a healthy life.
  – making the right choices.

If you set your long term goals now your Creative Subconscious will entrench this image in your brain now and begin to notice opportunities which will lead you to your goal.

Example:

You want to become a surgeon someday. You want to earn a good salary, live in a lovely house, be happily married and retire at 50!

If this image is clearly formed in your thoughts your Creative Subconscious will know precisely what to look for to notice the opportunities which will lead you to your goal.

SET YOUR GOALS FIRST AND THEN YOU'LL NOTICE THE OPPORTUNITIES!!

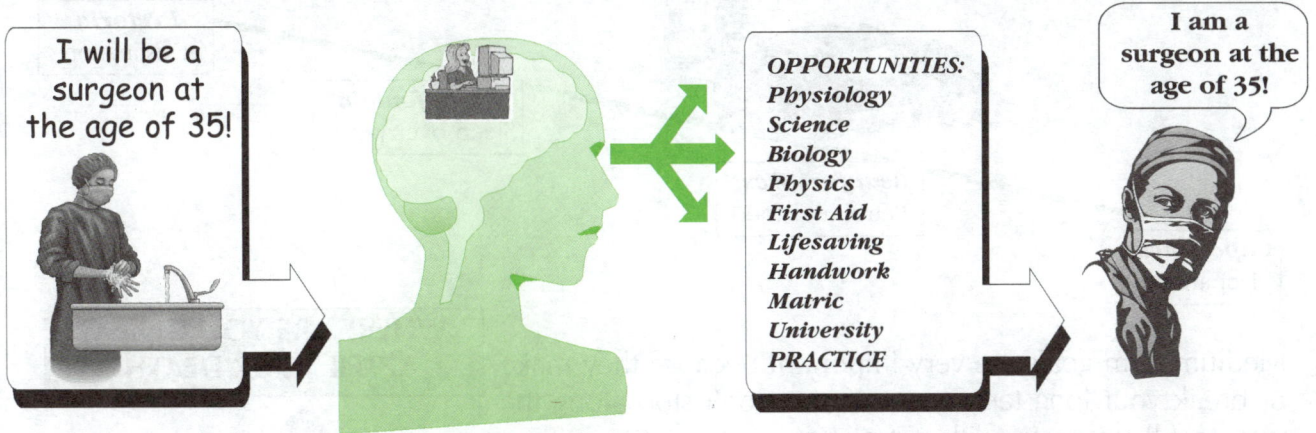

I will be a surgeon at the age of 35!

OPPORTUNITIES:
Physiology
Science
Biology
Physics
First Aid
Lifesaving
Handwork
Matric
University
PRACTICE

I am a surgeon at the age of 35!

The sooner in life you determine your goals the more OPPORTUNITIES you will notice to reach your goals!

However, if you have no goals your Creative Subconscious won't know what to look for and important opportunities will pass you by without you even realising it!

ARE YOU SLEEPING NEXT TO A POT OF GOLD?

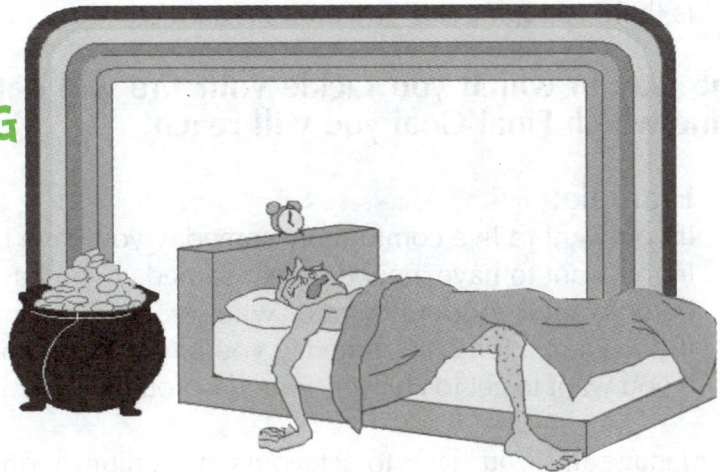

c) Medium term goals!

Long term goals can be compared to a long journey which you undertake to reach your final destination.
Your **medium term goals** are the **halfway stations** where you rest or stay overnight before you continue your journey.

Example:
You want to journey from Cape Town to Pretoria. Your final destination is Pretoria and the route you will follow is the long term goal you set yourself to get there. Since you cannot complete the journey in one day you break it up into parts with certain points where you will stop to stretch your legs, to rest, to eat and to put in petrol. These different parts are your medium term goals.

Cape Town
Departure

Beaufort West
Petrol and food

Bloemfontein
Sleep over/petrol

Pretoria
Destination

WHERE ARE YOU GOING AFTER YOUR DEATH?

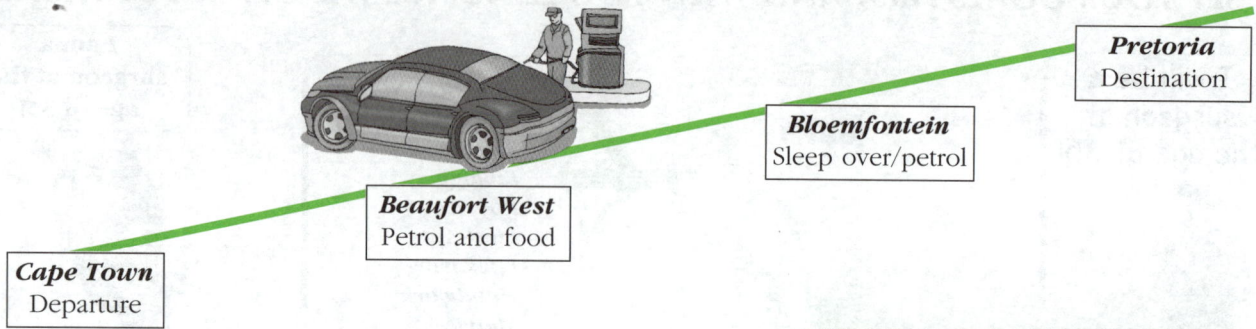

Medium term goals are very important because they make or break your long term goals. If you don't stop along the way to fill up again with petrol your car won't go. If you don't rest along the way you could easily have an accident.

The way in which you tackle your journey will determine which destination you will reach.
● Do you stick to the traffic rules?
● Is your car roadworthy?
● Do you get enough rest?
● Is there enough petrol in your car?

The way in which you tackle your life will determine which Final Goal you will reach.

Example:
● If you want to live comfortably someday you have to learn to handle money now.
● If you want to have a good career someday you have to study toward that now.
● If you want a good husband or wife someday you have to go out with such people now.
● If you want a long life someday you have to take care of your health now.
● If you want to get to Heaven someday you have to mend your relationship with God now.

To manage this you have to set yourself medium term goals for those things you want to achieve three to ten years from now.

You can already set your medium term goals today by:
☞ finding out who and what you really are.
☞ finding out who and what you really want to be.
☞ finding out what you have to do or change to become or be that person.
☞ finding out what your interests and talents are.
☞ finding out what study direction you should follow.
☞ making sure you are connected to God.

Long term goals and medium term goals, however, start with the short term goals you execute. If you want to build a wall it must be built **brick by brick**!

d) Short term goals

Short term goals are those things which you do every day as well as the things you plan to do for the following one to three years.

Long term goals and medium term goals often change during a person's life. This is normal. Remember, however, that you can never achieve success without having any goals.

REMEMBER:
Success is the constant reaching of goals which you have previously set for yourself and which you find worth it.

THUS SUCCESS IS:

Success is the constant reaching of goals which you have previously set for yourself and which you find worth it.

- That means that success begins **today** by the goals you set yourself today.

- Each time you set a goal and reach it you achieve success and you are successful. That also goes for the goals you set for today.

- The moment you stop setting goals for yourself, you stop achieving success. Then you'll only be able to speak of the success you achieved in the past.

I WAS FANTASTIC...!

Success is the constant reaching of goals which you have **previously** set for yourself and which you find worth it.

- The word **previously** means that you decided before the time what your goal would be. That also means that you have to work on the goals you have set for tomorrow today!

"If in the exams you want to do well,
open your books
and learn, my pal!"

- The word **previously** also means that you see this goal in your mind before the time and then take specific steps to reach it!

Success is the constant reaching of goals which **you have previously set for yourself and which you find worth it!**

CONGRAT MOM!

- You are only successful if you set goals **for yourself** and reach them yourself.

  If you get 80% because your mother or teacher wants you to, it is **their** goal. If you reach it, it is **also their success** and **not yours!**

  Are you really successful if your mother does your tasks and summaries for you, or must nag you all day long to go and learn, to do your homework, exercise your sport or clean up your room?

  Is it your success or her success if you then achieve?

  Does someone nag you or do you set goals for yourself?

  If you set **yourself** a goal of 80% and reach it, it is **your goal** and **your success. Then only are you truly successful!**

REPORT

Reading	A	A	A+
Writing	B	A	A+
Maths	A	A	A+

- If your goals are **not worth it to you**, you will not work hard at it to reach it.

  Ask yourself why you set that goal and why you want to reach it.

4. Foundations

No house will stand for long without foundations. It is these foundations which anchor your house to the ground and ensure that it is firmly constructed. Before you build a house you first have to dig the foundations and lay it firmly.

If you want to be successful, it is important that your goals rest on firm foundations.

These foundations are:

☞ The **principles** according to which you strive towards your goals!

☞ Your **knowledge** of your goals.

☞ Your **preparation** to reach your goals.

☞ The **requirements** which your goals have to meet.

Without these foundations, you will soon find that your goals were wrong, look useless or cannot be reached at all!

Without your foundations you are also easily forced off course, so that you don't reach your goals!

a) Principles

Are you prepared to do or sacrifice **anything** to reach your goal? Would you crib, steal, lie, step on others, abuse others or even murder to reach your goal?
Where do you draw the line?

Your principles are those things which are important to you and which you believe in. They are the laws according to which you live.

Your principles are the "rights" and "wrongs" according to which you live. Find out what God's principles are. He expects the same principles from you! Without these principles you are easily persuaded and then your choices are not based on what is right or wrong to you, but on how you feel at that moment!

EXAMPLE:

Is sex before marriage a sin or not?

It is easy to discuss this in class, but it's much harder to be in the moonlight with an attractive guy or girl and still feel it's wrong. This is where your principles will determine what you will do in such a situation. If you have very strong principles, you will quickly make a plan to get out of the moonlight! On the other hand, if you have no principles, your hormones will, most probably, tell you what you "should" do …

Can you leave the achievement of your goals to how you "feel" at any given moment?
Can you really let your future be decided by your emotions, hormones, peer pressure and the opinions of others? You will still experience a great deal of peer pressure. That won't stop, either, once you are no longer a teenager. Just watch a few adults and see how they yield to peer pressure and even pressure from teenagers …!
There are still going to be many temptations on your way. You will still have to make thousands of choices. Ensure that those choices and decisions depend on your **principles**.

Your principles are the cornerstones upon which you build your entire future.
Your principles help you to make responsible choices in life. The **stronger** your principles, the easier it will be to make these choices and the **easier** it will be to stay out of things which could destroy your goals.

According to which principles will your strive towards your goals?
Think carefully about the principles according to which you live.
Now write down your principles on the next page and **make sure that you live accordingly!**

It really doesn't help that you have wonderful principles, yet don't live according to one of them. If you believe that honesty is a principle, then see to it that you don't tell lies!

FIND GOALS WHICH MAKE YOU HAPPY!

Write down your own principles and live accordingly!

MY PRINCIPLES

Which part of an ice-cream cone do you like best?
Pretend that your goals are like an ice-cream that you eat. The best goals make you the happiest!

GOALS		How happy will it make me?
Your spiritual connection to God **FAITH, HOPE AND LOVE**		
What I do to make others and myself happy **THINGS FOR YOUR SOUL**		
That which I have. (My sport, possessions, certificates) **THINGS FOR YOUR BODY**		
Basic things such as food, clothes, water, heat, shelter **THINGS FOR YOUR BODY**		

b) Knowledge of your goals

Mount Everest is the highest mountain peak in the world and is a challenge to many to climb. Would you venture onto this mountain without knowing how high it is, what the weather is like or what gear you require? That could surely lead to your own death!

If you wish to reach a certain goal, it is important for you to find out as much as possible about that goal, so that you know what you're in for!

Since life, careers, your goals and needs can change in time, it is important that you have as much knowledge as possible about **everything** in life!

Knowledge is power – the power to make more and better choices!

Do you now understand why every school subject and everything you learn in life, is important? That is one of the main reasons why you have so many school subjects!

Each school subject forms the foundation of a career you may want to follow someday. There really is not a single school subject which you will never again use in your life, once you have left school!

Even the singing class can prepare you for a career as a pop star or, at least, help you to sing better in the bathroom!

INSTRUCTIONS

Write down your school subjects in the first column below.
Now write down all the careers and possible uses you could have for it in ten years' time.

SCHOOL SUBJECTS	WHAT I CAN USE THEM FOR IN TEN YEARS' TIME
Which career would you like to follow someday?	
Which subjects will help you to be successful in your career?	

IMPORTANT!

Remember that many of the careers which you could follow 20 years from now, don't even exist today. Never say: "I will never use this subject (type of sport, advice or knowledge)…!" Several important people's remarks have been proven wrong.

"The earth is the focal point of the universe"

Ptolemy, Greek Astrologer in the second century.

"Aeroplanes are interesting toys, but are useless for military use"

Fieldmarshall Ferdinand Foch, military strategist and First World War Commander, 1911.

"Go to reception and get rid of the crazy guy there! He says he has a machine through which you can see with wires – maybe he has a knife on him!"

Editor of the *Daily Express*, 1925, speaking of John Logie Baird, the inventor of television.

"Television will not sell after the first six months. People will soon get tired of watching a wooden box every day!"

Darryl F Zanuck, Head of 20th Century Fox, 1946.

"Radio has no future"

Lord Kelvin, President of the Royal Society, 19th century.

"X-rays are a farce!"

Lord Kelvin.

"In spite of all future scientific development, man will never reach the moon"

Dr Lee de Forest, Inventor and Scientist, 1967

"We don't like their sound. Groups with guitars are on the way out."

Decco Records about The Beatles whose music they turned down in 1967 and refused to market.

"There is no reason why any person should have a computer at home!"

Kenneth Olsen, President and Founder of Digital Equipment Corporation 1977.

c)   Preparation to reach your goals

Before someone is allowed to climb Mount Everest, they first have to produce proof of their involvement with and experience of mountaineering. These mountain climbers first attempt several other mountains before they venture onto Mount Everest. Thereafter they still have to spend months at the foot of the mountain to acclimatise and then wait for weeks for the right weather condition to climb up the mountain.

Everything in life requires preparation
- The mountain you want to climb.
- The sports medal you want to win.
- The homework you have to do.
- The tests you have to write.
- The exam mark you want.
- The career you want to practise someday.
- The goals you set for yourself.

The better your preparation, the bigger are the odds that you will reach your goal. Your school career is the preparation for the day you have to stand on your own feet. Are you using it to test a new hairstyle in front of the mirror or to hang around with your friends to the point of boredom?

Just as it would not be possible to descend from Mount Everest alive without first preparing thoroughly, so you will also not

- win the sports medal if you are unfit.
- be able to do homework if you keep on postponing.
- pass the test if you don't learn.
- get your exam mark if you don't revise.
- be able to follow your career without the necessary qualifications and hard work.
- reach the goal if you don't know what it is.

If your wish to be successful in reaching your goals, you have to prepare for it and regularly set goals so that it becomes a habit. If you want to be successful someday, you have to start by handling today successfully.

Life is full of mountains which have to be climbed before you reach the highest peak (your final goal).

Start today by setting clear goals for yourself which lead to the right final goal!

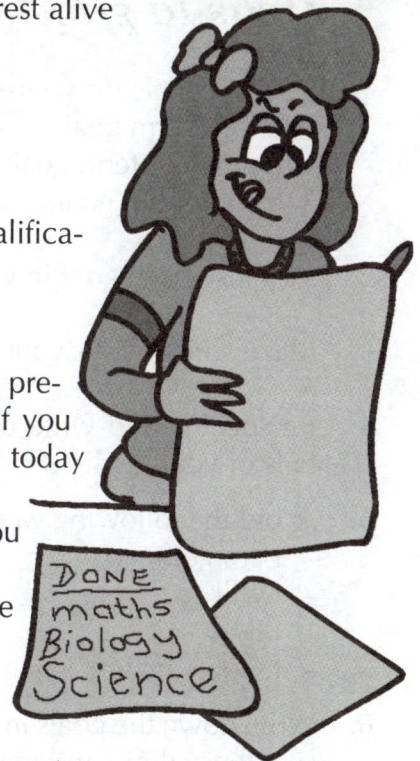

d) Requirements for good goals

In order to set good goals, your goals must confirm to the following requirements:

☞   Goals must be set by **yourself and in conjunction with God.**

☞   Goals must be **visualised**.
(See the picture in your head.)

☞   Goals must be **well planned**.
(Plan each step you have to take to reach your goal.)

☞   Goals must be **written down in advance**.
(Write it down and make a promise to yourself that you will keep it.)

☞   Goals must have **deadlines.**
(Give yourself a time or the date when your goal should be completed.)

☞   Goals must be **realistic**.
(Break your goal down into smaller tasks which you are capable of coping with.)

☞   Goals must make you **happy** and must never be reached at the cost of yourself, your health, your soul or other people.

5. Steps to good goals

1. Set final goals for yourself, then break it up into
   – a long term goal.
   – a medium term goal.
   – a short term goal.

   Every day I learn the work I did in school, so that I can improve my marks from 55% to 65%.

2. Visualise each goal in your mind and then write it down on paper.

3. Make sure that it's your own goal and write down why you want to achieve this goal.

4. Be specific and write down all the details of your goal.

   Every day I jog to become fit so that I can play for the first team.

5. Avoid the following words:
   – I am going to
   – I will
   – I'll try
   – I won't again …

   I make one person happy every day!

6. Write down the goals in the present tense (here and now).

7. Write down the advantages of each goal.

8. Write down the possible obstacles which could prevent you from reaching your goal:
   - postponement
   - stress and worry
   - fear
   - finances
   - time
   - lack of knowledge and skills

9. Write down solutions for each obstacle and problem.

10. Name all the people who could help you reach your goal.

11. Write down which skills or talents you need to reach your goals.

12. Set a date or time when you want to reach your goals.

13. Now break this goal up into
    ✔ goal for the year.
    ✔ tasks for each month.
    ✔ tasks for this month.
    ✔ tasks for each week of this month.
    ✔ tasks for each day of the week.

14. Write each task into your diary and mark it as if you have already achieved it.

15. Organise yourself and begin to work at your goal.

16. Reward yourself if you have completed the whole week's tasks in time.

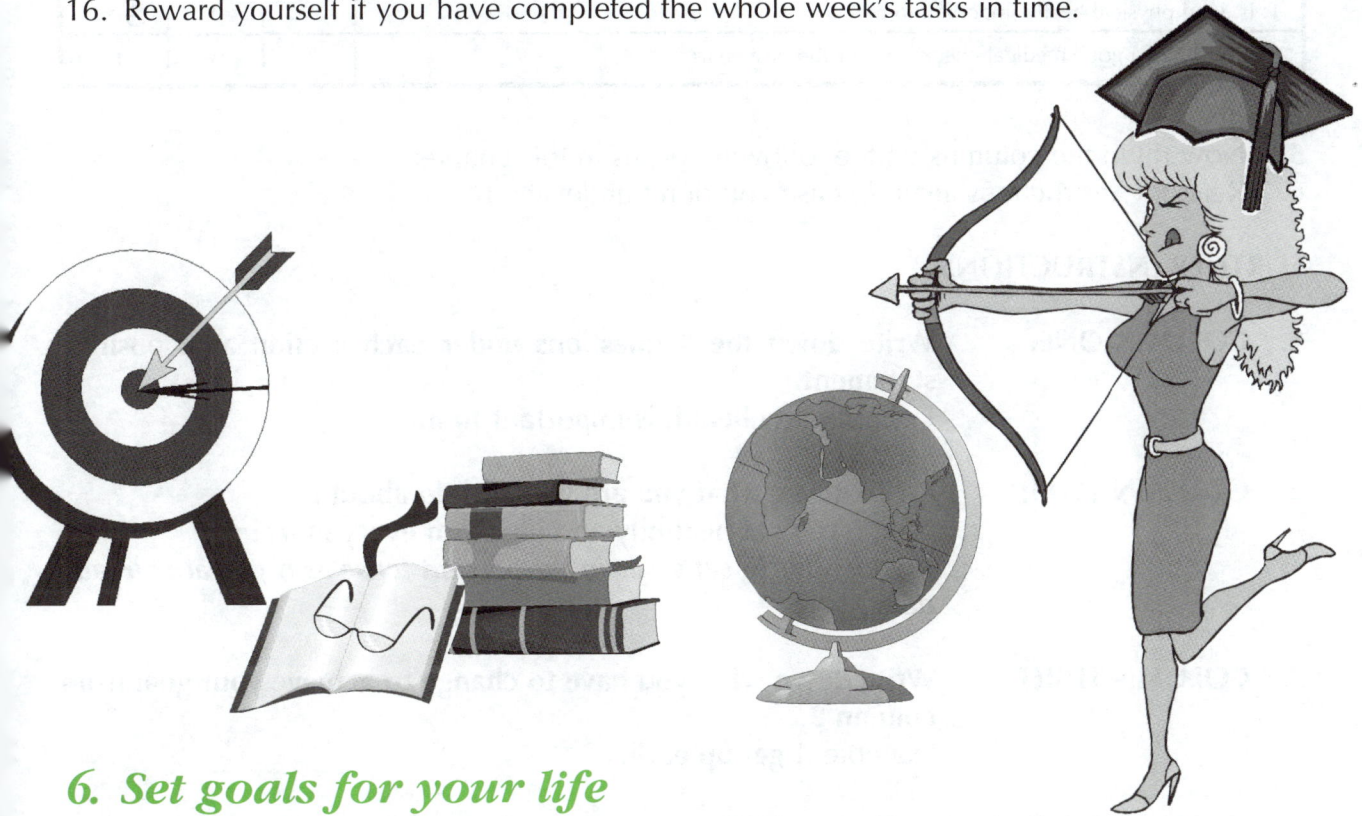

6. Set goals for your life

Page back to **CHAPTER 3** and once again look at the questionnaires you filled in.

INSTRUCTIONS:

1. Read each question of each questionnaire through carefully again.

2. Ask yourself:
   AM I SATISFIED WITH THIS?

3. Write down your answer in the third column.

   Make a PLUS SIGN if you are <u>satisfied</u> with your answer.

   Make a MINUS SIGN if you are <u>dissatisfied</u> with your answer.

   Now circle 10 MINUS SIGNS you would like to improve <u>in each questionnaire.</u>

4. Give a point FROM 1-5 for each MINUS SIGN with a circle, **which you would like to improve**.

   1 ⟶ 5
   Most important   Least important

Example:

QUESTION	YES	NO	+ OR –
1. Is good physical health important to me?		X	⊖ 1
2. Have I had a good medical check-up over the past year?	X		+

5.   Now fill in the columns on the following pages in this chapter.
6.   Read the instructions again in case you don't understand!

FURTHER INSTRUCTIONS:

1.   **COLUMN ONE:**   Write down the 5 questions under each section as a positive statement.
Example: **My health is important to me.**

2.   **COLUMN TWO:**   Write down what you are going to do about it.
Example: **I eat healthily and jog 5 km every morning.**
(Remember to set goals in the present tense as if you are already doing it.)

3.   **COLUMN THREE:**   Write down what you have to change to achieve your goal from column 2.
Example: **I get up earlier.**

4.   **COLUMN FOUR, FIVE, SIX AND SEVEN:**
Now mark one of these columns with a cross to indicate when this goal must be reached.

When you have reached these goals, you set new goals and start from scratch until you have reached all your goals!

1. MY HEALTH

NO	COLUMN ONE: STATEMENT	COLUMN TWO: WHAT CAN I DO ABOUT IT?	COLUMN THREE: WHAT AM I GOING TO CHANGE?	COLUMN FOUR: DO NOW	COLUMN FIVE: DO EVERY DAY	COLUMN SIX: DO THIS MONTH	COLUMN SEVEN: DO THIS YEAR
1							
2							
3							
4							
5							

2. MY SOCIAL LIFE

NO	COLUMN ONE: STATEMENT	COLUMN TWO: WHAT CAN I DO ABOUT IT?	COLUMN THREE: WHAT AM I GOING TO CHANGE?	COLUMN FOUR: DO NOW	COLUMN FIVE: DO EVERY DAY	COLUMN SIX: DO THIS MONTH	COLUMN SEVEN: DO THIS YEAR
1							
2							
3							
4							
5							

3. MY INTELLECT

NO	COLUMN ONE: STATEMENT	COLUMN TWO: WHAT CAN I DO ABOUT IT?	COLUMN THREE: WHAT AM I GOING TO CHANGE?	COLUMN FOUR: DO NOW	COLUMN FIVE: DO EVERY DAY	COLUMN SIX: DO THIS MONTH	COLUMN SEVEN: DO THIS YEAR
1							
2							
3							
4							
5							

4. MY SPIRITUAL LIFE

NO	COLUMN ONE: STATEMENT	COLUMN TWO: WHAT CAN I DO ABOUT IT?	COLUMN THREE: WHAT AM I GOING TO CHANGE?	COLUMN FOUR: DO NOW	COLUMN FIVE: DO EVERY DAY	COLUMN SIX: DO THIS MONTH	COLUMN SEVEN: DO THIS YEAR
1							
2							
3							
4							
5							

5. MY FINANCIAL MATTERS

NO	COLUMN ONE: STATEMENT	COLUMN TWO: WHAT CAN I DO ABOUT IT?	COLUMN THREE: WHAT AM I GOING TO CHANGE?	COLUMN FOUR: DO NOW	COLUMN FIVE: DO EVERY DAY	COLUMN SIX: DO THIS MONTH	COLUMN SEVEN: DO THIS YEAR
1							
2							
3							
4							
5							

6. MY FAMILY

NO	COLUMN ONE: STATEMENT	COLUMN TWO: WHAT CAN I DO ABOUT IT?	COLUMN THREE: WHAT AM I GOING TO CHANGE?	COLUMN FOUR: DO NOW	COLUMN FIVE: DO EVERY DAY	COLUMN SIX: DO THIS MONTH	COLUMN SEVEN: DO THIS YEAR
1							
2							
3							
4							
5							

7. MY VERY IMPORTANT PERSON

(If you answered mostly "no" to your questionnaire, you are not yet emotionally ready for a serious relationship!)

NO	COLUMN ONE: STATEMENT	COLUMN TWO: WHAT CAN I DO ABOUT IT?	COLUMN THREE: WHAT AM I GOING TO CHANGE?	COLUMN FOUR: DO NOW	COLUMN FIVE: DO EVERY DAY	COLUMN SIX: DO THIS MONTH	COLUMN SEVEN: DO THIS YEAR
1							
2							
3							
4							
5							

8. MY SCHOOLWORK

NO	COLUMN ONE: STATEMENT	COLUMN TWO: WHAT CAN I DO ABOUT IT?	COLUMN THREE: WHAT AM I GOING TO CHANGE?	COLUMN FOUR: DO NOW	COLUMN FIVE: DO EVERY DAY	COLUMN SIX: DO THIS MONTH	COLUMN SEVEN: DO THIS YEAR
1							
2							
3							
4							
5							

MY GOALS

Now write down those goals which are the most important to you in the following columns and stick it to a place where you will see it every day. Work out plans to reach your goals and mark those goals you have already achieved. Write down the date on which it was completed. Then set new goals and achieve them.

10 THINGS WHICH MUST BE DONE NOW			
NO	GOALS	ACHIEVED?	DATE
1			
2			
3			
4			
5			
6			
7			
8			
9			
10			

10 THINGS WHICH MUST BE DONE EVERY DAY			
NO	GOALS	ACHIEVED?	DATE
1			
2			
3			
4			
5			
6			
7			
8			
9			
10			

10 THINGS WHICH MUST BE DONE THIS MONTH			
NO	GOALS	ACHIEVED?	DATE
1			
2			
3			
4			
5			
6			
7			
8			
9			
10			

10 THINGS WHICH MUST BE DONE THIS YEAR

NO	GOALS	ACHIEVED?	DATE
1			
2			
3			
4			
5			
6			
7			
8			
9			
10			

Words of Wisdom

**To easily manage something which is difficult to others – that is talent.
To manage something which is impossible to the talented – that is brilliant!**

Henri- Fredric Amiel

If you think education is expensive, try ignorance!

Derek Bok

It is better to lose because of your principles than to win because of your lies.

Arthur Calwell

What really matters,
is not the size of the dog
in the fight,
but the size of the fight
in the dog.

*Dwight D Eisenhower
(left).*

8 Survive!

In prehistoric times people had specific tools and techniques to survive the cruel, wild world around them. Today we have concrete jungles and rivers of tar. Have monsters and cannibals really died out or do they simply look different from millions of years ago? This chapter will help you to survive in today's jungle...

1. In our midst …

a) Read carefully

Read the passage very carefully and write down your reading speed (number of words per minute).

In our Midst …

A small article recently appeared in a local newspaper in which mention was made of the latest research on **moles** appearing on the skin. **Professor Alexei Andropoloff**, who fled from Russia to South Africa during the communistic regime, found during his studies of several years that the appearance of moles on the skin held significant consequences for the human race.

As skin specialist, Professor Andropoloff examined about 1360 people over a 10 year period. According to his findings, the moles appear on the skin as raised brown spots and may differ in size or form. Following several experiments, he found that even more moles can appear on the skin if the person gets into the sun more often. Despite the fact that most moles seem to be harmless, many of them were the forerunners of the dreaded disease: **Skin cancer!**

The most important discovery Professor Andropoloff made, however, was that people with moles are not as clever as people without any of these marks on the skin. After several people were extensively questioned and examined, his suspicion was confirmed and he **published** it in the New World Medical Journal. **Dr Evans**, a specialist from America, immediately reacted to this and confirmed that he had come to the **same conclusion**! After several of his patients had been examined, he realised **that people with moles are in fact dumber than people without moles**. More studies showed that this skin condition was also **genetically transmittable**. Unfortunately the genes of people with moles are stronger than those without, with the result that the **children** in 90% of these cases would also have moles on the skin and thus already have an intellectual **backlog at birth**. The **government of the day** found that 50% of **criminals** in jails also have moles of the skin. They found that these people are not only unbelievably **dumb**, but also **clumsy**, often **careless** and inclined to **begging, theft** and even **murder**!

"The worst of this discovery …"according to Mr Ibrahim Rabinowitch of Greece, "… is that nearly **60% of the human population** have these moles on their skins in one form or another. This does not only have huge implications for combating crime, the development of technology and the stability of the economy, but **curbs** the natural **development** of the human race!"

People with moles are advised to stay out of the sun or apply a **sunscreen** to their skin to prevent **cancer** and stop further **intellectual deterioration**.

b) Answer the following questions:

Answer the following "comprehension test".

1. Who are the cleverest – people with or without moles?

   _____

2. What was proven in the research on moles?

   _____
   _____
   _____
   _____
   _____
   _____
   _____

3. What percentage of the human race have moles on their skin?

   _____

4. Do you know any person who has a mole on his or her skin?

   _____

5. Do you have a mole anywhere on your skin?

   _____

6. How do you feel about all the information you have just read?

   _____
   _____
   _____
   _____
   _____
   _____

I HAVE ONE!

NO WONDER ...

I HAVE ONE!

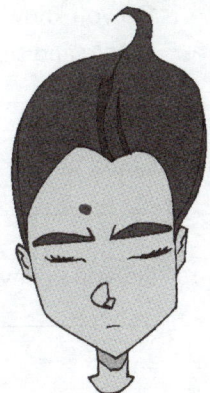

c) Can it be true?

Let us now have a critical look at the passages you have read:

a) In which newspaper or magazine did this article appear?

_____

b) In which local newspaper was the first article published?

_____

c) Who is Professor Andropoloff? Have you ever heard of him?

_____

d) Is he an authority in the area of human intellect?

_____

e) What would be the average number of patients visiting the professor's practice daily if he examined 1 360 patients in 10 years?

_____

f) Have you ever heard of the "New World Medical Journal"?

_____

g) Has the "Government of the day" really so much time that they would spend it examining criminals in jail for moles?

_____

h) Why did the other 50% without moles land in jail?

_____

i) How do you determine that 60% of the human race has moles?

_____

j) Do you know someone who has a mole on the skin – who is rather dumb, clumsy or careless?

_____

k) Do you know someone who has a mole on the skin – who is clever, supple and smart?

_____

l) Could a mole on the skin really be an indication of your intellect?

_____

m) Do you believe that there is any truth to this article, whatsoever?

_____

d) What was your reaction?

Your very first reaction to the reading this article was, possibly, one of the following:

!! Yes, I know that a mole could possibly be an indication of skin cancer!
!! What! Can't be! I have a mole on my back!
!! No wonder my brother/sister/mom/dad is so dumb!
!! It's my father's fault that I also have a mole.
!! No wonder I have such a struggle with Maths!
!! Oh! Luckily I don't have one!
!! I have seen so many people of other colours who have moles!
!! So, Mary is not as clever as she would like others to believe!
!! I have always thought so!
!! But Dad has one and he is clever!
!! No wonder there are so many stupid people in the world!

Just to put you at ease:

If you read *critically*, you would immediately have noticed that the information in the article on moles…

✘ **Is not completely true!**
✘ **THERE IS NO CONNECTION BETWEEN MOLES AND INTELLIGENCE!!**
✘ No such article has ever been published!
✘ The whole story is just a figment of the imagination!

Yet, perhaps you almost believed it, because:

▼ The article refers to "a newspaper".
▼ The statement over the connection between moles and skin cancer is discussed.
▼ Numbers and words such as "professor", "findings", "experiments", "research" and "specialists" appear in it.
▼ Other countries have been drawn into it.
▼ The "government of the day" is mentioned.

Perhaps you thought:

● It's ridiculous!
● It could only be unintelligent people who would make such statements!
● Where do they get this?
● Who publishes such drivel?

2. Bias and generalisation

Perhaps you had difficulty swallowing the previous passage and realised from the start that it was a load of nonsense. Yet, most people in our community take notice of this sort of unfounded bias and generalisation on a daily basis. Even statements which have never been researched or proven are believed, accepted and related.

From the time we are small, we place people in compartments and hang tags around their necks.

– Kids are "cool" or "nerds"
– Parents are "nice" or "old fashioned"
– "Teachers are stupid"
– Girls are "pretty" or "ugly"
– "Fat people are lazy".
– "Rich people are mean".
– The . . . . (any skin colour other than your own) are . . . . (any negative adverb)

This bias and generalisation perhaps have its origin at the dining table where you as a family discuss the rest of the country, or even on the school playground when the girls or boys are being discussed. Unfortunately it doesn't stop there, either. We carry our bias with us to school, the church, the workplace and to the grave. We carry this little seed with us and transfer it from one person to another, from parent to child and from generation to generation!

Yet all of us know of at least

– one "cool" kid who is also very hardworking.

– one set of parents who are totally "with it".

– one teacher who is really "terrific".

– one blonde who is "very clever".

– one fat person who works very hard and is both fit and friendly.

– one rich person who is generous.

– one person of another colour who thinks, feels and acts exactly like us.

– one person with a mole who is clever!

a) Bias

Bias means to *judge beforehand*. It means that a person is unfairly and negatively judged before you have taken the trouble to really get to know that person. Bias means that you send a certain image of someone to your brain where it is entrenched before you get to know that person. This is like someone who opens umbrellas and wears raincoats "in case" it's going to rain and not because it's raining.

Bias is usually based on the following:

*	Race	(e.g. Afrikaner, Englishman, Hollander, Zulu, Xhosa, Chinaman)
*	Faith	(e.g. Protestant, Roman Catholic, Jewish)
*	Association	(e.g. Different groups – sport, culture)
*	Sex	(e.g. Men and women)
*	Appearance	(e.g. Fat, thin, handicapped, short, tall, pretty, ugly)
*	Class	(e.g. Rich or poor)

When you are biased you deny that person, as well as yourself, the opportunity to start a meaningful relationship. Your bias is the cause that the person was *"weighed and found too light"* by you without having given that person the opportunity to even get onto the scale!

Bias is mainly a thought process. However, once your bias is converted into words and actions to hurt someone, to disadvantage or exclude them, it becomes known as discrimination.

b) Discrimination

Discrimination takes place when you no longer have biased thoughts only, but start to act accordingly.

Example:
You no longer only think that "people with moles are dumb". You refuse to speak to them, to play or even appear on the street with them. You don't mix with them and you see to it that they don't get the opportunity to mix with you, either. You openly declare that they make you "shudder" and how "simple" and "backward" they are. You will ridicule, slander, disadvantage, exclude or even harm them physically.

Discrimination means that you **knowingly "punish"** or **disadvantage** someone on the grounds of race, sex, religion or appearance.

The History of the World tells throughout how, in several countries, discrimination took place against people in the most horrific ways imaginable. The way in which Adolf Hitler acted against the Jews, is only one of many. Umpteen people were brutally murdered, tortured, abused, trampled and psychologically damaged because of it.

Regardless of the fact that several forms of discrimination were "allowed" in the past, it is **totally unacceptable** today. Such practices are poor behaviour and only serve to show your own fear and uncertainty. Today, discrimination in any form is AGAINST THE LAW in the workplace! Your thoughtless remark could very well cost you your job!

c) Generalisation

Generalisation means that you take the characteristics of certain people in a group and assume that everyone in that group has exactly the same characteristics.

EXAMPLE:

The teacher places you right in front in class, because your brother didn't pay attention in class.
One guy broke your heart, so all boys are pigs!

Generalisation causes us to link things which have no connection whatsoever, to each other.

Example:

"TYPICAL 'BLONDE'!"

"Boys are retarded!"
"Blondes are stupid!"
"Teenagers are lazy and rude!"
"People with moles are dumb!"

How could the number of moles on your body or the colour of your skin or hair, possibly have any connection with your intelligence?

"TYPICAL ...??..."

HOW DOES THE CLOTHING OF THE TWO GIRLS DIFFER IN ORDER FOR ONE TO BE CALLED A "TYPICAL BLONDE!"????

Generalisation is the cause of things being **magnified** and **worsened** and thereby intensifying our prejudices even further.

Example:

You already believe that "people with moles are dumber than others." If you then, in addition, also think that these people are "clumsy" and "careless" and, furthermore, are also capable of "theft" and "murder", you are worsening your bias. The poor person with the mole on his cheek now has to progress through another four obstacles before he can have a meaningful conversation with you.

How would you act towards a person if you know **beforehand** that that person regards you as "clumsy,", "careless,", "crooked" and "murderous"?

_____

_____

_____

_____

When everybody generalises and judges, we allow that to justify our prejudices and discriminatory behaviour to ourselves. Since "everybody" is like that, you don't have to trouble yourself to look for the **"exceptions" and get to know** them. Since "everybody" is like that and "everybody" thinks like that, we can carry on gossiping, slandering and setting obstacles for others as far as we go ...

With each repetition of your bias and generalisation, you don't just sharpen this image in your brain, but also in the brains of those around you. If you, furthermore, speak from a position of leadership, your worsen these acceptances, as people believe you and trust that you will really know what you're talking about!

3. *The dangers of bias and generalisation*

a) **Do we really have the right?**

Do we really have the right to make such statements about other people?

What does your Focal Point say about it?

Let us see what the Bible says ...

Genesis 1:27	So God created humans to be **like Himself**; He made men and women.	We are all created in the image of God. Do we have the right to belittle that image?
Psalm 8:5-6	You made us a little lower than Yourself and You have crowned us with **glory and honour. You let us rule everything ...**	Do we have the right to knock this crown of glory and honour with which God crowned us, from someone's head by our attitude and words?
Matthew 22:37-40	Love the Lord your God with all your heart, soul and mind. This is the first and most important commandment. The second most important commandment is **like this one**. And it is: **"Love others as much as you love yourself."** All the Law of Moses and the Book of Prophets are based on these two commandments.	Notice that God regards these two commandments as equal. They are equally important. The whole law and prophets (i.e. everything in the Bible) are summarised in these two sentences. Who is your "neighbour"? THE ONE WHO, AT ANY GIVEN TIME OF THE DAY OR NIGHT, SITS, LIES OR STANDS THE CLOSEST TO YOU!
Matthew 5:44-45	But I tell you to **love your enemie**s and pray for anyone who mistreats you. **Then** you will be acting like your Father in heaven.	Could you get to heaven if you are not a child of God ...?
Matthew 5:22	If you call someone a **fool**, you will be taken to court. And if you say that someone is worthless, you will be in danger of the **fires of hell**.	Here it clearly spells out what the final punishment is for such remarks.
Luke 6:37-38	**Don't judge** others and God won't judge you ... The way you treat others, is the way **you will be treated**.	By which measure will you be judged ...?
Luke 6:31	**Treat others just as you want to be treated.**	Would you like to carry a tag around your neck?

b) **What does it do to others?**

How did you feel at that specific moment when you read the words: "people with moles are, in fact, dumber than people without any of these marks on the skin"?

Glad? _____
Offended? _____
Angry? _____
Hurt? _____
Inferior? _____
Amused? _____

How would you feel if an important and trustworthy person in your life, made this statement while looking at your mole?
_____

How would you feel if you heard it constantly and from different sources?
_____

How does it feel to humiliate or judge someone?
_____

How does it feel to be humiliated or judged?
_____

Why do we then do it?
_____

_____

Many people's lives have been destroyed because of bias, discrimination and generalisation. What was your share in all this?

Do you BUILD or do you BULLY?
Do you cause others' tears and depression?
Is your tongue the fire with which others are burnt?
How would you feel if the situation was reversed and you were to become the receiver of your own sharp words and criticism?

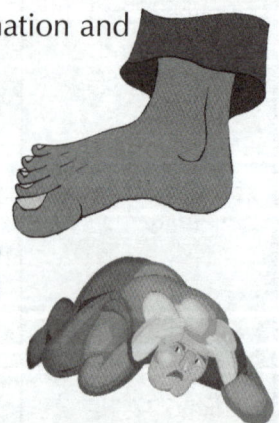

c) **What does it do to you?**

i) One of the biggest disadvantages of this bias and generalisation, is that you form ideas about people even before you have met them! Would you like to be friends with someone who is regarded as "crooked, lazy and dumb" by everyone?

You have probably already noticed that "first impressions" count a lot. You, however, have formed your "first impression" in the person's absence! Unfortunately for this person it no longer matters how clever, cute, generous, hardworking or honest he is, since you formed your own opinion long ago! Chances are that you won't even bother to get to know this person better, because you decided beforehand that it won't be worth the trouble!

ii) A further problem is that this person is now **"Guilty until he or she has been proven innocent"** instead of being **"Innocent until proven guilty"**.

There is quite a large shift of emphasis, since this person is now constantly in a position where he has to "prove" that he isn't this or that.

On the other hand you may, perhaps unconsciously, look for proof to confirm your perception of the person. You may possibly miss the person's good qualities and focus only on that which you heard beforehand of "such" people. Neither of you can then act normally!

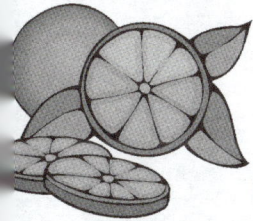

iii) We were all created for a specific purpose and in a specific way. Imagine how boring life would be if everybody looked exactly like you and felt and acted like you. *Do you really want to be friends with 30 clones of yourself?*

How would your food taste if you could eat oranges only and nothing else?

There is a reason for the variety of food you can eat. Each food type has certain proteins, vitamins and minerals your body needs to grow. You can eat all the oranges in the world and you won't find proteins in them! There are certain characteristics other people have which you don't possess. You can either live half a life without it, or you can learn and borrow from others and lead a full and happy life. **The choice is yours!**

4. *How do I overcome bias?*

a) Accept yourself
People with a low self-esteem tend towards bias and discrimination. Aren't you pulling others down because you yourself are sitting in the mud and do not have the guts to get out of it?

b) Admit that people differ
Thank God every day that we are not all the same and that there is such a huge variety of people with whom you can make friends. Use this variety as a source to develop yourself and learn more about life!

c) Focus on positive differences and similarities
Find positive similarities amongst people and appreciate the differences there are. Our heartache, pain, joy and happiness are often experienced in exactly the same way, regardless of our shape, size or colour.

d) Think logically about other people's remarks

Are these remarks true? Is it really true just because the teacher, my father, mother, grandfather, the minister or the government of the day say so?
USE YOUR FOCAL POINT AS YOUR COMPASS!
SO, LOOK FOR FACTS AND USE YOUR INTELLECT!

e) Walk in the other person's shoes

Ask yourself: "HOW WOULD I FEEL IF SOMEONE DID IT TO ME OR SAID IT ABOUT ME?"

f) Think!

Think before you speak, make a remark, laugh at someone or do something to someone. It's no joke if someone else is disadvantaged or hurt by it! Think of the consequences of that which you're busy with!
What consequences does it hold …
–   For the person to or about whom you speak?
–   For the person you are doing it to?
–   For yourself and others?

g) Choose the right friends

Do you move about with a group of friends who cannot see any good in others or the world? Get out as fast as you can! Would your friends sail past others drowning while there is more than enough space in the lifeboat? In that case they would probably push you over-board if the boat begins to leak or eat you if they become hungry …

h) Be proud

If you are proud of your own language, own culture and background, you will realise its value and not begrudge it to others.

i) Overcome your fear

Your fear of the unknown is often the reason for your bias. All people are not bad. Everybody is not out to do you harm. Grant people the opportunity to be themselves and get to know you. Give yourself the opportunity to get to know others.

j) Admit your faults

Ask yourself: Am I not like this, too? What am I doing wrong? Have I ever hurt someone else with my words and deeds? First remove the log from your eye before you look for splinters in other eyes!

5. Survival

One of the most important skills you can learn in life, is the ability to start good and loyal relationships with other people, to develop them and maintain them. This skill is important in your circle of friends, your relationship, your school and later also in your marriage and career.

We are dependent on others to lead healthy, balanced lives. We are dependent on others for everything we want from life and for that which we wish to achieve.

For …
– our food, clothes and safety
– help and advice
– education
– love and caring
– fun and pleasure
– self-fulfilment

Without the skill to build and maintain good relationships with others, you will never be truly successful or happy. Now that you have, hopefully, rid yourself of all bias, you can tackle the wonderful journey toward effective human relationships …

REMEMBER:
"No man is an island" and even if you sometimes feel angry or sad enough to wish that you could live on one, you would soon long for someone to talk to. Just think of what Robinson Crusoe would have done without his friend Friday and what Friday would have done without Robinson Crusoe.

YOU NEED PEOPLE TO SURVIVE!
THE MORE PEOPLE THERE ARE ON EARTH, THE CLOSER WE GET TO EACH OTHER AND THE BETTER WE HAVE TO GET ALONG WITH ONE ANOTHER!

6. What is interaction?

From the time you get up in the morning to the time you go to bed, there are people in your life. When you speak to each other, there is interaction. Yet when you have nothing to say to each other, there cannot be any interaction. Good personal relationships depend on that interaction!

You can compare this interaction to a tennis match where the ball is the words and the players are the communicators!

You speak to a person	
	The person listens to you
	The person considers it and decides how to react to it
	The person reacts to it
You listen to the person	
You think about it and decide how to react to it	
You react to it	

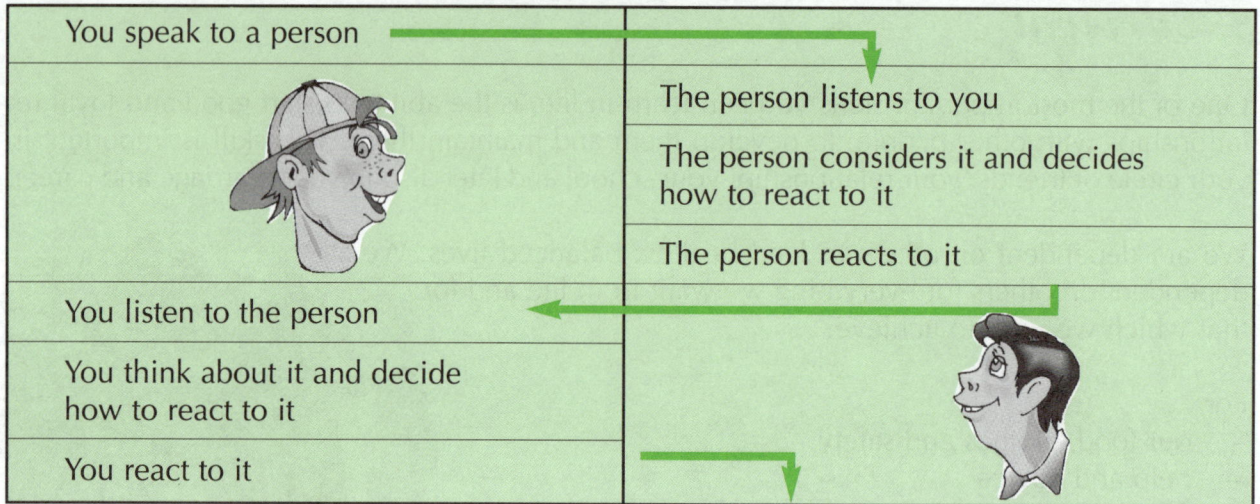

The game continues until one of the players misses the ball or both decide to stop the game.

The same happens with interaction between people. As soon as one person stops listening, interrupts the conversation or walks away, the interaction stops. A good game of tennis depends on how you and your opponent can handle the ball. A bad match takes place when the players get cross with each other and attack each other with their racquets! ***Do you hit the ball or the person?***

7. *What does interaction consist of?*

When you meet someone for the first time, you have to keep in mind that there is far more to this conversation than just the words spoken by you two! What else do you bring to this conversation?

a) Purpose
You chat to someone with a certain purpose in mind. You want to become or remain friends, you want advice, you want to fight, you want to buy or sell something.

b) Your mood
You're in a certain emotional state when talking to someone. You are angry, excited, glad, sad, in love or depressed.

c) Your body
Your body tells a great deal about what you feel or think. It shows whether you are tense, miserable, feel proud, feel unworthy, glad or sad.

d) Your role
You speak from a certain role. You are the learner who speaks to the principal, the sister who speaks to her brother, the son who speaks to his father, the friends who speak to each other or the shopkeeper who speaks to a customer.

e) The rules

They are the way in which you speak to someone, your principles and values, the language you use and the manners you exhibit.

f) The place and event

You don't speak into an air pocket to someone, but in a specific space and at a certain time. This conversation takes place in the classroom, at home, at a party, on the sports field or in the street.

The closer these aspects are to one another, the better you and the person you are speaking to, will get along. The further these aspects are from each other, the more difficult the conversation will flow. When you, therefore, speak to someone, first clear the following for yourself:

What is my **goal** with this conversation?	What is the other person's **goal** with this conversation?
What **mood** am I in?	What **mood** is the other person in?
What am I saying with my **body language**?	What does the other person's **body language** tell me?
What is my **role**?	What is the other person's **role**?
According to which **rules** do I speak?	According to which **rules** does the other person speak?
Where does this conversation take place and what is the **event**?	**Where** does the conversation take place and what is the **event**?

How do you think the following conversation
will progress and what could the consequences be?
Create your own dialogue if, however, Sally and Adrian
like each other …

SALLY AND ADRIAN'S BLIND DATE

ADRIAN	SALLY
Goal I like you and want to steal a kiss.	**Goal** I don't like you! What are you scheming …?
Mood I'm in the mood for fun.	**Mood** I am tired and want to go to bed.
Body I'm moving closer …	**Body** I'm moving further away …
Role You're visiting for the first time tonight …	**Role** I'm visiting for the first and last time tonight!
Rules I have no manners.	**Rules** WHAT PART OF "NO" DON'T YOU UNDERSTAND??
Place and Event Your father's lounge and it's a blind date!	**Place and Event** My father's lounge and it's a blind date.

8. Keep in mind ...

Keep the following in mind when you have a conversation with someone:

a)   PEOPLE SEE THINGS DIFFERENTLY.

.   What you see and what really happens, are not always the same.
You may perhaps think that someone is unfriendly and rude, while that person is actually shy, sad, tired or unhappy.

b)   THINK BEFORE YOU SPEAK OR ACT

Your actions determine the reaction of others. What you say or do, touches others around you. Think of your words and actions as a pebble you throw into a dam. The larger the pebble, the bigger the ripple effect on the water. If you shout, the other person shouts. If you stay calm, the other person will also stay calm!

c)   YOUR MOOD INFLUENCES THE CONVERSATION

Nobody wants to talk to someone who moans and groans all the time. Positive and cheerful people usually have more friends than those who always complain and are negative.

d)   MAINTAIN RESPECT

Never lose your dignity and values during any conversation. Once people have lost their respect for you, you will struggle to get it back again.

e)   PAY ATTENTION TO FEEDBACK.

Do you really listen to what people say to you? Pay attention to people's words, what they say, how they say it and what their body language tells you.
Know when to speak and also when to keep quiet.

f)   YOUR ACTIONS AND REACTIONS DETERMINE THE INTERACTION

It is not so much what is done to you, as what you do about it, that determines the success of the conversation.
If someone yells or screams at you, you can yell back, walk away or smile and calmly continue speaking. The choice is yours!

9. The importance of good personal relationships

A life without friends or people who love you, is no life. To be truly happy, you need other people. **Good relationships with other people are a necessity and not a luxury!**

Why are good human relationships so important?

● **It prevents loneliness.**
Loneliness causes you to:
–   stop growing as a person
–   regard yourself as a failure
–   feel as if life has no meaning
–   become anxious, tense and depressed
–   live in the past instead of the present.

● **It helps you to develop as a person and to form your own identity.**
Your identity is built up by your interaction with others.
– You come into contact with other people.
– You react to what they do and say.
– They react to what you do and say.
You learn how to act, who you would like to be and how people will accept you, from the reactions of others.

● **It is one of the most important skills enabling you**
– to be taken into service
– to be productive
– and to make a success of your career.
If you don't get along with others at work someday, you will not be in that job for long.

● **It gives quality and meaning to your life.**
You are only truly happy once you make others happy. What gives you more pleasure: A conversation with yourself or a conversation with others?

● **It keeps your body healthy.**
Loneliness can kill you. Research has proven that people who have supportive friends, live longer and recover faster from illnesses.

● **It keeps your spirit healthy.**
Loneliness causes a vicious cycle of depression, anxiety, frustration and a feeling of hopelessness and failure.
Positive supportive relationships, on the other hand, relieve stress, make you laugh, give you a good self image and help you to handle life and make a success of it.

● **It helps you to deal with stress in a positive manner.**
When life treats you badly or when things are not going well, it's the positive relationships that give you the necessary advice, direction, support, soothing and feedback you need to handle the situation and stress correctly.

● **It helps you to be the person you would like to be.**
Good personal relationships keep you in the present with what matters here and how.
Because people love you, accept you, care about you, understand and encourage you, you can live according to your values and principles and reach for your goals.

● It helps you to be humane.
If you accept others, you will be accepted.
If you forgive others, you will be forgiven.
If you show mercy to others, they will be merciful towards you.

IMPORTANT!

All relationships are not positive and constructive. Stay out of relationships with people who degrade and hurt you! Only enemies will wilfully put your body, soul and spirit in danger …

10.   *What do good personal relationships consist of?*

Would you like to get along well with others? In that case, there are a few basic rules to follow. If you follow these rules, chances are that you won't only make good friends, but will get on well with anybody!

Good human relationships are based on the following:

GIVE AND TAKE

RESPECT

HONESTY

TRUST

ACCEPTANCE

The success of any relationship – regardless of whether it is a love affair, a relationship with your parents, brothers and sisters, teachers, or, at a later stage, with your colleagues and employer – relies on these characteristics:

● **Respect**
● **Trust**
● **Honesty**
● **Acceptance**

Should one of these legs of the table be missing, chances are that the relationship will not stand the test of time.

Can you really have a good relationship with someone …
● for whom you have no respect?
● whom you cannot trust?
● who is dishonest?
● who does not accept you for who and what you are?

If you try, all the same, you will soon realise that your heart is not in the relationship and that you or the other person will eventually think of any possible excuse to get out of the relationship.

Relationships are built on the principles of **GIVE** and **TAKE**.

If you show no respect toward another, are dishonest, unreliable and do not accept the other person, you can expect the same treatment from them.

a) Respect

Respect for others begins with respect for yourself. This respect includes:

- *Respect for your own body.*
  If you believe that your body is a temple of God, you will treat it with respect, expect others to treat it thus and will also respect and handle the bodies of others accordingly. How do you behave when in a temple or church?

- *Respect for your own intellectual abilities.*
  If you believe that you have been appointed as representative of God here on earth, you would realise that God has very high expectations for the way in which you use your brain. If you really regard man as the crown of Creation, you won't underestimate someone else's abilities, but will see them as a source from which you can learn!

- *Respect for your own emotions.*
  If you believe that emotions are part of man's make-up and that everybody will, at some time or another, be hurt, feel frustrated, love and be happy or feel hopeless, you will not only be able to recognise your own emotions and constructively deal with them, but will recognise the same emotions in others.

b) Honesty

No relationship can ever be maintained sensibly if one or both parties constantly hide things from one another or lie. Lies breed lies!

One small lie soon snowballs into a huge deception. If you lie about **where** you were, you have to lie about who you were with, you have to lie about what you did there, you have to lie about what happened, you have to lie about what you ate and drank and you have to lie about **how** you got home!

- *Honesty begins with yourself.*
  If you lie to yourself, you will certainly lie to others about yourself.
  If you pretend to be someone else, your whole life is one big lie! Don't tell a guy that you like cricket if you hate it! He will soon realise it and then know that you lie about foolish things!

- *Be honest about your feelings.*
  Learn to put your emotions into words. Don't yell if you are sad. Don't be angry if you are hurt. Learn to say: "This hurts!" or "This makes me happy!"

- **Be honest about your actions.**
  Nothing that you do, goes unnoticed. There is no action that does not come to light sometime or other. The deeper you hide something, the bigger the consequences become when it comes to light.
- **Be honest about your goals and motives.**
  Be honest about the reasons why you do things. Don't give someone the impression that you are interested in him or her as a person, while you are, in fact, after her body, his money, her sister, his status, her friends or his job! If you are not honest, you are consciously MISLEADING and EXPLOITING someone!

c) Trust

In order to trust people, you have to ...

- **Take trouble to get to know others.**
  Knowledge of humanity is a skill. To really get to know people, you have to get rid of bias and generalisation. Still, you have to take trouble to get to know the person really well. Is this person wearing a mask? Is he really what he pretends to be ...? Can you respect him? Is he honest and above-board? Is he trustworthy? Can you accept his behaviour?

- **Allow people to trust you.**
  Could somebody trust you if they know absolutely nothing about you? Allow people to find out who and what you really are, what your principles are, which goals you are striving for and according to which rules you play the game of life. In this way you eliminate many unpleasant surprises.

- **Be trustworthy yourself.**
  Trust also works on the principle of GIVE and TAKE. You can't demand trust if you are not trustworthy yourself. You can't become angry if someone mistrusts you, when you are the cause of it yourself. Can you really blame someone who mistrusts you if you regularly lie, arrive late, forget or postpone appointments, gossip and never keep your word ...?

d) Acceptance

- **Accept yourself!**
  Acceptance begins by accepting your own faults and disabilities. If you accept yourself, you will be able to accept others. If you can't make peace with your life and your body, you will constantly wonder what others think about it and before long you compare and criticise people! In your effort to be accepted, you start judging others!
  Do you really think that people have all day to watch whether your stomach is bigger today than yesterday? Is that really all that life is about?

I AM FAT!

- **Accept that people make mistakes.**
Everybody makes mistakes. Everybody takes the "wrong road" at one time or another. Everybody has disabilities and no one is without sin. Mistakes are there to be learnt from and not to stone others with. When a group of people wanted to stone a woman because of her infidelity, Jesus said: "Let the one who is without sin, cast the first stone." Everybody turned around and walked away …

- **Forgive and forget.**
We easily "forgive", but usually struggle to "forget".
We easily throw it into the rubbish bin, but put the black bag in the cupboard until we fight or are hurt and then throw it back in the person's face!
1 Corinthians 13:5 says: **"Love doesn't keep a record of wrongs that others do."**
It doesn't make lists of that which someone has done to you. To forgive, does not mean "to turn over a new leaf". **Forgiveness means**: *It is forgotten! It is out of your mind! It is out of reach! It does no longer exist!*

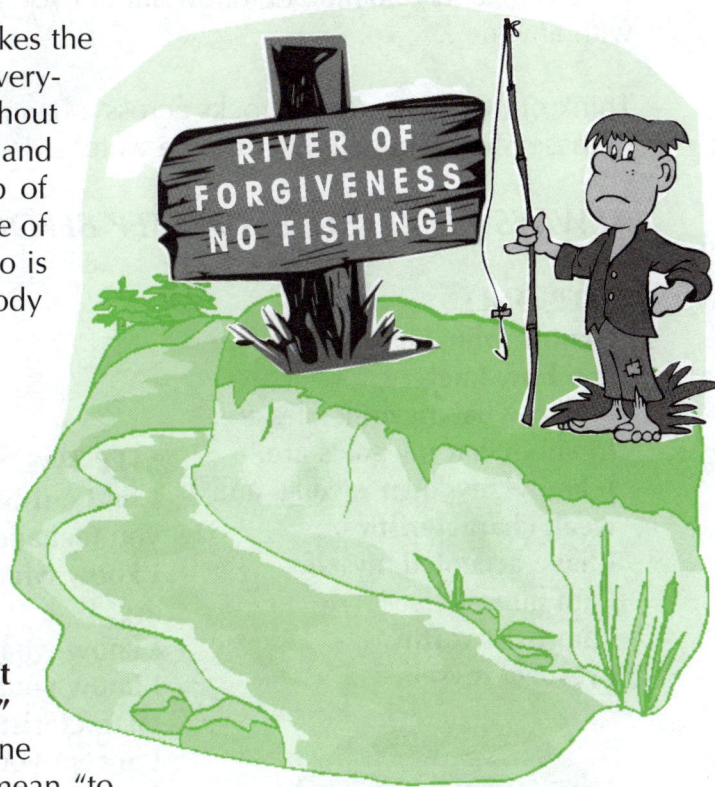

11. How are good human relationships formed?

We all like to have friends. Without friends life would lose a lot of its glitter. It is vital that we have friends! Yet, a lot of us struggle to make friends! We are sometimes so afraid of being rejected or disappointed, that we don't want to dare making friends.

While there are several ways for you to make friends, the best way is still to **offer your friendship first and to be a true friend!**

At the beginning of every relationship people often struggle to set the boundaries within which the relationship will take place. Do we remain acquaintances or do we become friends? Do we remain friends or do we become more than just friends?

Sometimes we give too little of ourselves and in this way cause the relationship not to develop. At other times we are again so over-eager to make friends and be accepted, that we give, show and tell things about ourselves about which we are extremely sorry later. Where do you draw the line?

Here is a good guideline to follow should you again wish to start a friendship or relationship with anyone …

Think of these steps as the rocks across a dangerous river you have to cross. If you miss one of these rocks, you will fall into the water …!

ALWAYS COMPLETE EACH STEP BEFORE MOVING TO THE NEXT!!!

STEP ONE:
I know who I am, how I feel and how I act.
I know what my principles are.
I know what my goals are.
I know my own strong and weak characteristics.
I have accepted myself.
I am honest.
I am trustworthy.
I respect myself.

STEP TWO:
I find out who you are, how you feel and how you act.
I know what your principles are.
I know what your goals are.
I know your good and weak characteristics.
I accept you.
I respect you.

STEP THREE:
I am trustworthy enough to accept you, to support and stand by you and to be honest with you.

STEP FOUR:
You prove that you are trustworthy enough to accept me, support and stand by me and to be honest with me.

STEP FIVE:
I am interested in your ideas, thoughts and emotions and I respect them.

STEP SIX:
I open myself up to you.
I am open and honest about my own thoughts, emotions and ideas.
I allow you to get to know me further as a person …

Processed from: **Reaching Out …**

12. Rules for good communication

When you speak to someone, you don't only want that person to receive your message but also to understand what you are trying to say. It often happens that you say something you don't mean at all or that which you wish to say, is not understood at all! Here are a few guidelines you can use so that people can really understand what you are trying to say!

Use the following guidelines to work out how to discuss something that has bothered you for a long time with your parents.
Then use the same guidelines to work out how to discuss something with your teacher. ...

a) First be willing to listen.

First become a good listener before you expect others to listen to you. Be prepared to listen to other people's point of view. Then listen attentively so that you will understand exactly what the other person says. Finish listening first before you begin to think what your reply will be.

b) Think before you speak.
Decide on what you want to say and how you want to relate it. Ask yourself:
What do I want to say? Is it **true**? It is **friendly**? It is **necessary**?
Why do I want to relate this message?
Who do I want to say it to?
What is the best way in which to relate this message?
What is the best time to relate this message?

c) Reason with yourself and get answers to your questions.
Think of the questions the person could ask and have answers ready. Try to put your viewpoint in such a way that the other person will understand. Put your words in such a way that you can reach your goal by way of the conversation.

d) Be organised.
Don't let your thoughts jump about. Start at a certain point and allow your thoughts to follow one another logically, so that the other person can understand. Don't speak round about. Don't take it for granted that people know what you're talking about, how you feel and what you want to say. The other person cannot see what's going on in your head. Explain how you feel, what you feel and what you want.

e) Make sure that the person is listening.
Relate your message so positively that someone likes to listen to you. Make sure that the person gives you his or her full attention. Make the person inquisitive enough to listen to you and in the end also grateful that they did listen to you.

f) Speak from the receiver's viewpoint.
Put yourself in the shoes of the person who will receive the message. How would he or she like to hear this message?

g) Keep your message simple and specific.

Don't be longwinded or say something in a roundabout way. It becomes boring if you can't get to the point. Put the message in such a way that someone can understand what you are saying.

h) Choose the best method to relate your message.

Ask yourself how the message can be best related and understood. Do you have to chat about it, phone, write a letter or rather keep quiet?

I) Ensure that your message is understood correctly.

Ask whether the person heard and understood the message. Ensure that the person knows exactly what you mean. Clear up misunderstandings. Repeat your message or put it another way. Misunderstandings often occur when people understand each other wrongly – even if both heard correctly!

j) Watch your language and the way you speak.

Always speak a language the other person can understand. Use words which that person would use. Watch the way you speak. Do you speak with head hanging down? Do you mumble? Do you speak too softly? Do you regard yourself as better than the other person? Are you aggressive, forward, taunting? Speak properly, loud enough and clearly and look the other person in the eye while you speak.

k) Watch the other person's body language.

What is the other person's attitude? Does it look as if the person wants to listen to you? Your body reveals much more than words can say!

l) Make the person feel important.

People like to listen to someone who treats them with love and respect. No one likes to listen to someone who makes you feel like a dirty rag!

m) Watch the time and place when you relate the message.

The right message can sometimes be completely lost because you chose the wrong time and place to relate it. Remember that there is a time and place for everything. Make sure that you relate the right message at the right time. Rather wait and choose a time which suits the receiver of your message. If that time does not come along, make a specific appointment!

n) Create a win-win situation.

Nobody likes to give or lose all the time. If you constantly want to win the case you will eventually lose the person. Make sure that there is an advantage to the other person in the conversation as well. Put your arguments, reasoning and requests in such a way that you both gain by it!

13. Conflict

A person is likely to think that conflict is something harmful which should be avoided at all cost. If you have ever seen two people fighting, you will admit that it's definitely not a pleasant experience. Yet conflict is part of life.

Think of a lot of apples in a box. The more apples you put in and the closer they get to each other, the bigger the odds are they will bump against each other. If you then shake the box, chances are good these apples will collide with each other.

The same happens with people. The closer we get to each other, the bigger the possibility that conflict will emerge. If life then adds to it by giving us a few jerks at that moment, the likelihood of conflict becomes bigger still. We tend to fight with those who are closest to us. You surely wouldn't stop a stranger on the street and promptly start fighting with him!

There are mainly two types of conflict, namely:

- **Negative conflict**
  (scream, yell, swear, manhandle, degrade, get personal, slam doors and walk away)
  Negative conflict does not only destroy the relationship between people, but even the people within that relationship.

- **Positive conflict**
  (reason, give facts, stay calm, argue, does not get personal, maintain respect)
  Positive conflict helps us to know each other better, learn from our mistakes and come up with new solutions.

LET US SEE HOW CONFLICT CAN BE TURNED INTO A POSITIVE EXPERIENCE …

14. The winning recipe for handling conflict

a) How do you handle conflict?

Determine how you usually handle conflict. If that didn't help you much in the past, you should try another way. Also note how the other person handles conflict. If this person always walks away when you always start screaming, a new method is necessary if you two want to save the relationship.

b) Ascertain why there is conflict.

Sometimes we fight about things so petty that it is actually laughable. Unfortunately these "small foxes" could easily destroy a good relationship. Constant fighting over small things is usually a sign that there is a bigger problem that should be sorted out. Sit with the person and first try to ascertain what it is **really** about.

c)   Choose the right time.

Don't fight with someone when you or the other person are tired, busy, late or feel very frustrated. Choose a time when neither of you can be interrupted and when both are calm enough to discuss the matter. Why, for instance would you want to argue with a drunk person when he can't even remember, the next day, what he said?

d)   Handle conflict as a problem.

Always handle conflict as a problem which must be solved calmly. Would the problem be solved if you swore and yelled? Will your father lend you money if you slam the doors? Ask questions and give facts which will bring you closer to the solution and not aggravate the problem. Do you extinguish a fire by standing over it and screaming?

e)   Think WIN-WIN.

Look for a solution which will satisfy both. Sometimes you actually have to lose a few pawns in order to win the match. Always ask yourself if it is that important to win the argument that you would risk losing the person's respect and friendship as a result of it.

f)   Make sure of your facts.

Consider your arguments before you tackle the problem and make sure that your facts are correct and cannot be twisted in any way. Don't accuse people unjustly. It only worsens the situation.

g)   Look into each other's eyes.

Don't turn your back on someone, walk away or stare at the television while someone is trying to sort out a problem with you in a positive way. Look at the person and give your full attention to solving this problem. Can you really be furious while someone looks you in the eye and even holds your hand?

h)   Listen to the other person.

Listen precisely to what the other person is trying to tell you with his words and body language. Don't be so busy forming counter arguments in your head that you don't follow the conversation at all!

i)   Put yourself in the other person's shoes.

How would you think, feel and act if you were in the other person's situation? Read the newspaper and try to understand why your mother goes crazy if you're a few hours late …

j)   Stay calm.

You lose the argument as soon as you lose your temper! The fact that you shout louder and throw more things around **does not mean that you have won the argument.** Remember that tension shuts down your brain. As soon as you become angry, your thoughts and actions become illogical and thoughtless!

k) Stick to the point.

Talk about here and now and about that which is a problem now. Forget about things that happened in the past or that has nothing to do with the issue. Your girlfriend's hairstyle, for instance, has nothing to do with the fact that you forgot the appointment. Don't scratch in the rubbish bin and throw each other with rotten peels!

l) Don't become personal.

Do you hit the ball to someone or do you hit that person with the racquet? Stick to what the person does that makes you unhappy and don't make personal remarks that you may not be able to take back.

m) Don't take everything personally.

Don't take it as a personal attack if people criticise you for something you have done wrong! People often say things they don't mean at all during a fit of anger.

Learn to differentiate between that which you have to listen to and that which you have to forgive and forget for the **sake** of the **relationship**.

n) Talk honestly about how you feel.

Anger is actually a form of frustration or pain. Learn to say: "I feel …………." and then use the right words to describe what you feel.

o) Find a solution.

Decide on a solution together and on how such conflict situations will be avoided in future. It's amazing how much time is wasted by constantly fighting about the same things. It becomes monotonous, dulls your feelings and damages the whole relationship. After a while, nobody listens to someone who threatens, screams, yells or moans and groans all day.

p) Apologise.

Learn to say: "I AM SORRY." MEAN IT SINCERELY AND DO SOMETHING ABOUT IT. FORGIVE COMPLETELY and FORGET ALTOGETHER.

L isten – always
E mpathy – show it
A ssertive – think win-win
D epersonalise – focus on problem
E quality – never talk down
R espect – earn it
S olutions – find them

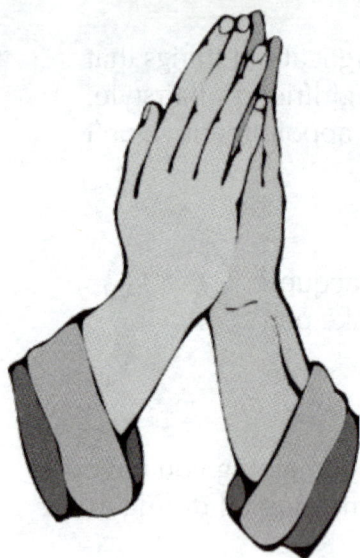

PRAYER FOR TODAY

Lord, make me an instrument of Thy peace.
Where there is hatred, let me show love;
where there is injury, pardon;
where there is doubt, hope;
where there is darkness, light
and where there is sadness, joy.

O, Divine Master, grant that I
may not so much seek to be consoled,
as to console;
to be understood as to understand;
to be loved, as to love;
for it is in giving
that we receive,
it is in pardoning
that we are pardoned,
and it is in dying
that we are born
into eternal life.

*Prayer of
Saint Francis*

9 Liberation or destruction?

We are all born to be free! We strive toward it all our life and soon revolt if our freedom is restricted. Ironically enough, most people throw away their own freedom because of the choices they make. Do you know the rights and responsibilities that form part of your freedom? Read here by all means! Read Paul's letter to Romans to find out what freedom really means, as well.

1. Freedom

The Statue of Liberty stands on Liberty Island in the harbour of New York. This statue is 93,5 meters high and was erected as a symbol of freedom. The statue consists of a woman with a long robe and a crown of thorns on her head. In her right hand she holds a torch aloft and in her left hand a book. The broken chains *on her feet symbolise the* **liberation** *from tyranny through the ages and still in the current life. This freedom* is fought for in several countries and by many people.

Individual freedom means that you have the right to do as you please. To any teenager it may immediately sound as if this statue definitely has a bearing on you. Wherever you go, you are restricted by rules and regulations and people who tell you what to do and what not to do. Perhaps you feel more like a puppet with everybody pulling your strings, than an individual who has any freedom. Why then should there be so many rules and laws if you are supposed to be FREE?

There are about 6000 million people on earth and it is calculated that this number will increase to 9800 million by the year 2050. These people all differ from each other. You won't even find identical twins who think, feel and look exactly the same. If everybody could come and go as they like, make and break as they like, say, mess, take and kill as they like, chaos and war would be the order of the day.

Your freedom can only be called TRUE FREEDOM if it is not threatened or disadvantaged by others and if you yourself don't disadvantage or threaten the freedom of others.

The laws of our country, the regulations of your town or city, the principals of the community, the rules of the school and even the rules in your home, **are set to ensure this freedom for everyone in the community.** Whenever somebody's words or actions cause others to lose their freedom, these laws, rules and regulations come into being to force that person (who harms other's freedom) to abide by the rules and respect the freedom of others in future.

EXAMPLE:

Any person with a valid driver's license has the freedom to drive his vehicle on the roads of the country. That person first had to earn his driver's license by knowing the rules of the road before the license was issued to him. The person therefore first had to prove that he is responsible and trustworthy enough to earn his freedom. Now that he has the license, he can drive the car where and whenever he wants to as long as he follows the rules. If, however, this person abuses this freedom by speeding through a town at 180 kilometers per hour, he disadvantages the freedom of others to cross or use the road safely. If the person is caught, he is punished and his freedom to drive his car (his driver's license) can be taken away.

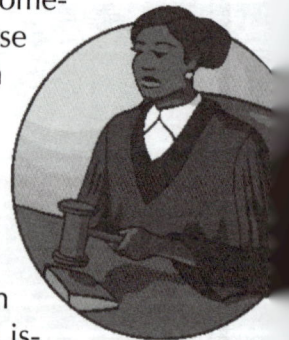

Let us use an example you may have experienced yourself:

You have the freedom to go out on Friday nights. For your own safety there are certain rules you have to adhere to however. When you get home late, you are not only threatening your own safety, but are also abusing the freedom of your parents who wanted to go to bed ages ago. Now they're sitting up waiting for you because they are concerned about your safety. You are curbing their right to sleep as well as their right to relax!

Laws, rules and regulations protect everybody's freedom and rights!

> **WHERE IS MY CHILD THIS LATE AT NIGHT...??**

2. *What protects your freedom?*

The Constitution of South Africa was accepted as law on 10 December 1996. According to this Constitution the rights and freedom of all people in South Africa are protected. It is important for you to know what these rights entail. Here is a brief summary of these rights:

a) The Constitution of South Africa

Summary of The Constitution of South Africa.

Every person has the right to:
- Equality and equal treatment in respect of sex, race, marital status, sexual preferences, age, disability, religion, values, culture, language, and birth.
- Respect and humane treatment.
- Life.
- Freedom and protection if your freedom is taken from you or threatened unlawfully.
- Protection against slavery and forced labour.
- Protection of your right to privacy.
- Freedom in the exercising of his or her religion and religious belief **(THAT IS WHY YOUR VIEW MAY DIFFER FROM THE FOCAL POINT OF THIS BOOK).**
- Freedom of speech **(THAT IS WHY I MAY GIVE YOU MY VIEW OF FOCAL POINT).**
- Freedom to gather about issues and even protesting peacefully.
- Freedom of association.
- Political freedom.
- Citizenship.
- Freedom of movement.
- Freedom to work.
- Reasonable and fair labour practices.
- A safe environment to be conserved for posterity.
- Protection of their property.
- Suitable housing.
- Health services, food, water, security and first aid.
- Children have special and specific rights (SEE NEXT PAGE).
- Training and education.
- An own language and culture.
- The exercising of an own culture, religion and community life.
- Access to information.
- Fair administration.
- Access to courts.
- The right to reasonable and fair arrest and confinement procedures.

The government has the right to:
- Maintain these rights.
- Limit these rights in a democratic, humane, equal and fair way.
- Announce emergency circumstances if the rights and freedom of citizens are threatened.

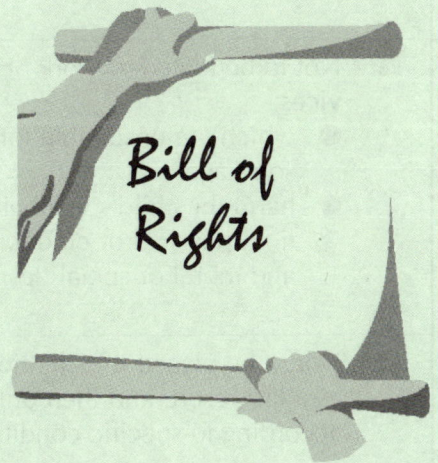

Bill of Rights

b) The rights of children

Since children grow up mainly in the care of parents and other adults and are not always in a position to protect themselves, special provision has been made for their rights. You must, however, remember that your rights always include certain responsibilities.

Rights of children	Responsiblity of children
Every child (person under 18 years) has from birth the right:	**Every child (person under 18 years) also has the following responsibilities:**
☞ To a name and nationality.	Be proud of your own name nationality and treat other people's names and nationality with the same respect with which you would like to be treated.
☞ To family and parental care or suitable alternative care if the child is removed from the family environment	Help with the care of everyone in your family. Help when someone is ill or tired or weaker or younger than you are.
☞ To have basic food, shelter, basic health services and welfare services.	Don't waste food. Regularly visit your doctor and dentist. Take care of you own health by bathing regularly, washing your hair, dressing neatly, brushing teeth and eating right. Avoid alcohol, cigarettes and drugs and ask for help if you have problems.
☞ To be protected against maltreatment, neglect, abuse or humiliation.(any form of molestation).	Don't maltreat, bully, neglect, abuse or humiliate anyone in your community. Don't delight in others pain and heartache. Don't cause wounds. Rather be the one who applies the ointment.
☞ To be protected against exploitive labour practices.	Give voluntary help in the home and community you are part, of the family and school. Don't leave work for others that you can do yourself.
☞ Not to be forced to work or deliver services ● which are unsuitable for the person's age. ● harm the child's wellbeing, education, physical or emotional health and moral or social development.	Homework is suitable for everyone. You won't go mad, drop down dead or become sick from it. Everyone is supposed to help clean the house and keep it neat, prepare meals and help with tasks in and around the house. You are perfectly capable of seeing to your own room, wardrobe or homework.
☞ Not to be placed in detention, unless as a last resort, and then only according to specific conditions.	See to it that you stay out of trouble by not overstepping the laws of the country, school rules or house rules. Rights always have rules which must be followed and punishment which will be meted out if these rules are not obeyed.
☞ To obtain legal representation in respect of matters relating to the child.	Get to know your rights and ask for help when you need it.

☞	Not be brought into armed conflict and to be protected under such circumstances.	Don't bully, frighten, hurt or clash with others. Learn to solve conflict with words and not with fists. Don't carry dangerous weapons or forbidden substances on your person. It is against the law.
☞	To basic and further training.	Go to school regularly, do your homework, learn and do your best!
☞	To love and care.	Show love in the right way and help to take care of others.
☞	To a safe home and shelter.	Help to maintain your home. Don't constantly ask for money to satisfy your personal needs. Your mom and dad work for it and must pay and maintain the house with it.
☞	To regular meals.	Eat regularly and healthily. Don't starve or fatten yourself and then try to undo the harm with a strict diet or pills. Don't use your eating habits to attract attention. It is infantile and you only harm yourself by it!
☞	To be treated with dignity and respect.	Treat your parents, grandparents, brothers and sisters, friends and strangers, teachers and figures in authority with dignity and respect.
☞	To expect time, patience and understanding from their parents.	Spend time with your family. Be patient and regard family time as something precious. Try to understand your parents if you wish to be understood.
☞	To self-respect and a life free of physical, emotional and sexual abuse.	Respect yourself. Love yourself. Don't abuse others physically, emotionally or sexually!
☞	To privacy.	You may insist on privacy in your bedroom, the bathroom and in respect of your possessions. Keep it neat and orderly and don't leave your things around everywhere. If others don't have to clean or tidy on your behalf, no one will scratch in your property.
☞	To culture, relaxation and games.	Enjoy sporting facilities, parks and playgrounds. They are, however, not there to be vandalised or messed. Neither is it a place where you may do those things you're not allowed to do at your own home.
☞	To express your own opinion.	Listen before you expect others to listen to you. Treat others as you would like to be treated.
☞	To free association.	You may choose your own friends, but listen to advice if people try to warn you against bad influences. Human knowledge is a skill which is learnt as time goes by. When your parents warn you against certain friends there are usually good factual reasons for it. Listen to them by all means!

c) Children and trials

Have you ever been called to the office for something serious you have done wrong or been accused of? Remember that all adults have to adhere to the Bill of Human Rights and therefore it is important that the correct procedures be followed if anyone, including children, are accused, found guilty or have to be punished. It is important that you know these procedures to ensure that you are not only treated reasonably and fairly, but also because these procedures will be followed in your career later in life.

SUMMARY OF RULES AND PROCEDURES

☞ It is forbidden to discriminate unfairly against a person on the grounds of race, sex, age, pregnancy, marital status, ethnic or social origin, colour, sexual preference, religion, conscience, culture, language or birth.

☞ Everybody's dignity must be respected and protected.

☞ The right to freedom and security must be protected.
- Violence is unacceptable.
- Maltreatment is unacceptable.
- Punishment in a cruel, inhuman or degrading manner is unacceptable.

☞ The right to physical and psychological integrity must be protected.

☞ The right to privacy must be protected.

☞ The person's home, possessions and property may not be searched in his or her absence.

☞ You have the right to be informed
- of your right to remain silent.
- of the consequences if you don't remain silent.

☞ You may not be forced to confess.

☞ The trail must take place as soon as possible after the charge (48) hours.

☞ You have the right to a reasonable and fair trial.
- You have to be informed of the charge against you with enough information to answer it.
- You have to be granted enough time to prepare your defence.
- You may be present during the trial.
- You may be represented by someone if you cannot handle your own defence properly.
- You are regarded as innocent until proven guilty.
- You may call witnesses to defend your cause.
- You may cross examine the prosecutors witnesses.
- The trail has to take place in a language you understand or an interpreter has to be present.
- You cannot be found guilty a second time on a charge for which you have already been heard and found guilty or innocent. (It can, however, count as incriminatory against you).
- The punishment must fit the crime.
- You have the right to appeal against the judgement of the trial so that it can be tried by a higher authority.
- You have the right to information about the case in a language that you understand.
- Evidence that is obtained in an unlawful manner, cannot be used as evidence.
- It is important that minutes be taken at the trial!

REMEMBER, HOWEVER, TO ACT AT ALL TIMES WITH DIGNITIY – EVEN IF YOU ARE FOUND GUILTY AND PUNISHED!

d) The rights of parents

Just before you run to your mother or father to complain about your lot on the "unreasonable labour practices" when they are possibly guilty, you need to remember that you are part of a family or household and that others have rights too. Parents, therefore, also have rights!

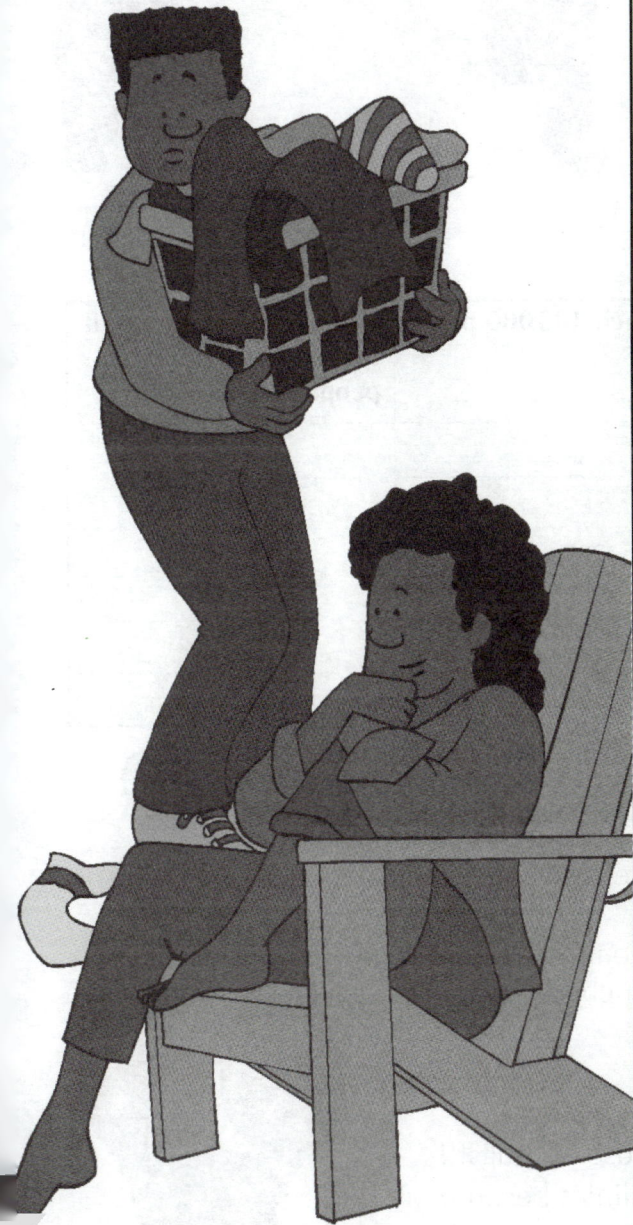

The rights of parents

1. **Parents have the right to humanity – nobody is perfect!**
   If a parent, however, has acted wrongly or made mistakes, he or she should be willing to admit it towards the child (If your parents smoke or drink, it doesn't give you the "right" to do it too.)

2. **Parents have the right to – in as far as possible – lead a relaxed life.**
   Be considerate and try not to stress out your parents unnecessarily by e.g. coming home later than the agreed homecoming time or by doing things which your parents don't approve of.

3. **Parents have the right to sleep.**
   They have the right not to be kept out of their sleep by loud music or as a result of their worry over their children's comings and goings.

4. **Parents have the right to relax and be happy in their own home.**
   It is their house. (They pay the maintenance, bond repayments or rent.) Everybody in the house should therefore make an effort to keep it clean and tidy.

5. **Parents have the right to be unafraid of their children or not to be maltreated, insulted or threatened by their children.**

6. **Parents have the right to expect help from their children** for tasks to be done in or about the house.

7. **Parents have the right to obtain information and to hear the truth.**
   Think about the fact that the truth has a way of coming to light at one time or another. You damage the relationship of trust between you and your parents and just limit your own freedom once they realise you are lying!

8. **Parents have the right to obtain help if their children experience problems.**

DO YOU RESPECT EVERYBODY'S RIGHTS?
ARE ALL YOUR RIGHTS BEING RESPECTED?
By all means read the Bill of Human Rights and ensure that your rights are respected and that you respect the rights of others!

3. When freedom is threatened

With so many laws, rules and regulations to protect everybody's rights, a person would think that all of us would live in a safe country and that everybody would enjoy a safe and relaxed existence. Yet it doesn't happen and we are living in one of the most violent countries in the world.

The statistics are, to say the least, shocking:

The following statistics are supplied by the South African Police on the Internet (http://www.saps.co.za):

Crime 1997–1998	1 for each 100 000 peple	Calculate the number if there are 48 million people in our country
Murder	58.5	
Attempted murder	69	
Aggravated assault	207.6	
Rape	115.8	
Drug related crime	93.6	
Driving under the influence of alcohol or drugs	60.2	

(See if you can fill in the latest statistics as well!)

☛ It is calculated that 1 out of every 3 women in South Africa is raped.
☛ The kidnapping of children is a reality! There really are syndicates who kidnap and sell children.
☛ The abuse and maltreatment of children is common and happens every day. According to SAFCA 250 cases of child abuse are reported daily!
☛ Children are murdered and tortured.
☛ Child pornography and child prostitution are reality!
☛ Primary schools test children these days for use of drugs!!!
☛ Girls as young as 12 years of age report to clinics because of unwanted pregnancies.

So, the next time you become angry because your parents want to know "where you are going" or refuse to let you go to some or other place, remember that your **safety, rights and freedom** are being protected by exactly that!

4. Protect yourself

Although the laws of each country and the legal system of that country are maintained and the defence force and police protect the citizens of the country, the protection of your rights begin WITH YOURSELF: **Your freedom and rights are your responsibility** – make sure that you have done everything in your power to protect and look after it! Why not start with a few lessons in self-protection?

Hints to protect yourself

1.   Never walk around alone – especially not at night!
2.   Always make sure that someone knows exactly where you are and when you will be home.
3.   Give contact numbers where people will be able to reach you.
4.   Don't walk or drive with strangers.
5.   Never get into a car if the driver is under the influence of alcohol or drugs.
6.   Lock doors and windows when you are at home or in the car.
7.   Don't trust all people without reservation.
8.   Keep your eyes open for danger signs and learn self defence techniques.
9.   Know all emergency numbers off by heart.
10. Immediately contact your parents, teacher or the police if you notice something suspicious, or if somebody intimidates, molests or threatens you.
11. Make sure that nobody tampers with your cool-drink or "spikes" it while you are looking away.
12. Don't go to isolated places where you won't be able to cry for help.
13. Stay away from groups where you feel afraid, unsure of yourself or intimidated.
14. Stay away from things which are dangerous, wrong, against the law or your values, your goals or against your parents' approval.
15. Stay away from something which can destroy your future.
16. Make sure that your words, actions and principles agree.
17. Don't give your home address or telephone number to strangers or someone on the internet.
18. Don't allow yourself to be forced or persuaded.
19. Make sure of your facts and don't believe everything that is dished up to you!
20. USE YOUR COMMON SENSE AND LEARN TO SAY "NO"!

5. Are you throwing your freedom away?

Your freedom and rights begin with yourself. Yet, there are many people who throw away this freedom unconsciously or with intent!

INSTRUCTION

1.   Read through the various tables on how to protect your rights again.

2. Now read the instances given in the following table and write down the right thrown away by these teenagers through their own actions!

EVENT		RIGHT THROWN AWAY BY IT
1.	Mary goes out with a guy who cheats, humiliates and belittles her.	
2.	Drugs are sold on the sly in front of the school. Themba also wants to try some of the "stickers".	
3.	Peter doesn't speak to the new boy in class because he is afraid of losing his friends if he does.	
4.	Jerry steals his father's car and crashes into a bridge while under the influence of alcohol. He breaks his neck and is paralysed.	
5.	Suzie oversleeps every morning and loses her job as a result.	
6.	A group of kids uses "Ecstasy". Sally has a seizure and dies.	
7.	John's dad is an alcoholic. John and his mother are regularly assaulted. Yet, they keep quiet about it.	
8.	Nicky's mom gives her 3 healthy meals a day – yet, she refuses to eat and becomes anorexic.	
9.	Nadia becomes drunk one night. A week later, naked photos taken of her that night, are plastered to the school notice board by someone …	
10.	Pierre gets a pamphlet on the dangers of smoking. He throws it away without reading it and lights another cigarette.	
11.	The children in school are given a talk by the Narcotics bureau on the dangers of drugs. The kids laugh it off since "nothing" has happened to Peter yet!	
12.	Liza is 16 years old. She plans to become a doctor. She becomes pregnant and has to leave school.	
13.	One night Tina meets a sexy guy at a party. She sleeps with him. Months later her blood tests are HIV POSITIVE. She later dies of AIDS.	
14.	Carla is so angry at her strict parents that she runs away from home one night. Two strange men give he a lift and rape her.	
15.	Patrick tells his girlfriend that no one becomes pregnant "that easily". A few months later she's pregnant. Patrick doesn't like her so much any more, but her father forces them to get married.	
16.	Simon buys marijuana from a pusher, who tells him that he will never become addicted to it. The pusher says the same when Simon later has to buy LSD, because marijuana is too weak and no longer gives him a "kick".	

Perhaps these examples sound too far-fetched and maybe you don't know anybody who is that "stupid"! Perhaps you are fully convinced that adults and the media exaggerate these cases and apply everything out of context so that you can have no pleasure in life! Maybe you have heard or read of such cases and still don't believe that it could happen to you! Every day newspapers, magazines, hospitals, institutions and prisons are full of cases of children it actually happened to. These are children from all cultures, classes and races, of all sexes and all sizes!!

IT CAN HAPPEN TO YOU TOO …

6. *Open your eyes!*

Statistics tell the sad tales of children who also thought that the many warnings about drinking, smoking, drugs, sex, AIDS, kidnappings and rapes are exaggerated and used out of context. These statistics are quoted from the **Executive Summary** of the **World Health Report 1995**, as well as several other sources on these topics which are mentioned in the list of information.

In 1995 there were approximately 5 720 million people on earth.

EVENT	STATISTIC
Accidents	2,2% of all deaths are caused by road accidents. Every 12 minutes someone dies in a car accident, while someone is injured every 14 seconds.
Deaths	7% of all deaths are of children between 5-19 years of age. SUICIDE is the third highest cause of deaths amongst youths between the ages of 15-24. 13 of each 100000 children commit suicide every year.
Teenage pregnancies	Approximately 1 million teenagers become pregnant each year, of which half give birth. The rest lose their babies as a result of miscarriages or abortions. Nearly 4 out of every 100 girls between 15-17 have a baby.
Sexually transmitted diseases (excluding HIV/AIDS)	333 million new cases of sexually transmitted diseases were recorded in 1995 and the number is still growing. 529000 cases of cervical cancer are caused by sexually transmitted diseases.
AIDS **In April 2000 AIDS was classified as an International Safety Risk!**	34 million people have been infected with AIDS. 43% of carriers of AIDS are women. 14% of all women who visit South African clinics, are HIV POSITIVE. (Men usually don't visit clinics and are, therefore, not so easily traced). Every minute 11 men, women and children across the world are infected with HIV. One tenth of all new cases of HIV appear amongst children under 15 years of age.
Smoking	6,6 million people died in 1995 as a result of cancer. (most of them because of smoking) In 1997 15,3 million died of heart disease. 500 million smokers who are presently alive, will eventually die because of it. 1 out of every 2 people who smoke, die from this habit. Smokers die approximately 7 years sooner than non-smokers.
Alcohol	3.1% of all teenagers between 12-17 years are heavy drinkers. 1 out of every 13 adults abuses alcohol or is addicted to it.
Drugs	83.2% of all teenagers have smoked marijuana. In America, more than 8000 people die every year as a result of drug abuse.

REMEMBER
The statistics mentioned here are not always the full picture. If you consider that 90% of all rapes are never even reported, you could say the same of the number of children who smoke, drinks, use drugs and are sexually active.

7. Are you gambling with your life?

Are you gambling with your odds?

Have you ever taken a dice and tried to throw a "six"? What are the odds that you will throw a "six" the first time? Gamblers calculate these odds by using the law of averages.

The law of averages

The law of averages is based on the principle of probability. (WHAT ARE THE ODDS?)
This theory is based on the principle that the average outcome of independent repetitions of a certain event will come **ever closer** to the expected outcome as these repetitions continue unlimitedly. The same principle can be explained when a dice is thrown. The more times you throw the dice, the higher the odds are that you will throw a "six".

What are the odds?

When you measure a probability, you can do a statistical calculation by asking: What are the odds that you will throw a "six". How many "sixes" can you throw if you get 36 chances to throw the dice?

$$\text{Probability that a "six" will be thrown} = \frac{6}{36}$$
$$= \frac{1}{6}$$

REMEMBER HOWEVER:

You can never determine your "odds" by looking at previous outcomes or statistics! The dice, car accident, drug, alcohol, sperm cell or broken heart do not have a memory. It does not do its own sums and decide who should become a statistic and when! Although statistics are therefore calculated on percentages and fractions by looking at the whole, you cannot do a sum on your own and think that you will be overlooked. **It can happen the first or only time!**

The possibility or "odds" that AIDS, addiction, pregnancy or pain and heartache could hit you is the same every time regardless of how many times you repeat your "experiment".

By all means take a dice and regard the following figures as:

1 = PAIN AND HEARTACHE (the guy or girl leaves you, car accident, illness)
2 = ADDICTION
3 = PREGNANCY
4 = SEXUALLY TRANSMITTED DISEASE
5 = AIDS
6 = NOTHING

Now throw the dice 36 times and see what your CHANCES are that NOTHING will happen to you! Do you really want to make sure that NOTHING will happen to you? Then, leave the dice alone altogether!

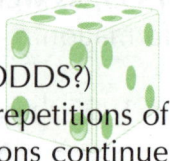

10 Let's talk about sex!

By this time you are probably familiar with the story of the birds and the bees! Sex is no longer a word not to be used in public. This chapter looks at sex and love from a biblical perspective. It gives you honest answers to possible questions with regard to the dangers as well as the right and wrong of love, being in love, and sex.

1. Know your facts on love and sex

Clever, successful people make sure of their facts before making a decision or attempting anything. These facts are not meant to spoil your fun or life, but to give you the true facts so that you can make the right decisions to reach your goals in life.

a) Love and sex

A group of American teenagers between the ages of 16 and 17 years was asked, during an experiment, to name all the words (including obscure and vulgar words) that they associate with the word SEX.

Boys used words which especially refers to the anatomy (breasts, penis, mouth) or the deed (penetration, kiss, positions), while girls used more emotional words (nice, sore, romantic, trust) and places (bed, car, park, party).

After the whole blackboard had been filled, the facilitator said: "There is one word that was not mentioned." No one in class could think of another word.

"What about this word?" the facilitator asked. She erased everything from the board and in big letters wrote the word LOVE.

Why couldn't the teenagers associate the word LOVE with the word SEX?

During puberty (11-18 years) the human body grows from that of a child to an adult. Girls complete the growth process by the age of 15 to 16 years while the boys complete the process only approximately 2 years later.

During puberty your physical development enjoys preference over your emotional and intellectual development. Your physical growth and development are therefore faster, more constant and controlled, while your emotions and moods are often erratic and unpredictable during this time. One moment you are head over heels in love and you can't stop touching each other and two months later you can't stand each other.

As a result your body is, at this stage, ready to be sexually active, while your Intellectual Quotient (IQ) and your Emotional Quotient (EQ) have not yet fully formed or understood the concept of true love. The fact that boys and girls focused different words, can also be explained by looking at the different stages of development through which both sexes would go at that stage.

In other words, when the romantic words "I love you" are used or heard at that stage of your life, your own brain cannot yet understand the full meaning, impact or responsibility thereof. Although you may use the words, you don't really understand what you mean by it, as your brain has not yet formed those concepts!

Can you really promise something to someone if your brain cannot yet form an understanding thereof? Would you really believe a promise by someone who is unable to really understand what he or she has promised?

Your brain must first form the concept of true love before you become sexually active. Teenagers are often disappointed in their sexual experiences precisely because their brains cannot convert what their bodies are doing! Sex without love is an emotional disappointment!

Unfortunately this "short cut" soon also becomes a habit. When one sleeping partner no longer satisfies you, you bounce to the next and the next and the next. When you become older someday, you may struggle to really understand adult love because you confuse the concepts of being in love, sex and adult love with each other.

When everything you receive in life is free, you will never understand the value of money and also never learn to appreciate what you receive. This is exactly what happens when you experiment with sex before you are emotionally ready for it.

When you confuse sex with love, you may miss true love altogether – even it sits on your nose like spectacles! When you meet someone who really loves you and cares about you, you don't even notice it, because you don't know what love really means.

You can take the sex out of love if you are not married. It is completely possible to truly love somebody without being sexually involved with that person. **However, you can never take love out of sex.** The moment you do that, you are definitely not making love, but are, in fact, destroying lives. Think about it!

b) Loving and being in love

Remember: There is a difference between loving and being in love. People normally first move through the phase of being in love (which lasts about 2 years) before they really begin to love one another. Many people never learn to love each other and find out that they don't even like one another after a few months!

Let us find out what the differences are between:

LOVING	BEING IN LOVE
Love grows with time. Anything that grows, needs time. You can only love someone if you have seen and accepted him or her for a long time under various circumstances.	Falling in love happens very quickly. You can fall in love by seeing someone only once!
Love accepts the person as a whole. The good and bad characteristics. When you love someone, you love his or her whole personality and being.	Falling in love takes place – in spite of the fact that you don't know the person well and do not know his or her characteristics. Falling in love accepts only certain characteristics of a person.
Love cares. The other person's needs and wishes are important to you. Love gives and shares.	Falling in love is self-centred. It's about what makes you happy and feel good. The other person must satisfy you and make you feel better about yourself.
You cannot love two people "equally" at the same time.	You can be in love with more than one person at a time. You easily swop partners and easily fall in love again.
If you love someone, you will do the things that make the other person happy and are advantageous to you both. If you love someone you won't neglect your health, studies or interests.	If you are in love, you easily neglect your health, appetite, activities and studies and you are happy only when you are close to that person.
Two people who love each other handle their problems openly and try all possible means of finding a solution. All obstacles become opportunities to get to know each other and develop as people.	People in love tend to ignore problems, sweep them under the carpet, act as if they don't exist or find excuses for them. When their problems become too big, they walk out of the relationship.
Love remains the same. Distance and problems won't cause the whole relationship to be wrecked.	Being in love is not constant. One day you hate and irritate each other and the next day you can't stay away from each other.

Love never does anything to harm, endanger or possibly destroy the person's future.	Being in love holds certain risks and experiments, even at the cost of the other person's safety, health or future. It keeps that "feeling" on the go.
When you love someone, you don't hide it. You show it to that person and to every one who knows you.	When you are in love with someone, you may perhaps deny or disregard it if someone asks you about it or teases you This is a sign that the person is not important enough to you to put him or her first.
LOVE: GIVES	BEING LOVE TAKES.
LOVE IS AN ACT.	**BEING IN LOVE IS A FEELING.**
LOVE BUILDS A HOME WITH THE PURPOSE OF LIVING IN IT TOGETHER, FOREVER.	**BEING IN LOVE PUTS UP A TENT WITH THE PURPOSE OF TAKING IT DOWN IF THINGS DON'T WORK OUT.**

2. *Why wait?*

Waiting for sex until you are married, does not only prevent unwanted pregnancies, sexually transmitted diseases and AIDS, but gives you and your partner the opportunity to develop the concept of true adult love and to understand it so that sex and love can be enjoyed, experienced and understood as a whole.

The message that goes out to today's teenagers in general, is:
"SEX BEFORE MARRIAGE IS SIN. WAIT FOR IT UNTIL YOU ARE MARRIED. IF YOU CANT, USE A CONDOM!"

What a contradictory message!

If you think that AIDS, sexually transmitted diseases or an unwanted pregnancy are the only things that can happen to you, **think again**. The reasons for suicide and emotional pain can often be derived from intimate relationships which were shipwrecked.

Condoms may possibly protect you against AIDS, sexually transmitted diseases or pregnancies, but if premarital sex is sin, then no condom can guarantee you a place in the Kingdom of God!

Let us try to answer 10 important questions very honestly:

a) **Is premarital sex a sin – or not?**
   Yes! God warns you that you will not enter His Kingdom!
   Please read Corinthians 7: 8-9 Romans 1: 18-32, Galatians 5: 19-21, 1 Thessalonians 4: 3-8, Ephesians 5:3-5, Revelation 22: 15, 1 Corinthians 5: 6-13.

b) **When does a marriage really begin?**
   Adam and Eve stood before God when he instituted the first marriage on earth. Man then took an oath of faithfulness before God! (*Genesis 2:24*) From that moment on husband and wife are no longer two people. With this oath the marriage is fulfilled. The bond between God and two people may not be broken. (*Matthew 19:1-2*)

c) **Where does sex fit into the picture?**
   God gives man a body. This body belongs to God. It is His temple where the Holy Spirit will live. When Jesus dies at the cross, He pays a price (His blood and suffering) to liberate your body and spirit so that His Holy Spirit can live within you. (*Corinthians 16-20*)

When two people have lain down an oath of faithfulness before God and towards each other, God gives these two people a gift. He allows them to share their bodies with each other (flesh of one flesh) on condition that this union may not be broken. God regards this severing of the union as violence. (*Malachi 2: 13-16*)

d) What is adultery?

Any act or thought which breaks or harms the bond of the oath which a man and a woman lay down before God is regarded as infidelity. (*Mark 10: 11-12*)

Think of the bond of marriage as a circle within which God allows them to enjoy and respect each other's bodies. The condition for being allowed into the circle, is that the man and woman will lay down an oath of faithfulness (marriage) before God and towards each other. (*Ephesians 5: 21-33*)

e) How do you commit adultery if you are not married?

When you and your partner do something outside the circle which belongs inside the circle several of God's 10 commandments are broken. Think about this carefully!

Do not worship any God except me (Exodus 20: 2-7) Can you really kneel together before God just before or after you have done "that" and thank him for the love he has given you, or do you shift him aside for that moment?

Be faithful in marriage (Exodus 20:14) Sex and sexual activity belong inside the circle of marriage. This is where it is protected against diseases, pain, heartache and misery. If you take something out of this circle, you are committing adultery.

You may not steal (Exodus 20:15) When you do something outside the circle, which belongs inside the circle, you are taking the gift which God gave to two married people. You are therefore taking someone's body for which you haven't paid (marriage) and which does not belong to you but to God. That is stealing!

Honour your father and your mother (Exodus 20:12) Your parents give you advice. They warn you against the dangers that follow once sex is practised outside the circle of marriage. Often your parents learnt this knowledge the hard way and are trying to prevent it happening to you. Do you honour your parents by listening to their advice or do you follow your own head?

Do not tell lies about others (Exodus 20-16) Sex outside the circle of marriage is often hidden under lies. Jesus calls Satan the beginning and father of all lies. Think about it!

You may not want anything that belongs to someone else (Exodus 20:17) Your guy's or girl's body and soul and spirit belong to God. Paul says: "It is better to marry than to burn with desire" **(Corinthians 7:9)**. Jesus says: "If your right eye causes you to sin, poke it out and throw it away **(Matthew 5:29).** If this relationship makes you desire things you cannot afford and makes you do things which will keep you out of God's Kingdom, you have to end it no matter how much it hurts! Weigh your relationship against the eternal life God promises you and see which is more important …

Do not murder (Exodus 20:13) What happens to the person when you "drop" him or her? God regards divorce as violence. Read Malachi 2:14-16. God speaks here of what you did in your **youth**!

f) Do you consider abortion if you become pregnant? *(Jeremiah 1:15)*

Please first visit the website *http//www.abortiontv.com* and make sure of the facts! By all means look at the viewing material *"The Silent Scream"* so that you can understand why many doctors refuse to do these operations!

g) How far is far enough?

Jesus Himself says even your thoughts are far enough! (*Matthew 5:7*) Are you willing to stay together through illness and health, poverty and prosperity until death parts you? Are you willing to lay down the oath of gratefulness before God before you "go further"? If not, stop immediately when it harms the Temple of God! Sexual organs with or without clothes are sacred. Use your "undies" as a good guideline as to where you should not be touched.

h) But we love each other!

Is sex proof that you love each other? **Think again!**

Abigail Vanburen writes: *"You need to prove your love through illicit sex like a moose needs a hat-rack. Why not prove your love by sticking your head in the oven and turning on the gas? Or how about playing leap-frog in traffic? It's about as safe. Clear the cobwebs out of your head! Anybody who asks you to prove your love is trying to take you for the biggest, most gullible fool that ever walked. That 'proving' is one of the rottenest lines ever invented."* (*The Word for Today* – February-April 2000)

Do you love each other? It doesn't sound like it! Would you expose someone you love to:
– fear, depression and feelings of guilt?
– the risk of losing his/her reputation and self-respect?
– the risk of an unwanted pregnancy?
– the possibility of a forced marriage or single parentage?
– the pain, agony and misery if things don't work out?
– sexually transmitted diseases?
– AIDS?
– exclusion from God's Kingdom?
Somebody who loves you, wants the BEST for you! Please read 1 Corinthians 13!

i) Why do you have to "buy" the cow if you can get the milk for free?

Is this how you feel about sex? Then you are really still very immature and you have a serious self-image problem:

"Don't be immoral in matters of sex. That is a sin against your own body in a way that no other sin is." (*1 Corinthians 6:18*)

If you plan to throw away the cow after you have drunk your fill of the milk, you should remember the following:
– That "cow" was created by God – in His image.
– That body is a Temple of God.
– Jesus died on the cross for that body – it belongs to Him.
"So if you don't obey these rules, you are not really disobeying us. You are disobeying God, who gives you His Holy Spirit." (*1 Thessalonians 4:8*)

j) But everybody does it!

➢ 34 Million people already have AIDS and still we say: "But everybody does it!"
➢ 333 million people were already diagnosed with sexually transmitted diseases because "everybody does it!"
➢ 4 out of every 100 girls between 15-16 years of age have a baby because "everybody does it!".
➢ 126 000 aabortions are performed every day in clinics across the world because "everybody does it!".
➢ Would you play Russian roulette because EVERYBODY does it?

k) **But it's impossible to wait!**

Quite right! It is impossible if your body is in control! A well-known pop song encourages listeners:

> *"You and me baby are nothing but mammals*
> *Let's do it like they do it on the Discovery Channel."*

When your channel is not tuned in to God, it is indeed impossible to stop the train when it is at full speed. It is impossible to stop once you have gone too far and that's why you can't stop until you have gone all the way. Each time a little further and further and further …

Yet, you are not an animal.

God created you "a little less than a heavenly being" – in His image – as His representative!

God gave you the power to make choices.

God gave you a spiritual channel.

♡ a spiritual channel in which the Holy Spirit can live.

♡ a spirit which respects the other person so much that you would put his or her place in God's Kingdom above your own desires.

♡ a spiritual channel which puts your relationship with God above your relationship with your partner because it's the only way to ensure that this relationship will remain sacred and have God's blessing.

♡ A spirit which is willing to break off the relationship rather than destroy you and your partner's lives.

It is love. It is possible.

3. *We have gone too far!*

So stop!

"You surely don't think much of God's wonderful goodness or of His patience and willingness to put up with you. Don't you know that the reason God is good to you is because He wants you to turn to Him? But you are stubborn and refuse to turn to God. So you are making things even worse for yourselves on that day when He will show you how angry He is and will judge the world with fairness. God will reward each of us for what we have done." (Romans 2:4-6).

Realise that Christ died on the cross for this.

"But God showed how much He loved us by having Christ die for us, even though we were sinful." (Romans 5:8))

Admit that you have sinned.

"I have sinned and done wrong since the day I was born. But you want complete honesty, so teach me true wisdom." (Psalm 51:5-6)

Ask God for forgiveness.

"Forget each wrong I did when I was young." (Psalm 15:7)

Ask your partner for forgiveness.

If you have sinned, you should tell each other what you have done. Then you can pray for one another and be healed. The prayer of an innocent person is powerful. (James 5:16)

Forgive your partner.

If you forgive others for the wrongs they do to you, your Father in heaven will forgive you. (Matthew 6:14)

Be reborn.

"Turn back to God! Be baptised in the Name of Jesus Christ, so that your sins will be forgiven. Then you will be given the Holy Spirit." (Acts 2:38)

Believe that God has given you a new turn and a new life!

I will treat them with kindness, even though they are wicked. I will forget their sins. (Hebrews 8:12)

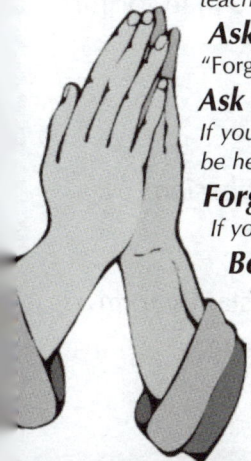

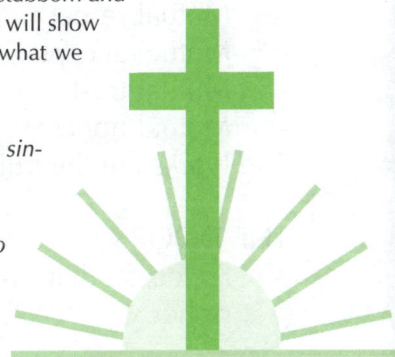

Stay away from temptation!
"You may go now, but don't sin anymore" (John 8:11).
"People's desires make them give in to immoral ways, filthy thoughts and shameful deeds. They worship idols, practise witchcraft, hate others and are hard to get along with. People become jealous, angry and selfish. They not only argue and cause trouble, but they are envious. They get drunk, carry on at wild parties and do other evil things as well. I told you before and I am telling you again: No one who does these things will share in the blessings of God's Kingdom." (Galatians 5:19-21).

Bear the fruit that suits your rebirth!
"God's Spirit makes us loving, happy, peaceful, patient, kind, good, faithful, gentle and self-controlled. There is no law against behaving in any of these ways. And because we belong to Jesus Christ, we have killed our selfish feelings and desires. God's Spirit has given us life and so we should follow the Spirit." (Galatians 5: 22-25)

4. Build the house right!

When two people start a relationship, it can be compared to a house they start building together. They can build the house according to God's plan or according to Satan's plan.

God's House
God has a specific plan with which two people must start a relationship. This plan has been tested through the ages and clear guidelines for it are given in the Bible. An experienced builder, who knows what he's doing, builds his house from the foundations upward and puts the roof on last.

THE FOUNDATIONS – God is the foundation *(Psalm 127:1)*
The foundations are dug first.
God's will is put first.
The building plan is the Bible.

THE FOUR WALLS – Two rows of bricks with provision in the middle.
– Mutual respect
– Mutual acceptance
– Mutual trust
– Mutual honesty
The bricks are the fruit of the Holy Spirit which are described in Galatians 5:22.

THE DOORS AND WINDOWS
– Space, so that every person can grow and develop fully according to God's plan for him or her.

THE ROOF
– Sex
– The roof is fixed to the walls of respect, trust, honesty and acceptance. *(Ephesians 5)*

MAINTENANCE
God doesn't want us to move from one partner to the next, but wants us to constantly forgive, heal, correct and reconcile. *(Malachi 2:14-16)*

Satan's house

Satan is not very creative and will, usually adapt and twist God's plan. Remember Satan changes God's plan. Remember – Satan changes God's exclamation marks to question marks!

IS A FOUNDATION REALLY NECESSARY?
Is it really necessary for both of you to believe in God's plan?
Is it really necessary for God to become part of your relationship as well? (Remember! "Two is company – three is a crowd!")

ARE THE WALLS REALLY NECESSARY?
Won't it become too stifling?
What about your freedom?
Is the body not more important? Remember, you can't touch respect, but you can touch that body! Must the walls really be that thick? Good grief, who can wait that long?

> "Lets build only four scaffolds before we add the roof. Believe me, it works just as well! Look, we've had a whole date, day, week, month, year in which we have learnt to know each other well! I have so much **respect** for you that I am now going to be very **honest** with you. I can honestly say that I want to sleep with you – no strings attached. I **accept** your whole body. You are really very lovely! **Trust** me – nothing will happen. It is quite safe!"

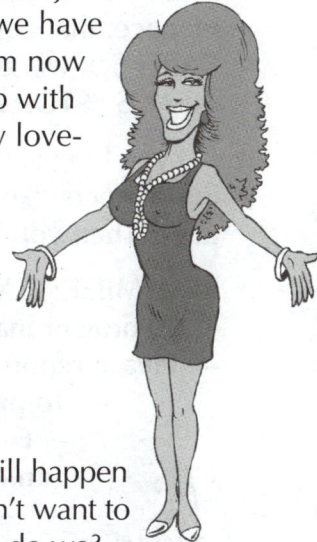

ARE THE DOORS AND WINDOWS REALLY NECESSARY?
If we don't build walls, then we don't need doors and windows, do we? OK – put in a back door – but please keep it open at all times in case it becomes too stifling inside …

SHOULDN'T WE START WITH THE ROOF?
Shouldn't we rather find out first whether we are sexually compatible? What will happen if we marry and find out too late that we don't "suit" each other? We really don't want to waste each other's time with a long relationship which could come to nothing, do we? Where does God say, in the Bible, that premarital sex is a sin?

Didn't God give Solomon riches, wisdom and knowledge? Heavens, the man had 700 wives and 300 concubines! In any case, those laws of olden days don't count anymore! (read 1 Kings 11: 1-13)

HOW CAN YOU FIX THIS MESS?
Is this relationship not "irreparably falling apart"?
Can it work again?
Isn't it better just to get out of the way?
Goodness there are plenty of fish in the sea!
Just remember your condom …!

5. Pornography

Pornography gives an extremely twisted idea of love and how a happy relationship really is. These films and images aim to take love out of sex. It is like a stupid monkey who throws away the banana to eat the peel!

What are you doing?

Jesus said: *"But I tell you that if you look at another woman and want her, you are already unfaithful in your thoughts"* (Matthew 5:27).

Remember: *"GARBAGE IN – GARBAGE OUT!"*

These pictures get stuck in your subconscious and before long you will also carry on like a monkey or machine without any love or emotions! Now, instead of measuring your relationship by the love, respect, loyalty, trust and acceptance in it, you start to measure it by the tricks you and your partner can perform! The roof becomes bigger and the walls can no longer bear the weight!

6. Molestation and rape

If you have to give your body to someone under pressure, blackmail, threat or menace, that person DOES NOT LOVE YOU – IT IS MOLESTATION AND RAPE! Sex without your explicit permission is rape! "**NO**" means NO! IT MEANS **"STOP IMMEDIATELY!"**

Do you brag about the number of sleeping partners you have? Do you switch sleeping partners like outfits? Do you deliberately entice men with your clothes or attitude? **Then you have a serious problem with your self image and you need help!!**

REMEMBER: SEX UNDER THE AGE OF 16 IS ILLEGAL!
– **To drug or make someone drunk with the intention of having sex with that person, is illegal!**
– **Please report rape! If someone gets away with it, it will happen to someone else!**
    – **To pin someone down and force sex on that person is rape!**
      – **Forbidden obscure and vulgar remarks and invitations are regarded as sexual molestation in the workplace – you could lose your job that way!**
        – **Don't look for trouble with your clothes or lack thereof!**

7. Sex

Many fallacies exist about sex and pregnancy. Your friends are not experts in that area and usually know as little or even less than you do. Many magazines simply answer people's questions and don't always paint the whole picture. Make sure that you know **the true facts** and that both you and your partner can bear the **consequences**.

FACTS

✔ Most teenagers are not sexually active. Almost 8 out of 10 girls and 7 out of 10 boys under 15 haven't done "IT" yet. Only 1 out of 5 teenagers over 15 are sexually active. **Therefore, you don't have to feel "out".**

✔ Nobody **has** to practise sex. You won't become ill or die if you don't do "IT". Nothing will **happen** to you if you and your partner wait with it. A quick jog around the block is enough to relieve the tension.

✔ **NO BIRTH CONTROL METHOD IS 100% SAFE**. Various factors (such as temperature, regularity, other medicines or illness) can cause it to malfunction! most birth control methods are used incorrectly or irregularly. Therefore know your facts about these **before** you want to use them!

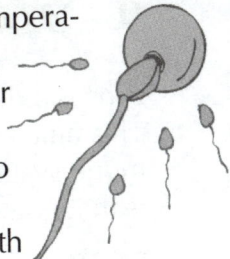

✔ Most teenagers who are sexually active, are sorry that they started so early.

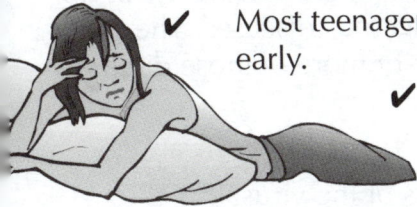

✔ Teenagers who are sexually active without using birth control have 90% chance to become pregnant within a year. 10% of all woman between 15-19 become pregnant every year. Nearly 4 out of every 10 teenage pregnancies end in abortions.

✔ It is **easy** to become pregnant if you're fertile. It can even happen the "first time", during menstruation or as a result of various forms of **sex**.

8. *Sexually transmitted diseases*

Sexually transmitted diseases can be transmitted by **any form of sex** –even if you have sex only once, these diseases are serious, dangerous and often incurable.

FACTS

✔ Approximately 1 out of every 4 teenagers *who are sexually active* – is infected with sexually transmitted diseases annually.

✔ If you have *unprotected sex even once only*, you have a 1% chance of getting Aids, 30% of getting genital herpes and 50% chance of getting gonorrhoea. Do you want to risk that 1% chance?

✔ More teenagers get gonorrhoea than sexually active men and women between 20-44 yrs.

✔ Sexually transmitted diseases start with the sexual organs, but can spread to the prostrate, uterus, testicles, nearby organs and the brain!

✔ Certain sexually transmitted diseases can cause infertility and even brain damage.

✔ Some sexually transmitted diseases like herpes can show no symptoms for a long time and then suddenly erupt!

✔ Condoms are made to keep in sperm and not to keep out viruses!

✔ **All CONDOMS ARE NOT SAFE!** At least 1 out of 250 condoms are defective. Condoms are often transported under unsafe temperatures which can cause it to tear. Condoms break 8% of the time and slip off 7% of the time.

SYMPTOMS OF SEXUALLY TRANSMITTED DISEASES

* Discharge from the penis or vagina, with an unusual colour or odour.
* Constant feeling of wanting to urinate.

DO YOU USE

Just remember ...

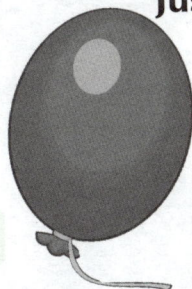

condoms?

balloons can burst...!

* Pain and itching during urination.
* Pain and itching in the area around the penis, vagina or anus.
* Painful sex.
* Rash, sores, blisters, warts on or around the penis or vagina.
* Fever.
* Swollen glands.

9. AIDS

Aids is a deadly disease which can be contracted when the HIV virus enters the bloodstream. This attacks the body's immune system, which protects you against illnesses. Once your immune system is destroyed, your body is susceptible to deadly dangerous diseases. The result is that you easily become seriously ill and eventually die from one or more of those diseases.

FACTS

✔ AIDS is contagious and is transmitted by the following:
- Any sexual contact. Women as well as men can be carriers of the virus.
- By sharing contaminated needles for drug abuse.
- By open cuts or sores which come into contact with the blood of someone who is HIV positive.
- From an HIV positive mother to her unborn baby.

✔ HIV can be dormant in a person's body for years without any signs of the disease. Although the person shows no signs of the disease, he or she can still infect others.

✔ **There is currently NO CURE FOR AIDS.** Once you have it, you will have it for the rest of your life and will eventually die from it. However, certain medicines can relieve or slow down the symptoms.

✔ HIV and AIDS cannot be transmitted by the following:
- normal contact
- air
- insect bites
- chatting

✔ **You can get AIDS even from your first sexual contact if the person is HIV positive.**

✔ All people of all races, male or female, young or old, poor or rich can get AIDS. This is not a disease limited to homosexuals or people of other colours only. AIDS DOES NOT DISCRIMINATE!

✔ Birth control methods are not a guarantee against being contaminated with Aids. Condoms can lower your risk but condoms are not always safe. The pill and other medications **don't help at all** against AIDS contamination!

✔ **The symptoms of AIDS include:**
First signs:
- Acute infections (swollen glands, fever, headaches, weight loss, perspiring and sore throat). Because it can be confused with other viral infections like "flu" or colds the person may be unaware that he or she has already been contaminated. By the time that he or she realises it others may possibly be already infected.
- *Serocon Version* (HIV can now be found in the blood). The person can live a normal life for 2 to 10 years without any symptoms.

Signs of HIV infection
- Rash – white spots on palate, gums and tongue
- Shingles – blisters and sores on the body
- Herpes – festering sores in and around sexual organs
- Inability of blood to clot
- Bruises and bleeding

General symptoms
– Chronic diarrhoea.
– Weight loss.
– Fever.
– Exhaustion.
– Perspiration.
– Depression.

Later symptoms and infections.
*   The body loses its defence against
     deadly diseases.
*   Pneumonia.
*   Tuberculosis.
*   Growths.
*   Parasites which affect the brain and causes fits.
*   Infections in all organs, especially the eyes.
*   Infections in the brain.
*   Diarrhoea.

✔ Blood tests can ascertain whether the person is actually HIV positive or has AIDS.
✔ Treatment to ease or prevent the symptoms, is extremely, expensive and comes to thousands of rands.
✔ If you are raped you should report it to the police **immediately**.
✔ TREAT PEOPLE WITH AIDS WITH DIGNITY, IT COULD HAPPEN TO YOU TOO!

10.   Abortions

In 1967 almost 60 scientists, researchers and experts got together during a conference on abortions which was held in Washington DC. The question "**WHERE DOES LIFE BEGIN?**" was discussed by all. These people were chosen on the grounds of their expertise and integrity. In order to find an answer the question was studied from all angles and study areas. The unanimous answer was the following:

"The great majority of our group could not find **any moment** from the fusion of the sperm and the egg and the birth of the baby where they could say: '**This is not human life.'** The altered stages from fertilisation, the six week embryo stage, the six month foetus stage, the one week old child to the adult person are **all just stages of man's growth and development."**

If you don't grant a person his embryo stage then you can presumably also not grant him his toddler, youngster, teenage, youth, adult and aged stages. If we could murder everybody who is an annoyance, untimely, troublesome or a bother, many parents would supposedly, also want to get rid of their teenagers. Think about it!

When fertilisation takes place, a life comes into being, which on its own, carries a genetic package which is entirely programmed to keep growing into an adult person. Nothing but time and food can be added.

Each stage of development – from fertilisation until you are old is simply the growth and development of **that which was already there from the beginning.** Birth only changes man's eating habits, the way in which he breathes and his allure …

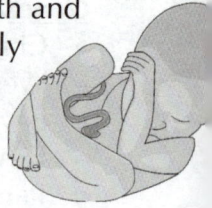

REMEMBER! YOU DETERMINE WHETHER SOMEONE WILL <u>CONTINUE</u> TO LIVE!

46 Million babies are aborted annually world wide.
THAT IS EQUAL TO THE ENTIRE POPULATION OF SOUTH AFRICA!
PLEASE VISIT THE WEBSITE: *http:/www/abortiontv/com*
Watch films of abortions
Read exactly how abortions are done.
Read what happened when abortions went wrong.
Read how baby organs are sold.
Read why many doctors refuse to do abortions.
Read what alternatives are available.

REMEMBER: God gives life. If you can't appreciate or afford it there are people who would welcome that baby with open arms. Speak to your parents immediately if you're pregnant and get proper help!

11.   Prevention

1.   The saying goes:

**"THE BEST LIBERATION
FROM SEDUCTION
IS EVASION!"**

Therefore, stay out of situations you can't handle. Get away from situations which become "too hot". Break the mood by suggesting something else then get up and do it!

2.   Don't get involved in a relationship where you would do *"anything"* that the other person expects of you.

3.   Focus on your FOCAL POINT your FINAL GOAL AND GOALS which you have set yourself. Would you really give up your life and career for 5 seconds or 30 minutes of pleasure?

4.   Learn self-discipline. If you can control your anger, frustrations and other emotions, you can also control your sexual emotions. If you can study for hours or practise sport, you can also bear not to be sexually active for hours.

5.   See to it that you are always fully aware. Alcohol and drugs dull your brain's ability to think logically, to reason and to remember! Stay away from drugs! The combination of drugs and alcohol causes you to lose your inhibitions and values.

6.   Find positive things to keep yourself busy with.

7.   Learn to say "NO". Nobody has the right to force you into anything you don't want to do.

You can say:

"I am not ready for this yet."

"I know it feels right to you and maybe you are ready for it, but I am not."

"… If you love me, you won't insist on it!"

"I don't want to mess up the future plans of both of us."

"What part of 'NO' don't you understand?"

8. You may insist that somebody be tested for AIDS before you become sexually involved with that person. No one will just tell another what diseases they carry while on the very first date.

9. Don't limit your sexual knowledge to letter columns in magazines and the information your pals give you. FIND AND READ THE TRUE FACTS!

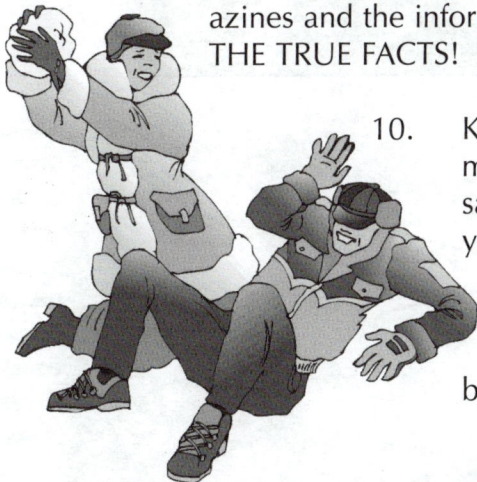

10. Keep sex for your marriage as God intended it. That is the most sensible and practical thing to do. Marriage is the safety net for tricks you do "in the clouds". If it is not there, you fall far, hard and very sore. It is the best, safest and most wonderful way to enjoy a gift from God. Sex is better and more pleasant when you are considerably older, physically as well as emotionally ready for it and able to bear the consequences!

11. The fact that you have been going steady with someone for five years does not mean that you will marry! You may drop each other the very next year …

12.   *Calculate your risks*

When you watch the soapies on television the soft music, beautiful bodies and candles which are all over the room look very romantic. Work out how many of these characters have so far jumped into bed with each other, and the reality should look very different. These people should by now be deadly ill!

It is alleged that the average sexually active teenager will have had two to four sexual partners by the time he or she leaves school.

WHAT HAPPENED WHEN EACH PERSON HAD MORE THAN ONE SLEEPING PARTNER ...?

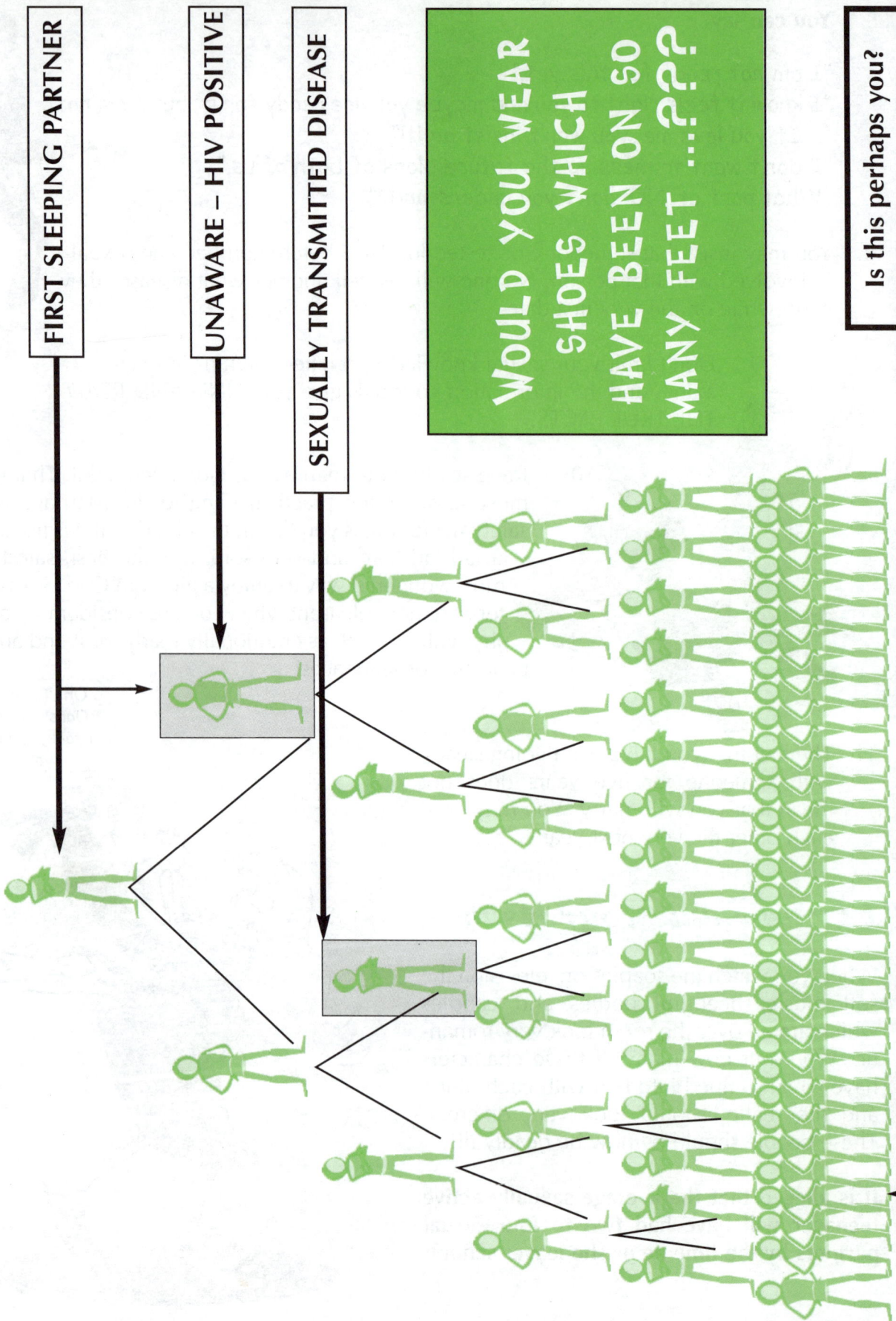

FIRST SLEEPING PARTNER

UNAWARE – HIV POSITIVE

SEXUALLY TRANSMITTED DISEASE

WOULD YOU WEAR SHOES WHICH HAVE BEEN ON SO MANY FEET ...???

Is this perhaps you?

11 Addiction ...

Do you know what a packet of cigarettes, a bottle of booze, a dagga zol and other forbidden substances cost? Think again! What is the price you really have to pay for it? The plan that God has for your life, was bought by the blood of Jesus. He paid so that you could be free – also free of addiction and dependence. Please read this chapter to make sure of the price you have to pay for drugs! By all means keep this chapter handy in case your paths should cross with these substances and first read the true facts before you try something which could destroy your life!

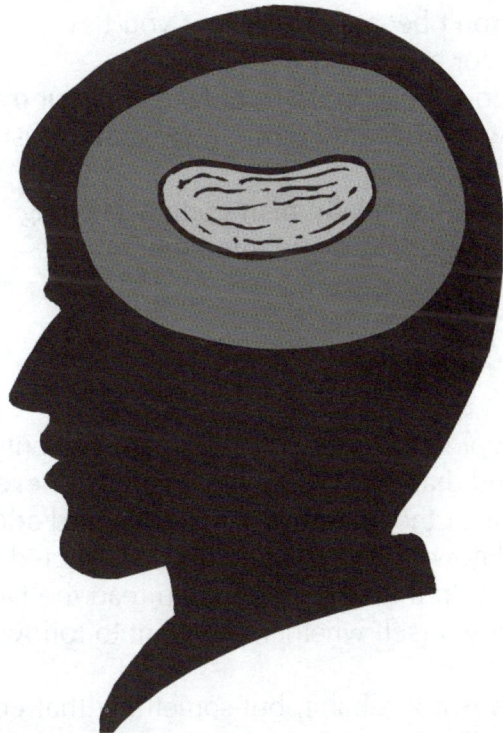

1. Habit or addiction?

All people on earth tend to form set habits during their life. Without this ability to form habits and develop set patterns, your life would be reasonably muddled. When you get up in the morning you have a certain routine you follow and when you go to bed at night you also follow a certain routine. These habits bring order to your life and help you to save time.

Example:

You are used to brushing your teeth. You brush them every morning, afternoon and at night after supper. You are used to it and feel uncomfortable and even guilty if you don't brush your teeth.

BUT:

✳ You put the **same amount** of toothpaste on your toothbrush every day.
✳ You don't brush your teeth **more and more**. You don't eventually squeeze out the whole tube into your mouth. Ten years from now you will still brush them three times a day.
✳ You don't **think** of toothpaste all the time and you don't suddenly **have a craze** for toothpaste.
✳ You don't brush your teeth **secretly** and don't **hide** the toothpaste.
✳ You don't **lie** about the **amount** of toothpaste you use and **why** you use it.
✳ You don't sit and **WAIT** all day long for an opportunity to brush your teeth.
✳ You don't become **irritable** if you haven't had the taste of toothpaste for a while.
✳ You don't go to **extra trouble** to get your **own kind** of toothpaste.
✳ You won't **become tense** if you can't brush your teeth every half hour.
✳ You don't **specially plan** certain evenings to brush your teeth without being disturbed **the whole time**!

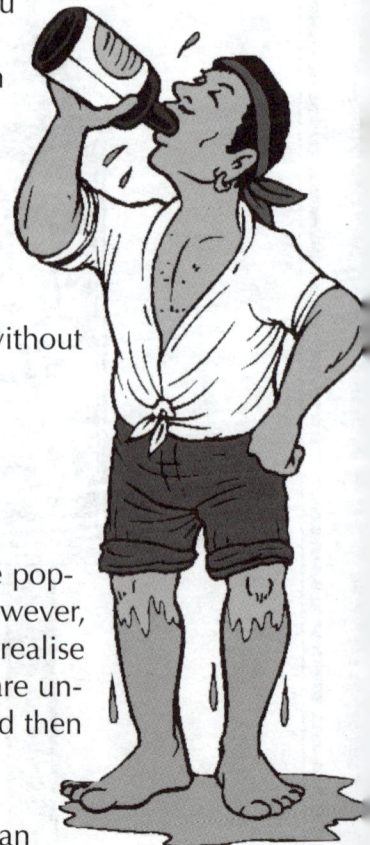

2. Addiction

Many people think that addiction happens only to the outcasts of the population and that "something like that" will **never** happen to them. However, if you look at the true meaning of the word **addiction**, you will soon realise that you know many people who are addicted to several things and are unaware of it! In this chapter you can read the facts about addiction and then decide for yourself whether you want to follow that road.

Addiction is not a habit, but something that controls your life and can destroy it. To understand addiction, you first have to realise that there is a **difference** between habits and addiction.

Unfortunately addiction is often confused with "bad habits". A habit – good or bad – remains just a habit. It does not become **more** and **larger**. It does not constantly take up more of your time, money or life. (You buy the same amount of toothpaste every time.) Unfortunately many people's habits turn into addiction, although they won't admit it.

They don't realise that these habits have become **out of hand** and have **taken over** their lives and thoughts. Because they can't or won't notice the addiction, they won't stop it until it's almost too late. Most people who are addicted to something, must first hit rock bottom and lose practically everything, before they realise what this addiction did to themselves, their lives and the people who really care for them.

WHAT IS ADDICTION?

Addiction is an **unnatural** and **harmful condition** which arises as the result of an interaction between a person and something else (e.g. alcohol, drugs, cigarettes, gambling …). This interaction usually has a certain effect on the person's behaviour and thoughts because the functioning of the brain is affected by it.

This interaction causes a **change in behaviour** in the person when the interaction happens, the interaction does not take place for a period or if the person wants to stop it.

HABITS ARE PART OF YOUR LIFE

LIFE CYCLE
TIME YOU SPEND

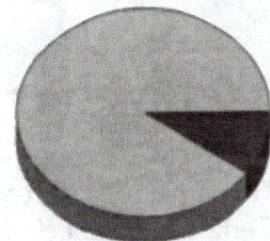

- REST OF YOUR LIFE
- HABIT

ADDICTION CONTROLS YOUR LIFE

LIFE CYCLE
TIME YOU SPEND

- ADDICTION
- REST OF YOUR LIFE

The person uses it *to control circumstances* (smokes a cigarette to remain calm), *to enlarge his power* (uses drugs that make you feel stronger and cleverer) or *to feel like the person he would like to be* (drinks at parties, to be more social).

Since this interaction often affects the brain, behaviour and nervous system the result is often that the person continuously requires **more and more** of this interaction to get the **same effect** he experienced at the beginning.

Addiction occurs when the person **loses control** of the interaction. He cannot control the quantity thereof or his behaviour over it. When the person wants to stop the interaction, he **struggles to stop**.

Addiction occurs when this person **continues** with the interaction in spite of the fact that he has been spoken to about it, it is harming his health, his life has been adversely affected or those around him have been harmed. Addicted people cannot stop the interaction and show **withdrawal symptoms** if the interaction does not take place.

Anything that makes you feel and act "differently", can cause addiction.

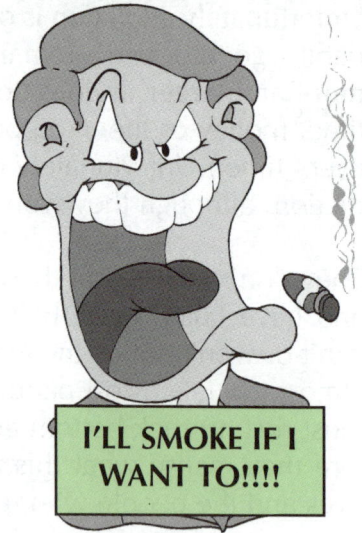

I'LL SMOKE IF I WANT TO!!!!

3. *When does addiction begin?*

ADDICTION BEGINS **WHEN YOU LOSE CONTROL** OVER THIS INTERACTION. YOU CAN NO LONGER CONTROL YOUR INTAKE OR BEHAVIOUR, THE QUANTITY THEREOF OR THE REGULARITY THEREOF.

WHEN DO YOU BECOME ADDICTED?

The exact time when you become addicted, is determined by:

❖ **The substance that you use or the action you perform.**
    Certain substances and actions are more addictive than others.

❖ **The length of time it takes for the substance or action to destroy your resistance against it.**
    Substances like "crack" are extremely addictive and you can immediately become addicted to it, while tea or coffee is not that addictive.

❖ **Yourself**
    The speed at which you become addicted, will depend on your sex, weight, size, personality, the way in which you use the substance and the quantity thereof. Your tendency towards addiction is even genetically transmittable.

❖ **Your capacity limit**
    Your capacity limit is the ability of your body to resist addiction. This limit differs from person to person. Unfortunately you never know what your capacity limit is until you have overstepped it. THEN IT IS TOO LATE!

    The problem is that people think they can stop before they become addicted. They believe that they are in control – even long after they have lost control. People often believe that they can **stop at any time** – even when they get withdrawal symptoms if they try!

4. Abuse and addiction

When is the boundary between use, abuse and addiction crossed? As already mentioned, the exact period of addiction depends on the substance, the addictive effect of the substance, your composition and your capacity limit.

Every time you abuse something (drunk, "high") you damage your body's resistance (YOUR CAPACITY) against the formation of addiction.

Capacity limit

EVERY TIME YOU GET THAT "EFFECT", IT BREAKS DOWN YOUR RESISTANCE AND DAMAGES YOUR CAPACITY LIMIT.

Capacity limit damaged – becomes drunk or drugged sooner

YOUR PERSONALITY AND THE SUBSTANCE YOU USE, DETERMINE HOW FAST YOUR CAPACITY LIMIT IS BROKEN DOWN.

Capacity limit broken. Cannot control intake and is addicted

ONCE YOU HAVE CROSSED THIS BOUNDARY, IT CAN NEVER BE MENDED!!

5. *When do you need help?*

It is very difficult to determine when someone really needs help. The biggest problem with addiction is that people **deny it**, find excuses for it and laugh off people who want to help them. Although their lives may have been a mess for a long time, they will still think that they have their habit **under control.**

If you use any substance or do something which is harmful, even a few of the following signs are DANGER SIGNS and you NEED HELP.

SIGNS THAT YOU ARE ADDICTED AND URGENTLY NEED HELP

☞ You cannot decide in advance when you use a certain substance whether you will become drunk or "high". Before you know it, it has already happened.

☞ You continue using or drinking certain substances to get a certain "feeling".

☞ You can't remember everything you did while under the influence. You can remember how the evening started but not how it ended!

☞ Your behaviour and thoughts change regularly when you drink or use any substance (drunk or "high").

☞ You do things you wouldn't do if you were sober and fully aware.

☞ You know what you're doing is dangerous, but you do it all the same.

☞ You have to drink or use more and more of the substance to get the same "feeling".

☞ You regard parties without alcohol or drugs as boring and don't want to go there. You begin to associate certain times, friends and events with your habit. You begin to organise events so that you can do it.

☞ You constantly talk to your friends about it, pretend that you know everything about it and "know all the facts".

☞ You believe that you can only really have fun if you can drink or use that substance. Without it you cannot relax, have a party, enjoy yourself or get rid of your frustrations.

☞ You begin to avoid people with whom you cannot do or use it. You will even gossip about them behind their backs and insult them.

☞ You choose new friends with whom you are allowed to drink or who use that substance and avoid those who don't approve of it.

☞ You put pressure on others to do it too. You spur on others to do it, doctor drinks when they're not looking and regard people who don't do it, as "nerdy" or beneath you. Teenagers, especially, start smoking and drinking as a result of this peer pressure.

☞ You look for excuses to justify your intoxication or abuse or make a joke of it.

- You take dangerous and uncalculated risks when you are under the influence. You sleep with someone, drive under the influence, become involved in a fight and do dangerous things.
- You lie about it. You deny that you do it or use it. You lie about the number of times you do it and about the quantity you take in or use.
- You get terrible cravings for it when your moods change and you become frustrated, are tense or sad, or feel helpless or unsure about yourself.
- You stop certain activities such as sport or music because you have lost interest.
- You begin to neglect your homework and struggle to concentrate.
- People warn you that what you do is dangerous and that you will have problems if you don't stop.
- You try to stop, but can't. You become irritable and moody. Sometimes you get headaches, panic attacks or hallucinations when you try to stop.
- You become secretive and sly to hide your addiction or to get your hands on the substance or alcohol.
- You become moody if you don't get it fast enough.
- You begin to organise your life in such a way that you specially make time for it where you cannot be disturbed by others.
- You make sure that you always have enough in supply.
- Your moods are very erratic. You go on a "high" and feel happy and then you "crash" into depression. Then you need something again to get you onto that "high" so that you can cope.
- You plan times in which you can chill so that people won't notice your symptoms.
- You often feel scared, anxious, tense, depressed and even consider suicide.
- You do something to your appearance to hide the signs of the previous evening's "high" or intoxication.
- You "sober up", spray deodorant or eat something before going home so that no one will notice what you have done.

> **SPORT AND HOMEWORK ARE FOR "KIDS"! I'M NOT A KID ANYMORE!!!**

- You get home late and sneak to your room so that your parents won't notice in what condition you are.
- Your eating and sleeping patterns change.
- You become untidy and don't care how you look.
- You regularly feel hangover, shaky, nauseous and become ill more easily.
- You experience problems at home, at school and other places.
- You begin to borrow money, sell things or even steal to get money to buy your "supply".

EVEN A FEW OF THESE SYMPTOMS INDICATE THAT YOU NEED HELP!

6. When so you have to start watching out?

When do the black spots in this block start? Would you risk touching this block if the least block spot can mean your death? Addiction works the same. When you can't distinguish any longer it is usually too late …

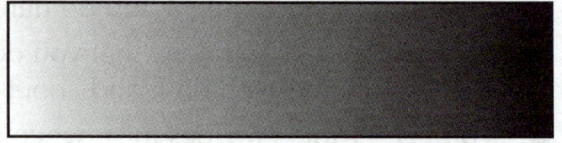

STAY AWAY FROM SUBSTANCES WHICH MAKE YOU FEEL FUNNY AND DIZZY AND INCREASE YOUR HEARTBEAT. THEY ARE ADDICTIVE!

7. Why do people become addicted?

We all have the capacity to become addicted. Addiction begins when your Life Cycle becomes imbalanced and one aspect, habit, substance or action starts to dominate your thoughts and behaviour.

Why does it happen?

REASONS WHY PEOPLE BECOME ADDICTED:

a) Poor self image

When you have a poor self image, are uncertain of yourself or feel uncomfortable in certain situations you could easily think that drink or drugs will give you the "guts" to handle a situation. We all want to be accepted and respected by others. However, when you do "anything" to be "in" you have a problem with your self image.

Often a poor self image is hidden behind an attitude of total confidence and many of the "cool" guys and "cool" girls at school struggle with the very same problems of acceptance that you experience.

THE FOCAL POINT OF YOUR LIFE will determine how good this self image of yours is. If you have a good self image you won't mind if "everybody" does something and you are the only one who is not partaking. If you choose the right FOCAL POINT, God's acceptance will be enough for you and you won't regard people's acceptance as the beginning and end of your life!

Imagine a cup and saucer. When water is poured in from the top the cup fills and runs over into the saucer, onto the tablecloth, over the edge of the table and onto the floor.

The Holy Spirit works in the same way when you invite him into your life, it fills your spirit, your self image (soul) and spills over into all your actions (body). Then it no longer matters what others say about you because you are connected to God and you need only His approval.

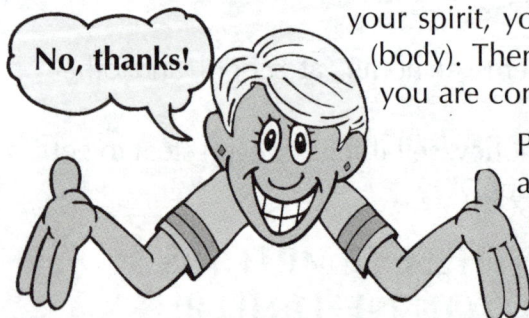

No, thanks!

People who have a good self image, accept other people as they are and don't try to persuade them to speak, think or act the way they do themselves. People who have a good self image like people who can differ from them, can do their own thing and think for themselves!

b) Peer pressure

Peer pressure is all about power. If you want to share in the group's power, you have to do what they say. If you read the previous section carefully, you will realise that people who egg you on or force you to sleep with them, drink with them, to smoke or use drugs, **have already lost their control and power over themselves.**

If this group can persuade you to join them, they can justify their actions to themselves and others. Then they can more easily practise their habit openly and get away with it by saying, "EVERYBODY DOES IT!!"

You possess a certain power which they have already lost. The more you refuse to play along the greater your power and the more powerless they feel. They will, therefore, use any lie and excuse to convince you that nothing will happen to you. They will, however, not tell you of their guilt feelings, their mood swings or the craving they get and even less about how much it costs them to simply function "normally".

You may perhaps think these people are the *"only people who really understand and accept you as you are …"*

?   Why then, don't THEY understand your "NO THANK YOU"?

?   Why do you have to *earn* their respect and acceptance by doing certain things that put your future and life in danger?

?   If they, then, "understand you" they would, in fact, accept you without conditions!

Remember that these friend's habit already controls and has taken over their lives. It has become their FOCAL POINT.

Their thoughts and motives are controlled by it.

When they have to choose between you and their habit, YOU ARE GOING TO LOSE!

Is this true friendship or love? Think again!

YOUR POWER AND THE FACT THAT YOU ARE IN CONTROL OF YOUR LIFE, ARE A THREAT TO THEM!

c) Excitement, experimentation and rebellion

All of us look for excitement in life and that's why people jump out of aeroplanes, cling to cliffs, sail down dangerous rivers and swing from ropes. All of us also have that urge within us to try something that will relieve the everyday routine and problems for a moment. All of us sometimes feel angry, frustrated, furious and sad. All of us sometimes just want to break away and forget about everything that limits us.

What is important, is to realise that every excitement has its own PRICE TAG. Everything has a price and also specific consequences which come with it.

Think about a beautiful jacket hanging in the shop. You would love to buy it. However, when you look at the price tag you see that it is hopelessly too expensive and that you won't even be able to save enough for it within the next ten years.

What are going to do?
* Would you steal money and take the chance of landing in jail?
* Would you steal the jacket and risk getting caught?
* Would you borrow the money from your mom and cook every evening and work in the garden every day for the next ten years?
* Would you borrow money at a shocking rate so that it costs you three times as much later and you have to pay it off for the rest of your life?

If you think about it carefully, any of these methods will mean that you will still be paying off on it, long after the jacket if out of fashion!!!

Look at the price tag of that which you want to try.
To determine the risk, you have to know your facts well. Most substances which are habit forming and lead to addiction have a destructive effect which only comes to light *after a period of time ...*

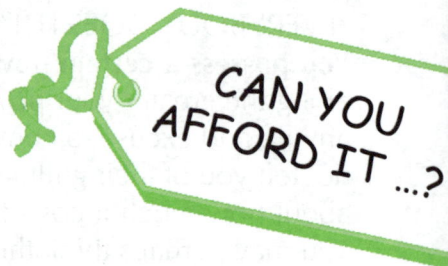

CAN YOU AFFORD IT ...?

8. Classification of substances

When you are offered drugs, you should not only look at the price and listen to what the person says, but know and understand the side effects and long term consequences.

THAT IS THE TRUE PRICE THAT YOU ARE GOING TO PAY FOR IT!!!

ADDICTIVE SUBSTANCES CAN BE DIVIDED AS FOLLOWS:

LEGAL SUBSTANCES	ILLEGAL SUBSTANCES
Caffeine.	"Dagga" (marijuana).
Cough medicine and painkillers.	Mandrax.
Diet pills.	Cocaine.
Tranquillisers.	Crack.
Household and industrial products.	LSD.
Tobacco.	Ecstasy and ICE.
Alcohol.	Shabu.
"Smart drinks" (energy drinks).	Opium and Heroin.
ALL THESE SUBSTANCES CAN LEAD TO ADDICTION IF USED INCORRECTLY, TOO LONG OR EXCESSIVELY.	THESE SUBSTANCES ARE ILLEGAL BECAUSE IT LEADS TO ADDICTION VERY QUICKLY AND CAUSES SERIOUS DAMAGE TO THE BODY.

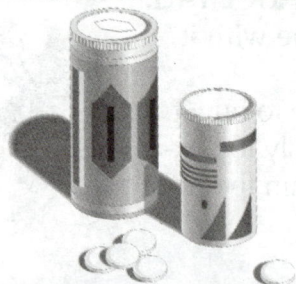

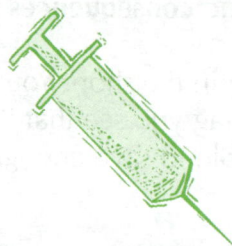

9. The true facts about these substances

Here are the true facts about excessive and serious abuse of the substances mentioned in the previous columns. These facts come from various sources of which the book *Getting High on Life* of the late Adèle Searll is the most important. GO AHEAD – READ IT!

A. CAFFEINE	
Occurs in:	"Regmakers", tea, coffee, cocoa, certain cooldrinks and some medicines.
Effect:	Stimulates the nervous system.
Addiction:	Non addictive if used moderately (3-4 cups of tea or coffee a day, or medicine according to the prescription). Excessive use can lead to addiction.
Side effects of addiction:	Insomnia, tension, panic, muscle spasms, palpitations, hyper activity, buzzing in the ears, poor concentration.
Serious consequences:	Central nervous system, the cardiovascular system, the digestive system are affected. Excessive adrenaline is excreted and muscles go into spasm. Teeth become yellow with brown stains.
Withdrawal symptoms:	Headaches, exhaustion, listlessness, trembling in the hands, depression and irritability.

B. COUGH MEDICINES AND PAINKILLERS	
Occurs in:	Cough syrup, headache and tension capsules, powders and pills.
Effect:	Drowsy or hyper-active, speaks slowly, poor co-ordination, poor concentration, muddled, tummy ache, confusion, nausea, constipation.
Addiction:	Addictive – stick to prescription.
Side effects of addiction:	Ages faster. Constant bladder infections. Health becomes poorer.
Serious consequences:	Damage to liver. Damage to kidneys. Causes stomach ulcers.
Withdrawal symptoms:	Headaches, trembling, irritation, moods.

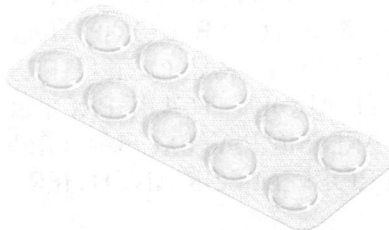

C. DIET PILLS ("uppers")	
Occurs in:	Appetite suppressants and pills which increase the metabolism.
Effect:	Suppresses appetite, increases metabolism.
Addiction:	Psychological addiction, stick to prescription!
Side effects of addiction:	Fits, convulsions death if an overdose is taken. Anorexia. Insomnia Depression. Aggressive behaviour. Hallucinations
Serious consequences:	Damage to important organs. Damage to thyroid which regulates metabolism. Changes heart rhythm and can cause heart attacks. Poor appetite causes poor health. Causes stomach ulcers.
Withdrawal symptoms:	Headaches, trembling, irritation, moods

D. TRANQUILLISERS ("downers")	
Occurs in:	Tranquillisers in tablet form or in capsules.
Effect:	Drowsy, speaks slowly, poor co-ordination, changing moods, depression, aggression, loses inhibitions, poor concentration, muddled confused.
Addiction:	Highly addictive – stick to prescription! DON'T EVER USE TOGETHER WITH ALCOHOL!
Side effects of addiction:	Nausea, headaches, feels faint, poor balance, personality change, low blood pressure, anxiousness and depression, irritation, emotional instability, impotence, trembling.
Serious consequences:	Brain damage. Spiritual and physical deterioration. Fits. Coma and death if overdose is taken.
Withdrawal symptoms:	Headaches, trembling, irritability, moods, fits, hallucinations, panic attacks, perspiration, insomnia.

CERTAIN TYPES OF DEPRESSION ARE CAUSED BY A CHEMICAL IMBALANCE AND THEN CERTAIN MEDICATION, WHICH SHOULD BE USED ACCORDING TO THE PRESCRIPTION, BECOMES ABSOLUTELY NECESSARY.

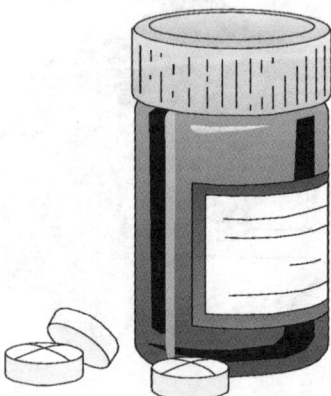

HOWEVER, LEARN TO SOLVE PROBLEMS IN A HEALTHY NATURAL MANNER. IF YOU BECOME ADDICTED BY USING TRANQUILLISERS TO FORGET ABOUT YOUR PROBLEM, YOU ARE SIMPLY EXCHANGING ONE PROBLEM FOR ANOTHER.

E. HOUSEHOLD PRODUCTS	
Occurs in:	Glue, petrol, cleaners, lighter fluid, nail polish remover, spray paint, paint removers, benzene, spirits, air fresheners, cooking spray, furniture polish, tippex. Snuffed or inhaled.
Effect:	Represses the central nervous system. Euphoria, loss of balance, light headed and loses inhibitions, lame feeling, inability to reason, irritation in eyes, nose, nausea, diarrhoea, chronic cough, double vision, speech affected, hallucination, aggression, violent behaviour, amnesia, serious depression and suicidal tendencies.
Addiction:	HIGHLY ADDICTIVE – STAY AWAY ALTOGETHER!
Side effects of addiction:	Personality changes. Chronic depression. Insomnia. Amnesia. Bleeding. Lead poisoning. Paralysis of nervous system.
Serious consequences:	Damage to kidneys, heart, liver, lungs. Damage to mucous membrane of the respiratory system. Damage to central nervous system and brain cells. (You inhale deadly poison which travels to your brain with the oxygen!!!) Death as a result of smothering or choking in own vomit. SSD (Sudden Sniffing Death) as the heart stops. Death as a result of spasms of the larynx.
Withdrawal symptoms:	SERIOUS WITHDRAWAL SYMPTOMS WHICH CAN BE COMPARED TO ALCOHOL AND DRUG WITHDRAWAL.

HELP!
I CAN'T
BREATHE!!!

F. TOBACCO	
Occurs in:	Cigarettes, tobacco, cigars, pipes – are smoked.
Effect:	Affects the central nervous system TWICE AS FAST AS AN INJECTION AND THREE TIMES FASTER THAN A LIQUID. It soothes and stimulates at the same time. **Other than other substances the symptoms become less after using a few times. THEN YOU ARE ADDICTED.**
Addiction:	HIGHLY ADDICTIVE – STAY AWAY ALTOGETHER. ONE THIRD OF CHILDREN WHO EXPERIMENT BECOME ADDICTED.
Side effects of addiction:	Loses or lessens ability to taste and smell. Poor breathing. Quick pulse. High blood pressure. Airway infections. Anxiousness. Insomnia. Irritability. Chronic cough. Yellow fingers and teeth. Restlessness. Exhaustion. Trembling hands. Chest pains. YOU STINK!!!
Serious consequences:	You age fast. Damage to the skin, which causes wrinkles. Possibility of lung cancer 25% higher. Possibility of throat and mouth cancer 10% higher. Possibility of deadly heart diseases twice as much. Serious damage to lungs and airways. Blood vessels narrow, which causes strokes and heart attacks. Emphysema in lungs. Damage thyroid, which causes Grave's disease and can make your eyes bulge. Yellow stains on skin. Yellow colour in skin. Yellow teeth with brown stains. Tooth decay. **EVENTUALLY YOU WILL DIE AS A RESULT OF IT – 7 YEARS SOONER.**
Withdrawal symptoms:	Tension, irritation, palpitations, insomnia, constant need to smoke, moodiness, aggression, eats constantly, hands tremble, exhaustion, weight gain.

MY GUY HAS DROPPED ME! HE SAYS I LOOK TOO OLD FOR HIM! WHY DO THE GIRLS IN THE ADVERTS LOOK SO YOUNG!? I SMOKE MORE THAN THEY DO AND I'M LOOKING OLDER AND OLDER!!!!

Nothing looks as stupid as a kid with braces on the teeth and a cigarette in the hand!!

G. ALCOHOL	
Occurs in:	All alcoholic drinks. The quantity is given on the bottle in % . Certain medicines.
Effect:	Affects the nervous system. CHANGES YOUR PERSONALITY. Poor co-ordination, poor reaction and reflexes, poor concentration, muddled thoughts, loses control over emotions and inhibitions, speech is affected and lips feel "dumb", poor balance, drowsiness or insomnia, becomes vulgar, swears and talks nonsense, feels bad and becomes nauseous, becomes aggressive and even violent, loses ability to judge.
Addiction:	**HIGHLY ADDICTIVE, THE LARGEST ADDICTION IN THE WORLD – NEVER DRINK UNTIL YOU FEEL DRUNK. SCHOOL CHILDREN BECOME ADDICTED WITHIN 6-8 MONTHS IF ALCOHOL IS ABUSED.**
Side effects of addiction:	Alcohol controls thoughts – knows all types of drink, talks about it, looks for opportunities to drink. Feels guilty and lies about drinking. Hides drink. Feels tense if there's no drink. Brags about how much can be drunk or pretends to have drunk only a little. Finds excuse to drink or why you drink and become angry if somebody speaks to you about it. Deny that you have a problem. Stay without drink for a time – then you drink a lot again. Smells of alcohol. Eats something to hide the smell. Drinks fast and gulps drinks down. Nausea, becomes nauseous in the morning, loses appetite. Hangover ("babalas") Alcohol poisoning can occur if person has drunk to much. Hands tremble.
Serious consequences: **Do you change into a monster when you drink? THEN YOU NEED HELP!!!**	PERSONALITY CHANGES PERMANENTLY. ***Brain:*** damage to short term memory, hallucinations, black outs, muddled, confused, irrational behaviour, aggression, fits of anger, inability to control behaviour and emotions. Later permanent brain damage. ***Heart:*** enlarges the heart and weakens the heart muscles. ***Lungs:*** infections like pneumonia, bronchitis and tuberculosis (TB). ***Abdomen***: Peptic ulcers, inability to digest food, inflammation of the stomach lining, diarrhoea. ***Kidneys:*** kidney failure. ***Liver:*** enlarged liver, liver failure, liver stops working and cannot excrete poisons from body. ***Sexual organs:*** Impotence, infertility. ***Muscles:*** muscles become smaller, weak and limp. ***Blood***: body loses ability to form blood clots. ***Skin problems*** such as veins, red nose, "potato nose" Vitamin shortage: increases susceptibility to diseases. Extreme depression. Suicide is common amongst alcoholics. The alcoholic's behaviour influences the lives of 15 people around him.

Withdrawal symptoms:	Serious withdrawal symptoms. Insomnia, anxiousness, trembling, palpitations, nausea, headaches, stomach problems, nervousness, irrational behaviour, aggression, tension. DT's = serious hallucinations and deadly fits. **ALCOHOLICS CAN NEVER AGAIN DRINK NORMALLY AFTER THEY HAVE BEEN REHABILITATED BECAUSE THEY WILL BECOME ADDICTED AGAIN. THEN ONE DRINK BECOMES ONE TOO MANY AND A THOUSAND TOO FEW.**

H. "SMART DRINKS"

Remember that these energy drinks increase your metabolism and in the long term can cause damage to your body if you abuse it.

Stay away from any drinks which increase your heartbeat or make you feel "funny"!!

Everybody needs vitamins but nobody needs an overdose of it.

Always read the label to see what the contents are!
"Smart Drinks" with the following contents should rather be avoided as they cannot be put above suspicion!

Pangamic Acid
Ma-Haung   – (E,g. in "Little Engine")
Kava-Kava   – (E,g. in "Dream")
Vasopressin Guarana   – (E,g. in "Ignition")
L-Phenylalanine   – (E,g. in "Cyber Tonic")

ALWAYS OPEN THE BOTTLE
YOURSELF AND POUR THE
QUANTITY YOU'RE GOING TO DRINK
INTO YOUR OWN GLASS.
DRINKS ARE OFTEN SPIKED
WITHOUT YOUR KNOWLEDGE.
SEVERAL WOMEN HAVE
BEEN RAPED BECAUSE OF THIS.

Illegal substances!!!

THE FOLLOWING SUBSTANCES ARE ILLEGAL AND YOU CAN RECEIVE A JAIL SENTENCE IF IT IS FOUND IN YOUR POSSESSION OR IF YOU TRADE IN IT. IN SOME COUNTRIES DRUG ABUSE IS A SERIOUS OFFENCE.

OFFENDERS WHO ARE CAUGHT IN THESE COUNTRIES CAN GET A VERY LONG JAIL SENTENCE AND EVEN THE DEATH SENTENCE FOR THEIR MISDEEDS.

THERE ARE THOUSANDS OF SOUTH AFRICANS IN JAIL OVERSEAS BECAUSE OF SMUGGLING DRUGS. THESE PEOPLE ARE SOMETIMES DETAINED UNDER SHOCKING CONDITIONS WITHOUT BEING ABLE TO UNDERSTAND THE COUNTRY'S LANGUAGE OR CULTURE.

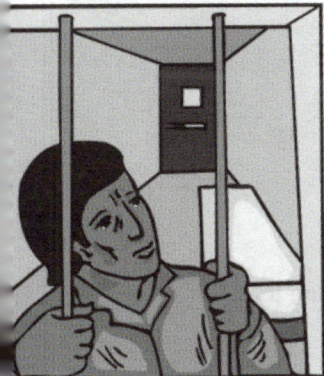

DRUGS ARE USUALLY BEHIND MOST CRIMES AND MURDERS AND PEOPLE WON'T HESITATE TO KILL TO BE ABLE TO AFFORD THEIR SUPPLY. MANY ADDICTED CHILDREN TURN TO THEFT AND PROSTITUTION TO GET THIS SUPPLY.

SINCE DRUGS ARE EXPENSIVE IT MAKES SENSE TO ADDICTS TO ADDICT OTHERS SO THAT THESE PEOPLE CAN THEN PAY FOR THEIR HABIT.

THEREFORE DON'T BELIEVE ANYTHING A DRUG PUSHER TELLS YOU. YOU ARE GOING TO PAY FOR THEIR HABIT TOO AND YOU WILL EVENTUALLY HAVE TO ADDICT OTHERS TO PAY FOR YOUR HABIT.

DRUG SYNDICATES ARE POWERFULLY RICH AND HAVE A LOT OF INFLUENCE. ONCE YOU HAVE LANDED IN THEIR CLAWS YOUR LIFE IS ALWAYS IN DANGER. THEY BECOME RICH AND IF YOU BUY THESE DRUGS YOU WILL LATER PAY FOR IT WITH YOUR LIFE.

IMMEDIATELY SEEK HELP AND REPORT PEOPLE WHO SOW THIS DESTRUCTION.

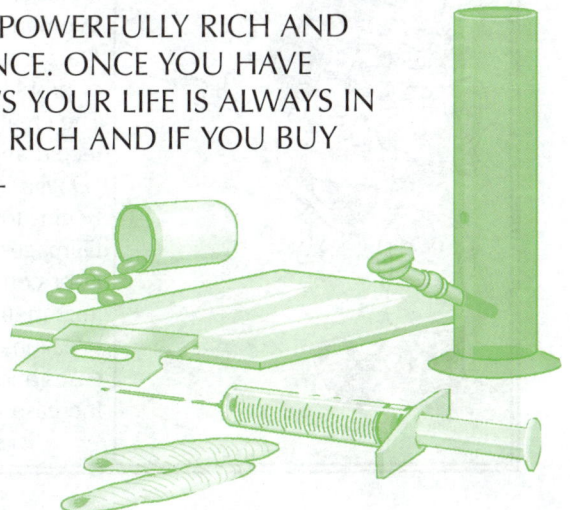

NARCOTICS

DRUGS ARE NOT COOL!

JUST SAY NO!

A. "DAGGA" (MARIJUANA)

Occurs in:	Leaves and flowers are smoked in cigarettes, pipes and bottle necks and are often mixed with other substance such as Mandrax.
Effect:	Works on the nervous system and the brain. Light headedness, relaxation, talkativeness, euphoria, increased appetite, feeling of independence and removal of reality. Blocks messages to the brain and twists messages from the senses, anxiousness, depression, panic attacks, confusion, paranoid fear, increased pulse, cold shivers, dry mouth and throat, red eyes, nausea. Loses inhibitions and co-ordination and often becomes violent.
Addiction:	IT CAUSES A PSYCHOLOGICAL ADDICTION AND IS THEREFORE ADDICTIVE – THE USER MUST USE MORE AND MORE TO GET THE SAME EFFECT. DAGGA LEADS TO THE USE OF OTHER STRONGER SUBSTANCES OR THE MIXING OF SUBSTANCES. DANGEROUS TO CHILDREN AS ORGANS ARE STILL FORMING.
Side effects of addiction:	Serious terror and panic attacks. Loses drive and initiative. Becomes aimless. Develops emotional and psychological problems. Dagga psychosis. Chronic cough. Bronchitis. Health deteriorates Heartbeat increases and heart is affected. Insomnia, loses ability to keep track of time. Impotence. Becomes psychologically addictive and needs more to get that "feeling". Aggravates existing emotional problems.
Long term consequences:	Affects lungs (the tar in 1 zol is equal to a packet of cigarettes). Causes lung cancer. Chronic diseases of the airways as well as asthma, emphysema and TB. Increased risk of contracting cancer. Cancer of the tongue and palate is common. Men – testosterone levels drop, lower sperm count and problems to father children. Women – testosterone levels increases, fertility drops. Dagga causes the slowing down of emotional growth, the processing of problems and challenges. The creative subconscious which gives you drive and motivation is affected and the person becomes aimless and apathetic. "Dagga" causes asocial behaviour. Begins to lie, steal, becomes lazy, neglects work etc. Damages brain – especially short term memory. Poor concentration and inability to work out solutions for problems (e.g. mathematical problems). Weakens immune system and makes user susceptible to serious diseases and infections. Increase and decrease of heart beat causes heart problems.

Withdrawal symptoms:	"Dagga" (marijuana) can remain in your system for weeks and is usually not eliminated before the next dosage is taken. Withdrawal symptoms are the same as for cigarettes: moodiness, shakes, headaches, perspiring, irritability, cough.

"DAGGA" SMOKERS ARE QUICK TO POINT OUT TO YOU THAT "DAGGA" IS A NATURAL PRODUCT AND IS, THEREFORE, HARMLESS.

THIS IS AN ABSURD EXCUSE AS MOST HIGHLY ADDICTIVE DRUGS ARE ALSO MADE FROM PLANTS.

SOME PLANTS LIKE OLEANDER ARE INDEED SO DANGEROUS THAT SMOKING IT WILL KILL YOU IF YOU INHALE.

B. MANDRAX	
Occurs in.	Tablet form. 80% of "dagga" smokers mix Mandrax with dagga" by making it into a powder and then smoking it with "dagga".
Effect:	Person falls over or faints. A lot of saliva forms and runs out of the mouth or has to be spat out, coughs, falls to sleep for long hours and wakes up drunk, heartbeat changes, fits, terrible headaches, coughing spells, stomach ache, drunkenness, restlessness, poor co-ordination, nausea, poor speech.
Addiction:	Causes extreme psychological and emotional addiction. Deadly and dangerous. STAY AWAY!!!!
Side effects of addiction	Fits. Diarrhoea. Vomiting and nausea. Drunk feeling. Light-headedness. Psychological and emotional problems. Stomach cramps. Terrible headaches. Deterioration of immune system. Infections and diseases such as pneumonia.
Long term consequences:	Deadly if taken with alcohol. Coma and DEATH as a result of overdose. Breathing and blood circulation are impeded. Brain damage especially to the memory. Personality changes.
Withdrawal symptoms:	Dosage must constantly be increased. It controls the addict's life and he loses all interest in other things. Withdrawal symptoms cause headaches, stomach cramps, coughing spells, depression, hallucinations, insomnia fits, irritation, aggression, stomach ulcers.

C. COCAINE	
Occurs in:	Powder which is sniffed or concentrated cubes which are smoked ("freebase"). Dealers often mix cocaine with other powders.
Effect :	Stimulates central nervous system. Works on the "pleasure" points of the brain. Sniffed up through nose to be taken up into the bloodstream immediately. "High" is of short duration (20-30 minutes) and person has to sniff more and more to get the same effect. The effect depends on the person's moods and environment. Cocaine prevents the brain from calming itself. "High" of energy and euphoria. **The person will be more talkative and believes that he is cleverer and stronger than he really is.** **He then does things which endanger his life!** Together with these feelings, the person feels anxiety and tension. The user becomes depressive, paranoid, extremely nervous, restless, scared and irritated. Other symptoms are dry mouth, spasms, shakes and sweat. Pulse increases and blood pressure rises. Person quickly moves from "high" of euphoria to "crash" of extreme depression and anxiety with withdrawal symptoms.
Addiction :	**One of the most addictive substances on the planet . You can become addicted from your very first sniff.** The psychological and physical breakdown is faster than with any other substances. IT IS THE MOST EXPENSIVE TO BUY, TO MAINTAIN AND TO TREAT. STAY AWAY! IT'S DEADLY!!!
Side effects of addiction:	Violent and inexplicable behaviour, nausea, dizziness, tingling in hands and feet.
Long term consequences:	Psychotic behaviour. Suicidal tendencies. Serious hallucinations. Damage to nasal passages and wall between nostrils is eroded. Cocaine psychosis –can be compared to paranoid schizophrenia. Terrible hallucinations – bugs on or under the skin, hears voices, fears and confusion. Becomes violent. Affects the lower brain areas– causes fits and shakes. Heart beats faster. Person starts to swallow air and gets heart attack. Fits. Nose bleeds. Heart stops Breathing organs stop functioning. Changes the chemical construction of the brain. DEATH!!!

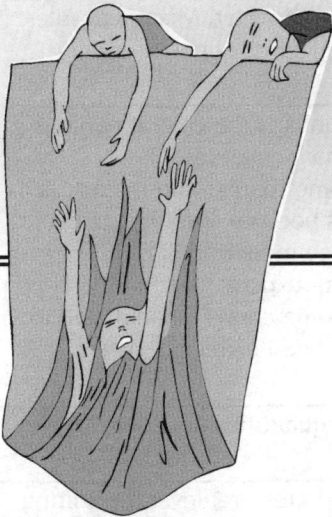

Withdrawal symptoms:	The person's life eventually becomes controlled by the habit. He will sell everything and anything to maintain his habit. It can cost up to R30,000 a month. The user never again reaches the same "feeling" that he had the first time. From the second time this wonderful feeling is replaced by depression and fear. To keep those feelings away for him he sniffs more and more.
	Withdrawal symptoms are eating disorders, nausea, vomiting, cravings, depression, shakes, sleeping disorders, muscular pains, irritability, Suicide attempts. Could take 1–3 years to rehabilitate.

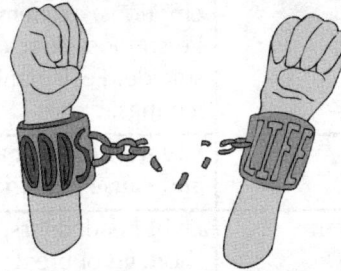

D. CRACK

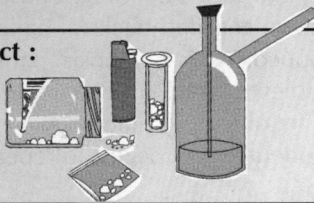

Occurs in:	Smoked in special pipes, bottle necks or cigarettes – sometimes fumes are inhaled. Concentrated cocaine.
Effect :	Gets into bloodstream faster than cocaine. Sets brain chemicals free, increases heartbeat and blood pressure. Euphoric effect is of short duration and is followed by depression, anxiousness and irritation. As a result of effect on brain addiction is practically immediate.
Addiction :	**HIGHLY DANGEROUS!** **HIGHEST ADDICTION!** **PRACTICALLY IMMEDIATELY ADDICTED!** **STAY AWAY ALTOGETHER!!!**
Side effects of addiction:	Same symptoms as cocaine, but much more intense. Terrible fury and aggression. Damages heart, blood vessels and other organs! Fits. Paranoia. Hallucinations. Insomnia. Weight loss. Chronic coughing spells.
Long term consequences:	Impotence. Amnesia. Strokes. Heart attacks and heart failure affects brain and causes attacks. You could become brain dead. Lung problems. Crack-lungs: Chest pains, breathing problems and high fever. Causes serious psychological problems. Will murder or commit suicide if person has no supply.
Withdrawal symptoms:	Same as cocaine, but much more intense.

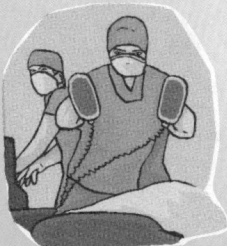

E. LSD	
Occurs in:	Tasteless odourless, crystals which dissolve in water. Mixed capsules, stamps, stickers, bits of paper soaked in LSD. Bits of paper usually have cartoon pictures on them.
Effect:	Hallucinatory – twists the important functions of the central nervous system, changes perceptions and causes hallucinations. Effect lasts about 8-16 hours. Senses become sharper and it appears as if objects move and change shape. Senses become muddled and send wrong messages to the brain. Quick change in moods, strong emotions, excitement, loathing, fear, are all experienced jumbled up. Person loses track of time, believes he's going crazy. It could lead to suicide. Feels panicky, develops paranoia and heightens existing feelings.
Addiction:	**Greatest hallucinator known. Only small quantities necessary to give and cause addiction. STAY AWAY!!!!!!!!**
Side effects of addiction:	Light-headedness, nausea, increased blood pressure, fever, perspiring, shortage of breath, hyperventilation, lameness, cold fever, shakes, insomnia, trembling, loses muscle co-ordination, speech is affected, inability to feel pain leads to serious injuries, spasms.
Long term consequences:	Psychological addiction twists the person's perception of his own abilities. You believe you can fly and could fall from a building. Causes terrible depression and anxiousness. Person gets flashbacks of hallucinations – even years after they have stopped. Toxic psychosis, panic attacks, coma, heart and lung failure, violent behaviour. Behaviour compares to schizophrenic paranoia. Catatonic syndrome occurs and person becomes mute, slow witted, disoriented and begins to repeat senseless movements endlessly.
Withdrawal symptoms:	Few physical symptoms but serious psychological withdrawal and depression. Hallucinations can persist for years after use.

F. ECSTACY and ICE	
Occurs in:	Tablet form, capsules, powder and crystals – usually at "Raves".
Effect:	Person becomes very friendly and social loses inhibitions and feels very sensual. Loses co-ordination, perspires, dry mouth, constant thirst, blood pressure increases and heartbeat becomes faster, affects vision, fever, tingling in body, muscles stiffen, loses balance.
Addiction:	HIGHLY ADDICTIVE – MUST USE MORE AND MORE TO GET SAME EFFECT AND OVERDOSE IS DEADLY.
Side effects of addiction:	Dehydration. Muscles spasm. Clenches jaws and bites on teeth. Anxiousness. Paranoia. Depression. Lameness. Violent behaviour. Heightens existing feelings.

Long term consequences:	Severe anorexia. Heart attacks. Blood clots on brain. Strokes. Paralysis. Psychological deviations. Is connected with Parkinson's Disease. Decreases fluid in spinal marrow. Liver damage. Damages brain cells. Heart attacks are common and can occur with first use. Fits and blood clots in lungs. Lung failure causes person's inability to breathe and can lead to death. Damages blood vessels in the brain which leads to strokes and brain damage.
Withdrawal symptoms:	Serious psychological withdrawal symptoms i.e. depression, paranoia, fear.

G. SHABU	
Occurs in:	Tablet form and sometimes disguised and sold as Ecstasy or other drugs. Looks like Ecstasy. Printed letters on tablet. SHABU can also be smoked or injected.
Effect:	Much worse, more dangerous and damaging than Ecstasy. Only one tablet can cause terrible changes in moods, uncontrollable aggressive behaviour, fits, shakes and uncontrolled speech.
Addiction:	UTTERLY UTTERLY DANGEROUS – IT WILL CAUSE YOUR DEATH. SHABU is a metaphetamine and is similar to amphetamines ("whizz", "speed", "sulphate" or "uppers") but with stronger side effects. Dealers are determined to make money and often mix their ingredients with washing powder and even rat poison. SHABU IS DEADLIER AND MORE ADDICTIVE THAN "CRACK-COCAINE".
Side effects of addiction:	Dreadful acne rash on skin. Short of breath, hallucinations, insomnia (up to 36 hours), terrible panic attacks, spiritual confusion, serious suicidal tendencies and attempts at suicide
Long term consequences:	Serious depression – users eventually try to commit suicide at all costs. Deadly lung diseases. Deadly damage to kidneys. Deadly damage to liver.
Withdrawal symptoms:	The same symptoms as for "Crack" but much more serious. THIS DRUG KILLS!!! Your withdrawal symptoms will probably be your last convulsions and the last breath you exhale … (Bliss, February 1999)

H. OPIUM and HEROIN	
Occurs in:	Brown or white granules which are sold in powder form or cubes. Odourless with a bitter taste. Injected in liquid from by way of needles or smoked.
Effect :	Suppresses the central nervous system. The "high" doesn't last long and the dosage must constantly be repeated which causes adduction. Heightens existing feelings. User experiences euphoria, staring eyes, constipation, mood swings, personality changes, loss of appetite, enormous weight loss, insomnia, impotence, speech is affected, poor reflexes, loss of co-ordination, aggression, withdrawal from people, loses interest in everyday tasks and relationships.
Addiction :	Highly addictive – physically as well as psychologically. Person struggles to rehabilitate for years. Rehabilitation not very successful.
Side effects of addiction:	Serious psychological and physical addiction. Injections which could lead to gangrene and amputations. Limbs which are affected. Lung problems, dehydration, runny nose, shakes, cramps, perspiring, convulsions. The drug becomes so important that the person neglects his health, appearance and whole life, because they are no longer important to him. Regular infections occur.
Long term consequences:	HIV – transmitted by needles. Hepatitis A. B. and C. Lung problems and lung infections. Heart failure. General physical deterioration. Gangrene in limbs. Impotence. Psychological deterioration and serious psychological problems. Coma or death from overdose.
Withdrawal symptoms.:	Hyperventilation, fever, cold shivers, fits, diarrhoea, constant urination, hallucinations, feelings of fear and terror, muscular pains, delirium, heart failure. Persons can usually not stop for long and become addicted again and again.

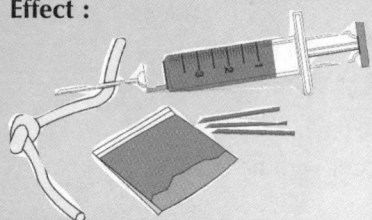

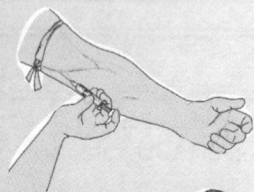

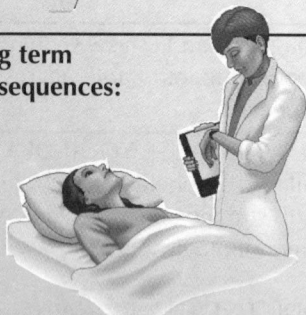

Visit the website

http://www.drugstv.com

for excellent information on drugs

10. *Somebody I know is addicted ...*

When somebody you know shows the symptoms of addiction it is important not to keep quiet about it but talk about it.
GET HELP – FOR YOURSELF AND THAT PERSON!

If one of your parents is addicted it could destroy your life as well. Children of addicts often have feelings of tension, frustration, anger and anxiety. If these problems are not handled, they could lead to psychological problems. Make sure that you receive help. To keep quiet simply worsens the problem.

Addiction is not a shame, but a serious disease.

The person is usually past the point where he can help himself. Would you keep quiet if someone is really very ill?

11. *I need help!*

1. GET HELP IMMEDIATELY. SPEAK TO SOMEONE WHOM YOU REALLY CAN TRUST!

2, DIAL ONE OF THE FOLLOWING ORGANISATIONS.
NUMBERS OF THE LOCAL BRANCHES ARE AVAILABLE IN THE TELEPHONE DIRECTORY OR CALL 1023 (ENQUIRIES).

3. CONTACT
    * CHILDLINE
    * LIFELINE
    * SANCA
    * SAPD
    * Alcoholics Anonymous
    * CYA
    * Youth groups
    * Coffee shops
    * Your minister, pastor or spiritual leader

4. CERTAIN SUBSTANCES HAVE EXTREMELY DANGEROUS WITHDRAWAL SYMPTOMS. DON'T TRY TO GET OFF ILLEGAL DRUGS BY YOURSELF. GET HELP FROM TRAINED PEOPLE WHO KNOW WHAT TO DO.

5. LIVE THE FOLLOWING TWELVE STEPS!

TWELVE STEPS TO LIBERATION

1 BE HONEST WITH YOURSELF AND ADMIT TO YOUR PROBLEM. Admit that this substance or habit is taking over your life. Admit that you feel powerless and that your life is out of control.

2 Believe that GOD who is greater than you can take away this helplessness and give you back your common sense.

3 Decide to give your own will and life to God – as you understood Him – trust Him to change your life.

4 Sit down and make a very honest list of all your fears, good points, bad points and everything that has happened in your life.

5 Then admit to GOD, to yourself and to someone else as well, exactly what your own faults and weaknesses are.

6 Allow God to then remove these faults from your life

7 Realise that you cannot remove these faults on your own and humbly ask God to do it for you.

8 Make a very honest list of everyone you have ever wronged and be willing to put matters right between you.

9 Go and fix what you have messed up. Ask for forgiveness and truly regret that which you have done to them. If your admittance of guilt is likely to do the person more harm then rather leave the matter with God and pray about it sincerely.

10 Keep making a regular list of what is happening in your life. When you are wrong admit it straight away, apologise and ask for forgiveness.

11 Keep praying. **Seek God until you find Him**. He is waiting for you. Then improve this relationship and pray that He will give you the knowledge to do His will, as well as the power to do so.

12 Live these principles each day in your everyday life and help people who have gone through the same struggle that you have.

These 12 STEPS are an adaptation of the 12 STEPS which were set up by ALCOHOLICS ANONYMOUS and have liberated thousands of people from their addiction to date. IT CAN HELP ANYONE WHO HAS PROBLEMS!!!

12 Is it time for order?

Do you have order in your life or does your life look like the room on this page? Disarray is one of the biggest reasons why your time is consumed to such a degree that you cannot reach your goals. This chapter teaches you to differentiate between order and disarray and helps you to get more order into your life.

1. Goals which are not reached

At this stage of your life you have probably realised that it does happen that all wishes and dreams don't come true and that not all goals are reached.
All of us fail at one time or another during our lives. This is normal and happens to everybody. Even the greatest discoverers had failures and disappointments.

- Nelson Mandela was jailed for 27 years before he became president and his dream of freedom came true!

  - The millionaire, Richard Branson, experienced serious learning problems at school. His principal said: "You will either get rich or land up in jail."

- Albert Einstein couldn't speak until he was four and is believed to have failed Grade 6!

  - Louis Pasteur was regarded as an "average" student in chemistry.

  - Marie Curie was almost bankrupt before she won the Nobel Prize for Chemistry and Physics individually.

- Thomas Edison did hundreds of experiments before finding the correct filaments which would make the light bulb burn. When he was asked about his "failures" at a later stage he replied that not one of his experiments ever failed, but simply brought him closer to the solution!

Making mistakes, making wrong choices and experiencing failures are not the worst that can happen to you. The worst that can happen to you is if you never learn from your mistakes. Think of a fly which keeps buzzing against the closed window in order to get out, while an open window is right next to him! Yet he would literally strain himself to death, rather that change direction!

2. Don't you have time for your goals?

Many of us never reach our goals because we just don't make time for it. We're busy all day long and yet we don't do much. When you would like to reach your goals and want to make time for it, it is TIME FOR ORDER.

When you go on holiday you pack your neatly ironed cloths into a suitcase. You neatly put the larger items in first and then you look for space for your underwear, toiletries and other items you want to take with. In this way you try to put as much as possible into the suitcase.

As your holiday progresses you put on and take off clothes, search the suitcase and clutter up the whole lot. At the end of the holiday you have to repack and now you can't close the suitcase at all! Have your clothes become more? Unfortunately not. It is only in disarray and because you have to pack hastily and have no time to wash or iron, you can't close your suitcase!

Your life can be compared to this packing of the suitcase. As long as your life is in order you reach your big and small goals. Since you first arrange time for your big goals you will soon realise that you also have time to complete the small tasks.

However, if your life is in disarray, if you want to please everybody, to enjoy your own life and to put everything off until the last moment, you will never reach your goal. Before you know it you will be desperately unhappy because you are in trouble everywhere and your life has become a race to nowhere.

Unfortunately many people live this way. Let us see whether you can recognise yourself as one of these types of people who are also described in Sean Covey's book ***Seven Habits of Highly Effective Teen***s and also in Gordon McDonald's book ***Ordering Your Private World.*** Mark those points where you feel guilty …

a) "Muddled people"

We all have rooms, cupboards and suitcases which have been jumbled at one stage or another. Sometimes this muddled way of life becomes a bad habit that eventually takes over your life. What do "Muddled people" look like?

☐ Flat surfaces in the "Muddled person's" life are usually full of clutter. It doesn't matter whether it's a shelf, the bedside table, desk or kitchen shelf – it remains cluttered!

☐ "Muddled people" mess up spaces. Wherever the muddled person sits or stands, it will be cluttered. They are constantly either cluttering or clearing up.

☐ "Muddled people" often don't keep appointments, make double appointments, don't phone back and don't hand in work or tasks in time. They are usually late for everything!

☐ "Muddled people" often spend a lot of their time on petty things and neglect those things that are really important (like the focal point of their Life Cycle) and which should be completed (like homework).

☐ Friends and family require a lot of patience with "Muddled people" because they make people angry with their unorganised way of life. To constantly clear up after someone else, always have to wait for them and listen to excuses as to why things haven't been done, is no joke!

☐ "Muddled people" often have a poor self image because they realise that their work, studies, relationships, time and life have become lost in the jumbled confusion of their lives.

Are you a "muddled person"? THEN IT IS TIME FOR ORDER!

b) "Postpone-Cancel people"

We have all done things that are unplanned and necessary. Life often delivers crisis situations where you have to drop whatever you're doing to attend to the crisis. Some people's lives, however, consists mainly of crises because everything they do and should do is postponed to the extent where everything has to be handled as a crisis at the last moment.

☐ The "Postpone person's" vocabulary consists mainly of the words: **"I will, just now!"** These words "just now" unfortunately means anything but "immediately".

☐ If the "Postpone person" opens his or her diary he or she usually does the less important and easier tasks first and all complicated, difficult, unpleasant or time consuming things are left for later.

☐ The "Postpone person" usually has excellent excuses as to why things cannot be completed straight away.
"The weather isn't right", "Maybe things will get better later", "I don't have time right now", "I'm tired", "I first want to rest because I have just …" "There's a lot of time left. What's the hurry?"
When the "Postpone person's" time catches up with him and the work has not been completed, the excuses become even better! *"I couldn't do it, because I first had to …", "I didn't have enough time", "I was too tired", "I overslept!"*

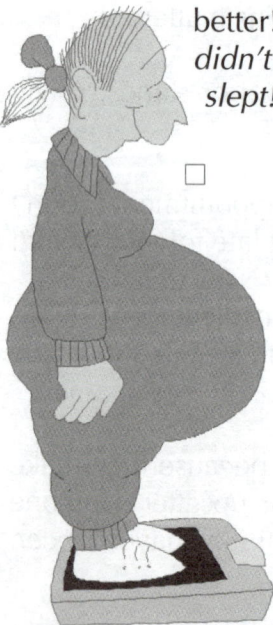

☐ "Postpone people" always need a lot of time to finish things. They take days and hours to complete small tasks and spend hours avoiding important things that have to be done.

☐ "Postpone people" make huge tasks out of small tasks since their way of postponing things to the last minute has become a habit. Small tasks have now become big tasks requiring preparation, planning and time. The bicycle's flat tyre has now also bent the bicycle frame. The untidy bedroom is now a "pigsty". The work task which normally takes half an hour has now become a few nights' work. The little rolls of fat have now become a tub of lard!

☐ "Postpone people" like their own comfort zone which makes them feel comfortable and safe and they often postpone, because it takes nerve, staying power and discipline to do things you don't like or which you haven't done before.

☐ Because "Postpone people" put off everything to the last moment and then quickly rushes through it, these people usually suffer from:

❖ Tension and worry
❖ Burn out
❖ Mediocrity
❖ Poor self image.

☐ "Postpone people" are usually also "Cancel people" because the work they postponed earlier now begins to clash with other work which has to be handled immediately. The "Postpone-cancel person" now has to choose between what has to be done and what not. Usually the "Postpone-cancel person" will do nothing because there was "not enough time" for the first task and for the second task there is "still plenty of time …"

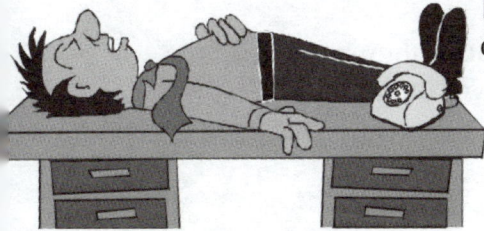

Do you recognise yourself as a "Postpone-Cancel person"? **THEN IT IS TIME FOR ORDER!**

c) "OK-fine-people"

Good friends are one of the most important investments you could ever make in your life. Friends and family make time for each other, bear each other's troubles and are there for one another when the rest of the world walks out of the door. If, however, your friends and family take up so much of your time and energy, your soul and peace, demand your life and begin to misuse you, you have possibly become one of the "OK-fine-people"!

☐ "OK-fine-people" are constantly busy with other people's "important matters". They like to help others to sort out their work problems and life.

☐ "OK-fine-people" can't say "NO". They are afraid that they will hurt the feelings of others and that people won't like them. They can't even say "NO" to the telephone when it rings while they're in the bath!

☐ "OK-fine-people's" lives are full of interruptions. As soon as they are concentrating on something (like work to learn for tomorrow's test), they will be interrupted by a "Muddled person" who doesn't have the notes or by a "Postpone-cancel person" who first wants to do something else. Because they can't say "No!" and like to help, they leave their own important work to help others.

☐ "OK-fine-people" often make promises they can't keep. They are trying to please so many people that, eventually they can please no one – including themselves!

☐ "Ok-fine-people" easily give in to peer pressure and usually do things they "later" regret deeply. They swim with the current because they can't refuse. Because they are not doing it with **all their heart**, they don't enjoy it anyway and usually end up in a place where they didn't want to be in the first place!

☐ "Ok-fine-people" usually suffer from
❖ a "sure bro!" reputation and people often regard him or her as spineless
❖ Exhaustion.
❖ A lack of discipline.
❖ A poor self image because he or she realises that they are often abused by others.

☐ "Ok-fine-people's" work is often late or incomplete because they were so busy helping others that there was no time left to give attention to their own work.

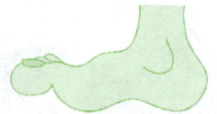

Do people walk all over you?
Then it is TIME FOR ORDER!

d) The sluggard

When you have worked hard and the holidays arrive, you spend a day or two just being lazy. You want to sleep and rest and do nothing. The difference between a person who is sometimes lazy and one who is always lazy, is that the Sluggard never wants to do anything and never wants to get up, while the ordinary person will become jittery if he does nothing for days on end.

☐ The Sluggard likes the "good" things in life. He loves sleeping, eating, hanging out, doing nothing, watching TV and blowing money. If, however, he has to work for it or help, he has hundreds of excuses.

☐ The Sluggard has only heard the first part of the saying "*Too much of a good thing…*" and applies it wholeheartedly. He *lives* from overindulgence. Too much television, too much sleep, too much hanging out, too much visiting, too much eating, too much talking … This is the way in which the Sluggard spends his day.

☐ The Sluggard is a master manipulator in getting others to do his work. His mother cleans his room, his girlfriend does his written work, his friends lend him their notes, his little sister brings his coffee, his teacher explains the work to him again and again … and yet he does nothing. He doesn't help, he doesn't fetch or carry, he doesn't clean up and he doesn't even try to think!

☐ The sluggard also has a multitude of aches and pains and excuses ready, in case someone gets to grips with him about his attitude, his habits or his unfinished work. He knows how to blame others for it and does it with gusto. In the same way as he takes no responsibility for the things he should be doing himself, so he also takes no responsibility for the things he hasn't done!

☐ The Sluggard lives like a parasite on other people's money, possessions, knowledge, sense of responsibility, friendship and loyalty. When people eventually tire of him and shake him off, he will look for the fault with them and immediately find someone else to suck onto.

☐ Sluggards' arms are usually too short to help and their hands too round to handle something. They are there quickly to join in the pleasures and comforts of life, but are usually conspicuous by their absence when it comes to packing right, packing away, helping, cleaning, carrying, picking up and learning.

"It's not my job (house, child, turn)!" are words often and without any hesitation used to get away from any responsibilities.

The adage **"Too much of a good thing …"** ends with the words **"… is no good!"** You will know when you start to overstep that limit of **too much**.

THEN IT IS TIME FOR ORDER!

3. How do I get order in my life?

Order in your life is as important as eating, sleeping and breathing. Without order you life will soon turn to chaos, which will become bigger as time goes by.

Just like the "Muddled people,", "Postpone-cancel-people", Ok-fine-people" and the Sluggards' bad habits changed into lifestyles, habits of order and discipline can also become a lifestyle.

Use the following hints to get order into your life!

a) Get order into your soul

If you really want order in your life forever, you first have to find order in your soul. See to it that your spirit is alive and that you connect with God every day. Go back to your Focal Point and ask what He expects from you.

–   What is your final goal?
–   According to which principles do you live?

When you look at the inner part of the earth, you will notice that it consists of various layers. The inner core of the earth is a boiling mass and when cracks appear in the earth's crust or when the earth's crust erupts due to tremors or earthquakes, you get destruction, volcanoes and sink holes.

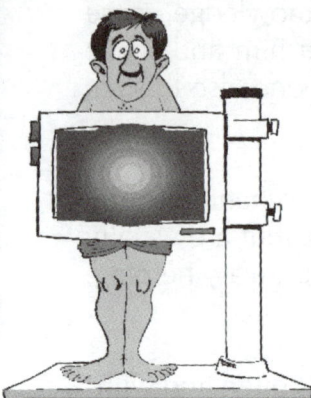

If you crop up everything that makes you sad and concentrate only on all the possessions, certificates, people and activities in your life, something is bound to give which makes your world fall apart.

If you don't have order in your soul, you will never have order in your life. If you don't make time for God every day, no diary, calendar or planning will help you when life's storms shake you to your foundations.

Gordon Macdonald writes in his book "***Ordering Your Private World"*** that there is a difference between people who are "**driven"** and people who are "**called"**.

Driven people

Driven people are spurned on by something outside themselves. Your possessions, friends, activities, schoolwork, achievements, status and power cause you to become a driven person. The more you achieve, the more you want to achieve, and the more you achieve, the harder you have to work to achieve that which you want to achieve. Doesn't this sound very much like a dog chasing his own tail?

Called people

Called people listen to what God expects of them. They know what their final goal and their own goals are. If a thousand storms explode around them they know who is in control of their lives and what is expected of them. These people remain calm and on course.

When the disciples were caught in a storm with their boat, Jesus lay asleep. They woke Him and called "Master, Master, we are perishing!" Jesus calmed the storm and asked His disciples:

"Where is your faith?"

Where is your faith?

Where are you heading?

b) Keep focused on your goals

"You lazy people can learn by watching an ant hill. Ants don't have leaders, supervisors or rulers, but they store up food during harvest season. How long will you lie there doing nothing at all? When are you going to get up and stop sleeping?"

"Sleep a little. Doze a little. Fold your hands and twiddle your thumbs. Suddenly everything is gone, as though it had been taken by an armed robber."   Proverbs 6: 6-11.

Have you watched a row of moving ants? Wet your finger and pull it along the ground between them. What happens? The ants run about in confusion for a while. Then they find a detour or one becomes brave enough to walk through the smell from your finger, and before long the row of ants is marching forward again – often with loads double their size.

These ants have a **final goal** – winter is coming and they have to replenish their supply in time.

If an ant doesn't need a leader, supervisor or ruler, then surely you don't need someone peeping over your shoulder all day long to ensure that you do your homework, clean your room, practise the piano or feed your dog.

Once you begin to feel guilty about beginning to emulate a "Muddled person", a "Postpone-cancel-person", an "Ok-fine-person" or a Sluggard, then it's time to have another look at your goals and final goal!

Ask yourself:
– What am I busy with now?
– Is it part of my final goal and goals?
– Is it taking me closer to or further from my goals?
– What am I supposed to do?
– Am I dumber than an ant for having to wait until someone tells me what to do?

c) Stop postponing

One of the main reasons why goals are not reached is because people have the habit of postponing (procrastinating).
Here are a few hints you can use to get rid of this bad habit!!

⇒   **Set priorities.**
Start with one task, focus on it and complete it before you start another.

⇒   **Divide the task into smaller sections.**
Divide your task into smaller sections and plan when you are going to do each of these small parts. You move the mountain by carrying away the rocks one by one.

⇒   **Set small specific goals.**
Work according to a timetable and set yourself a time limit in which to complete a specific task.

⇒   **Learn good timing.**
Teach yourself to guess in advance how much time a project or task will take before it's completed. This will prevent that you plan insufficient time to complete tasks correctly and well.

⇒   **Be realistic.**
Don't plan work for times when you will probably want to do something else. Do you study more over the weekend than during the week? Don't leave your work for the weekend if you know very well that you have never been able to work over weekends.

⇒   **Ask others for help.**
Ask for help if you get stuck. Don't waste hours by brooding over something you can't do.

⇒   **Note what you have already achieved.**
Don't keep staring at the heap of work still to be done but rather quickly scan what you have already completed.

⇒   **Reward yourself.**
Reward yourself for each small task you have completed successfully.

⇒   **Start.**
You can't begin to swim, until you are in the water. Remove "JUST NOW" from you vocabulary and start IMMEDIATELY!

d) Find a balance

Have you ever heard of wheel balancing? Without wheel balancing a car won't just use too much fuel, but the tyre tread will run down, the steering wheel will turn with difficulty and it could even cause an accident! Do a wheel balancing of your life cycle and stay out of the "dongas".

People with orderly lives have balance in their lives. They set priorities for themselves and arrange their lives accordingly.

Priorities are those things, which have to be done so that you can achieve your goals.

DUTY BEFORE PLEASURE!!

The secret of someone who's priorities are in order is that this person managed to:

☆ *reduce crises* by postponing less often and immediately finish work so that your work doesn't pile up and has to be rushed through. (Start to learn for the test immediately and work on the task or make your bed when you get up.)

☆ *spend less time on unimportant things.* (Remember the **too** of **too much** when you watch TV, visit, shop, sleep or rest.)

☆ *plan time for things that are important*
Study rosters and diaries help to make time for important things.

☆ *say "NO".* (Your friend who once again wants to discuss her problems for hours while you are ill or have to prepare for the exams.)

☆ *concentrate* on that which should be done and finished now. (Set your clock and concentrate to complete the work within a certain period of time.)

INSTRUCTIONS:

1) Note the goals you have set for yourself.

2) Check your homework book for work which must be done this week. Check on next week's work as well. (Preparation for tests tasks and projects.)

3) **On the next page write down the goals you have to reach this week.**

4) **In future make a list of goals every week, on what needs to be achieved for that week.**

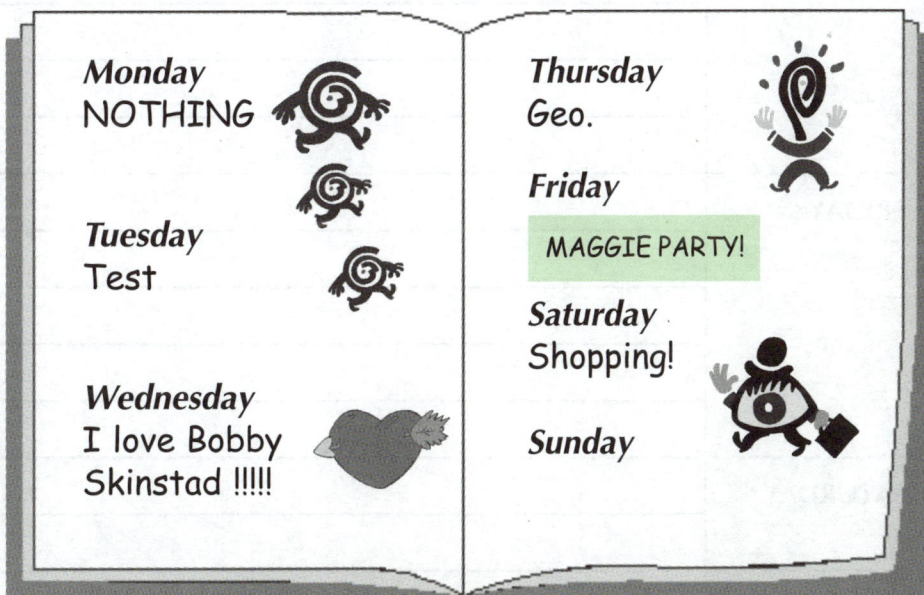

Monday
NOTHING

Tuesday
Test

Wednesday
I love Bobby
Skinstad !!!!!

Thursday
Geo.

Friday
MAGGIE PARTY!

Saturday
Shopping!

Sunday

Does your homework book look like this ...?

MY TASKS FOR THE WEEK

Or like this...?

DAY	TASKS	COMPLETED
MONDAY		
TUESDAY		
WEDNESDAY		
THURSDAY		
FRIDAY		
SATURDAY		
SUNDAY		

e)   Budget your time

How do you pack your suitcase for the holidays?
Large items which shouldn't be folded at the bottom or top of the suitcase.
Shirts folded on the one-side. Pants folded on the other side.
Undies and smaller items of clothing which are crease resistant in the gaps in between.

How do you spend your pocket money?
First budget for the large, important things you want to buy or want to save for, and then use the rest of the money for sweets and trivialities.

*When you **budget your time**, you do exactly the same.*

First do the big, urgent or unpleasant tasks, and then fill the rest of your time with the things which are less important or unimportant and not urgent!

Budget for every minute of your day!

MY DAY

6:30–17:30   **17:30–6:30**

0–14:00

20:30–21:00
20:00–20:30
19:30–20:00
19:10–19:30
18:40–19:10
18:30–18:40
18:00–18:30
17:30–18:00

21:00–21:45
21:45–22:15

6:30–7:30

16:30–17:30

15:00–16:30

14:00–14:30   14:30–15:00

22:15–6:30

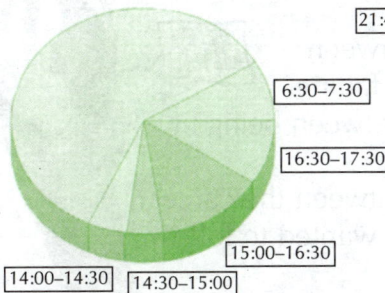

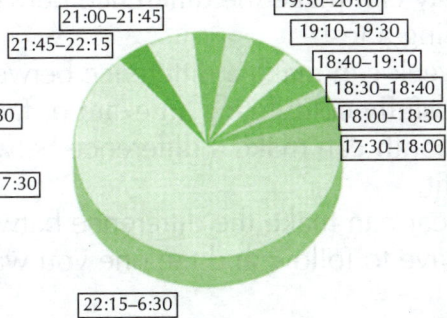

Rise
School
Eat
Rest
Hockey
Revision
Visit
Homework
Rest
Homework
Eat
Homework
Bath and room
Homework
TV
Soul
Sleep

4. Make time your friend!

All people on earth are given the same amount of hours per day for making a success or failure of their life.

Imagine time as a bank which pays R86400,00 into your account every morning. Whatever is not used on that day the bank takes back at closing time. What would you do? Use only R10,00 and leave the rest there? Certainly not! You would draw all of the R86400,00 before closing time!

God gives you 86400 seconds every day. You can't carry over any of it or borrow against it. You get it every morning when the clock is at oo:oo and it's taken away again when the 24 hours have passed. How do you use this time?

Although the appearance and price of clocks differ, all clocks are divided according to the same number of hours, minutes and seconds.

We all get:
→ 24 hours a day.
→ 60 minutes per hour.
→ 60 seconds per minute.

The child and the adult, the rich man and the beggar the housewife and the career women, you and your friends, your mom and dad – EVERYONE GETS THE SAME NUMBER OF HOURS EVERY DAY!

We all also receive
→   After every night a new day.
→   After every week a new week.
→   After every 4 weeks a new month.
→   After every 12 months a new year.
→   In every year 365 days.

It seems as if you have a lot of time if you think about it in that way, and yet …
→   one second can break a record.
→   one minute can save or lose a life.
→   one hour can make or destroy a life.
→   one day can make the difference between passing or failing a test.
→   one week can make a difference between successfully completing an exam or failing.
→   one month can make a difference between being fit or unfit.
→   one year can make the difference between the career you have to follow and the one you wanted to follow.

SUCCESSFUL PEOPLE GET TIME ON THEIR SIDE BY PLANNING!

5. How do successful people spend their time?

⇨ Successful people make appointments with themselves. They block out times in their diaries for all the different facets of their Life Cycle.

⇨ Successful people's lives are balanced!

⇨ Successful people plan on time. It's the guy who asks first who gets the girl. Successful people have learnt that "postponing" changes to "cancelling".

⇨ Truly happy successful people make time for God. They make sure that everything is still in order and keep in contact with Him.

⇨ Successful people control their time. Successful people are not controlled by others daily programmes, quirks and sulks and "crises".

⇨ Time is the successful person's best friend since he controls his time and plans in advance what he's going to do with it. It doesn't ever run out or become too little!

⇨ Successful people have enough self-confidence to say **"no"** and people respect and even envy them for it.

Who is in control of your life?

⇨ Successful people are never lazy – they will rest relax, sleep enough, enjoy life and even do silly things. However they do everything with their final goal and goals in mind.

⇨ Successful people are so positive about what they do that they can't wait to do it. They don't postpone because they enjoy everything they do!

⇨ Truly successful people are called and not driven. They follow the voice which calls them to their final goal …

WHAT DO YOU DO WITH YOUR TIME?

From the standpoint of everyday life ...
there is one thing we do know:
that man is here for the sake of other men –
above all, for those upon whose smile
and well-being our happiness depends,
and also for the countless unknown souls
with whose fate we are connected
by a bond of sympathy.
Many times a day I realize how much
my own outer and inner life is built upon
the labors of my fellow men,
both living and dead,
and how earnestly I must exert myself
in order to give in return as much
as I have received.

– Albert Einstein

God forgave you ...

God's

Riches

At

Christ's

Expense

When the One Great Scorekeeper one
day comes to write against your name,
He writes now how you won or lost,
but how you played the game.

– Gartland Rice

13 Manage your time!

Effective time management is an art that you can and must learn. This chapter helps you to organise your time and to plan in such a way that you won't just have time to reach your goals, but also to relax!

1. Lost time!

Have you ever in your life wished that you could turn back the clock to relive a wonderful moment or to right the wrongs you have done? Does the following situation sound familiar to you?

☺   You had a wonderful day with a "Very Important Person" and relive everything over and over in your mind and wish that you could relive the whole day!

☺   You win a prize and wish that the applause and congratulations won't stop!

or

☺   You sit in the exam hall or write a test and wish that you started learning sooner because you can't remember anything you tried to stuff into your head the previous night!

☺   You stand next to the sports field and wish that you had started practising sooner because you have been unable to make the team due to being unfit!

Many leading figures, top businessmen, parents and grandparents are today sitting with broken marriages, failed careers, rebellious children, poor marks or diseases as a result of time lost or wrongly spent. Regret over lost time and time unwisely spent must be one of the main reasons why people suffer from stress, depression and low self-esteem.

Children usually say:
"I will later when I'm older …"
"I will one day when I've finished school …"
"I'm still young and want to enjoy my life …"

Adults usually say:
"If I had only when I was younger …"
"If I had only earlier when I was still at school …"

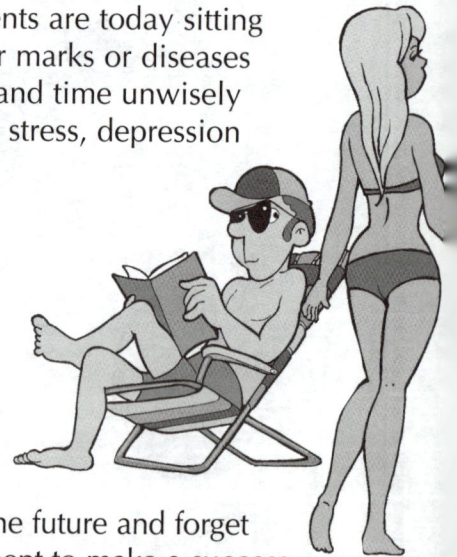

In this way we all live in the past or in the future and forget that we only have today and this moment to make a success or a failure of our lives.

Make peace today with that which is over.

Make peace with the choices you made and the consequences you have to bear. As long as you sit and brood about it you live in the past and waste the seconds and minutes given to you today to make a success of your life.

Don't postpone things to tomorrow or for when you are grown up someday. You are not going to start working someday. **You HAVE BEEN "WORKING" A LONG TIME.** Your school is your job, your homework is your job, your sport is your job, your tasks which you have to do in and around the house are your job. You certainly don't receive a salary for it yet but you do have a roof over your head, food, clothing, education and pocket money. Ask any person who earns a salary how much these things cost and what a salary is used for and you will soon find out that you have been receiving payment for these things for a long time.

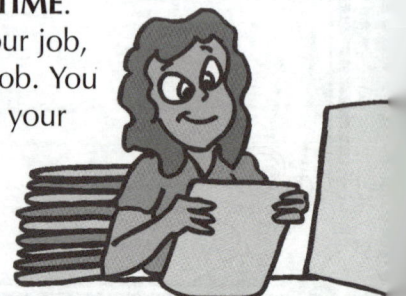

If you don't become the manager of your time, you will run behind the clock's hands for the rest of your life. The clock ticks away every second, minute, hour, day, month and year. You can turn your clock back but you can't ever make up for lost time.

Some people would be quick to say: *"I don't need a diary!"* or *"I don't want to be tied down!"*

Yet these people are usually slaves to time. They "never have time"! They are usually late and usually neglect important tasks and people. Their lives usually also end with the words **"If only I ..."**

Remember what Morrie Swartz said: **"Everybody knows they're going to die but nobody believes it! If they did we would do things differently."**

2. *How do I organise my time?*

Most of try hard to organize our time in such a way that we can do everything we should and want to do. Here are a few hints to organise your time.

a) **First create order!**

Maybe this is the last thing you need to hear, but except for the fact that a messy room gives the impression that the occupant's head is just as messed up, it is really difficult to work when you have to stop all the time to find something. It also takes much longer to tidy the whole room and all the cupboards than when you put aside ten to twenty minutes each day to clean your room.

Watch out for the "Muddled person's" habits. It usually starts in childhood with messy rooms ...!

Create definite spaces in your room:
- To sleep.
- To pack away your things.
- To do your homework.

b) **Divide your time!**

① **Determine your priorities and goals** for the year, the month and every week of the month. Don't choose a sport or activity just to be "cool" but choose activities that suit your own talents and goals.

① Get a **Year Planner** and write down important dates, tasks and priorities in it. Stick the Year Planner to the wall above your desk or next to your desk. Stick a **notice board** to your wall to pin important timetables, dates and letters to.

🕐 Use a **monthly planner** to write down important dates and priorities for the month. Keep it on your desk so that it can catch your eye when you sit down. It helps especially to plan for work tasks, revision, sports matches, tests and exams.

🕐 Use a **diary** to plan your week. Diaries which show all the days of a week at a glance and still leave enough space for written work are the best because your brain unconsciously starts to memorize the dates and tasks when you open your diary.

🕐 Work out a **timetable** for each day and stick to it. In the beginning you have to go back to your timetable several times, but after a month it becomes a habit and you do it as automatically as brushing teeth.

🕐 Remember that life cannot be planned perfectly and without adaptation from beginning to end. Schedules and planning can be changed, but take care that you don't spend all your time planning and re-planning your days.

🕐 Make **sure of your**:
–   limitations.
–   available time.
–   ongoing commitments.
–   needs.
–   goals.
–   the promises you make to others and yourself.
–   principles.
–   watch out for burnout.

🕐 Yearly planners, monthly planners and daily planners are there to help you to:

–   budget for time.
–   remember.
–   organise.
–   prioritise.
–   relax.

Regard thorough planning as something which frees you to do things you would like to do and not something that binds you!

c) Control your time

Try for a moment to think of everything you did yesterday. Can you account for every minute of your day? Try to fill in everything you did yesterday on this page.

PLEASE BE VERY HONEST!

MY DAY

6:30_____	19:00_____
7:00_____	19:30_____
7:30_____	20:00_____
8:00–14:00 SCHOOL	
14:00_____	20:30_____
14:30_____	21:00_____
15:00_____	21:30_____
15:30_____	22:00_____
16:00_____	22:30_____
16:30_____	23:00_____
17:00_____	23:30_____
17:30_____	
18:00_____	
18:30_____	

Can you account for every minute of your day?

Pierre acquired this habit. Let us see what his day looks like!

MY DAY

7:00 Rise	19:00-19:30 Eat
7:00 Dress and eat	20:00-20:30 Homework
7:30 To school	20:30-21:00 Practise guitar
8:00-14:00 SCHOOL	21:00-21:45 Television
14:00-14:30 Eat and rest	21:45-22:00 My soul & Focal Point
14:30-16:00 Rugby	22:30 SLEEP
16:00-16:15 Rest	23:00
16:15-16:45 Revise day's work	00:00
16:45-17:30 Visit	
17:30-18:00 Homework	
18:00-18:10 Rest	
18:10-18:40 Homework	
18:4019:00 Bath and room	

Time is Running Out!

Which activities does Pierre take part in? _____

How much time does Pierre spend on relaxation? _____

How much time does Pierre spend on daily revision of the day's work? _____

How much time does Pierre spend on studies? _____

How much time do you spend on your studies?_____

REMEMBER:

Every person's daily programme differs. Work out a programme which suits your circumstances.
Every day's activities differ! Therefore, work out a programme for every day of the week!

3. Why do I have to plan my time?

a) **Unplanned time is usually spent on your "weak points".**

You, for example, like computer games a lot. Because it's your "weak point" you soon find yourself on the chair in front of the computer and before you know it you have spent the whole evening in the chair!

b) **Unplanned time is often grabbed by other people.**

If you don't make appointments with yourself, your time will be filled by other people who have "nothing" to do! In this way you become an "Ok-fine-person" who spends all day trying to help others handle their crises.

c) **Unplanned time is often spent on trivialities which need to be done while the big tasks are left for later.**

Because the easy homework can be done faster and the content subjects require concentration, you sometimes spend more time on the first, while you postpone the difficult homework and revision, so that it has to be rushed through or cancelled at a later stage.

d) **Unplanned time is often spent on things which are linked to rewards.**

Yes, it's much easier to do the work of the kind teacher than that of the one you don't get along with …!

e) **Unplanned time causes you to fail in reaching your goals.**

So much time is lost, that you never get to your goals!

REMEMBER!
Time management is something you
have to learn.
Practise until you can do it!

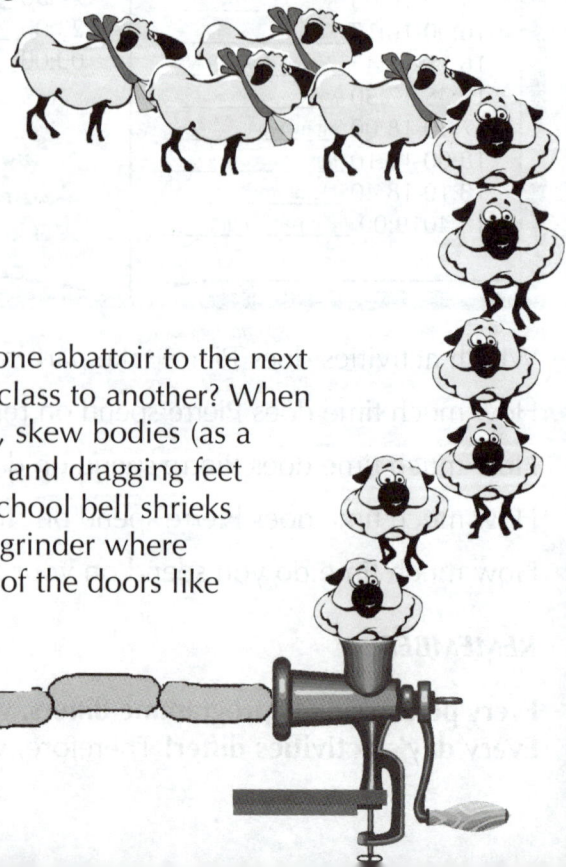

4. Why timetables?

Do you sometimes feel like a sheep being led from one abattoir to the next when the bell rings and you have to walk from one class to another? When you're standing outside, looking at all the sour faces, skew bodies (as a result of the heavy schoolbags balanced on one hip) and dragging feet which move from one class to the other, while the school bell shrieks itself into a coma, it strongly reminds you of a meat grinder where children are ground in the classes and then pop out of the doors like sausage!

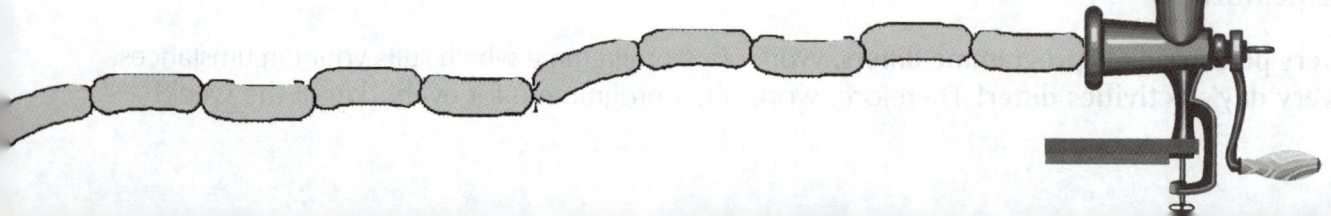

If, however, you take away the timetable and the school bell, the unavoidable chaos is unthinkable! Most probably, the kids will all come to school and then hang about on the playground because they don't know where to go or what to do!

School timetables, sports timetables, tests and exam timetables are set to:
- Inform you about what, when and how something will take place.
- Make sure that something will, indeed, take place and be completed.
- Save time.

However, the success of these timetables depends on the discipline and punctuality with which they are followed. It serves no purpose to set a school timetable if no one listens to the bell and also no purpose to sports timetables or exam timetable if no one turns up! A timetable for your other activities is as necessary as the school timetable, sports timetable and exam timetable.

Timetables help you to:
- Determine what must be done and what needn't be done.
- Utilise your time in the most effective way.
- Increase study time.
- Control the things that can distract you.
- Increase your effectiveness and lower your tension.

Without tension you can:
- Be more in control of what you do.
- Utilise your time better.
- Enjoy what you are doing without feeling guilty.
- Plan time for yourself to really relax and enjoy life!

Your attitude towards timetables will greatly determine the measure of success you achieve. If you regard the school bell as necessary to avoid chaos and save time, you may try to get to class sooner in future. If you regard your timetable at home as something which creates time for you to enjoy other things, you will stick to it!

Remember that timetables can be **adapted and rewritten**. It takes quite a time before you will be able to set a really effective timetable. Therefore, be patient with yourself and change the timetable if you can't stick to it.On the next page there is a time schedule for one week. Use this schedule to determine where your time disappears to during the week if you don't have a timetable to follow.

INSTRUCTIONS

1. Use this timetable or a copy thereof.
2. Write down exactly what you do every day and what time you do it.
3. Try to write down even when you walk to the fridge for a snack!
4. BE EXTREMELY HONEST IF YOU REALLY WANT TO MAKE MORE TIME IN YOUR LIFE FOR THINGS YOU REALLY ENJOY!

HOW DO I SPEND MY DAY?

TIME	MONDAY	TIME	TUESDAY	TIME	WEDNESDAY	TIME	THURSDAY	TIME	FRIDAY
	RISE		RISE		RISE		RISE		RISE

INSTRUCTIONS

1.   Write down every activity and action that you wrote down in the previous column, in the ACTIVITY column of the following table.

2.   Write in the second column, how much TIME you spent on it ALTOGETHER for the WHOLE WEEK.

3.   Draw a cross in one of the next columns to show whether you've spent too much, too little or enough time on it.

HOW DID I SPEND MY TIME?					
	ACTIVITY	**TIME SPENT**	**TOO MUCH**	**TOO LITTLE**	**ENOUGH**
1					
2					
3					
4					
5					
6					
7					
8					
9					
10					
11					
12					
13					
14					
15					
16					
17					
18					
19					
20					

DO YOU NOW SEE WHY ...

● SOME OF YOUR GOALS ARE NOT REACHED?
● YOU ARE PERHAPS OVERWEIGHT OR UNDERWEIGHT?
● YOU ARE UNFIT?
● YOUR ROOM DOES NOT STAY TIDY?
● YOUR HOMEWORK DOES NOT GET FINISHED?

The following hints will help you to set up your timetable correctly and to keep to it.

5. *Importance of timetables*

When you want to set a timetable you have to keep the following in mind:

a) Get results

The main aim of timetables is not to fill your time, keep you out of harm's way or away from your friends, but actually to achieve real results. It doesn't help to plan 2 hours per day for studies and then get lower marks. If this happens, it means that you have used those 2 hours incorrectly and didn't really achieve anything. Read **"Surivive your Studies"** for hints on study methods.

b) Ask important questions

When you plan or execute activities or studies, you should always ask yourself:

Do I spend my time correctly?
?   What do I waste time with?
?   What would I like to spend time on?
?   How do I know that I used my time well?
?   What do I want to achieve?
?   Was I successful with it?

c) Routine tasks

Certain tasks like sleeping, combing hair and brushing teeth are routine tasks which must be done every day. Complete these tasks thoroughly but as fast as possible. Don't stare into the mirror for too long after you have brushed your teeth. Your face could look like a battlefield when you eventually walk away.

d) Daily necessary activities

Certain tasks like going to school or eating, must be done every day. See to it that you are punctual. Pack your bag the previous night and put out your clothes, ready for school the night before. Eat at the right times and don't skip meals. Nor should others have to sit and wait for you at the table. Except for the fact that it's not only extremely bad manners towards the person who had to prepare the meal, nobody likes cold food, either!

IMPORTANT

☞ **Sleep** at least **8-9 hours** per night.

☞ Eat **three** healthy **meals** per day and don't constantly nibble in-between.

☞ Drink **eight glasses of water** per day.

☞ Don't study straight after you've had a heavy meal, The blood is now in your stomach to digest the food and not in your brain!

e) Your own rhythms

If you kept a record of everything you did the whole week, you will be able to determine certain patterns in your behaviour. People differ from each other and not everybody likes to get up early in the morning. At certain times of the day you have more energy than at others.

IMPORTANT!

☞ Your body is like a machine and your energy levels usually diminish when you need more food or rest.

☞ You can stretch these times by eating right, getting enough sleep and to alleviate tension!

☞ Use the time of day when you can think best for studying. Don't study very late at night!

f) Unforeseen events

You can't control everything in your life. Neither can you avoid all the crises in your life. To prevent crises and events from disarranging your life, you have to make provision for it. Illness, accidents, interruptions and problems are part of life. Live in such a way that it doesn't completely catch you unawares.

IMPORTANT!

☞ Don't ever leave important tasks to the last moment.

☞ If a crisis arises, you won't have time to handle it. Make provision for it.

 – A power failure just before you write a test …

 – An illness which downs you just before the exams …

 – A computer virus which destroys your project …

g) Large projects.

Learn to estimate in advance how long it will take to complete certain tasks. You know how long it takes to brush your teeth, but do you really know how long it takes you to complete your science task?

IMPORTANT!

☞ Make summaries **within 72 hours** and file for revision.

☞ Begin to learn for **your test** at least **2 weeks** before the time.

☞ Begin to revise for **your exam** at least **2 months** before the time

☞ Begin at least **2 months** before your have to hand in your task or project.

h) Postponement

Tasks are usually postponed for the following reasons:

i) *Paralysis after Planning* – You plan tasks in detail, but don't do anything about it!

ii) *Perfectionism* – You keep fiddling with tasks which have already been completed well and correctly. You don't have to comb your hair for 2 hours!

I'M MAD ABOUT A CRISIS!

iii) *Boredom* – The tasks bore you and that's why you can't get started or complete it.

iv) *Negativity* – You don't like the work or the person who gave it to you and that's why you postpone it.

v) *Crisis adrenaline* – You get addicted to the adrenaline flowing through your veins when you experience a crisis and eventually can only work when you're sufficiently stressed out to get going with your work!

IMPORTANT!

☞ Ask yourself: **"Is what I'm doing now …"**

Urgent and important? (Tomorrow's test, your tooth that's aching)
Important but not urgent? (Next week's test)
Unimportant but urgent? (Your friend phones and cries because her boyfriend has forgotten yet another date)
Unimportant and not urgent? (Your favourite soapie)

☞ If your life is well planned, most of your tasks will be completed when they're IMPORTANT, BUT NOT URGENT. This means that you are handling tasks before they become urgent and important! Don't wait until all your teeth are aching before visiting the dentist!

i) Interruptions

There will always be people who disrupt and change your timetable. The trick is not to avoid these interruptions altogether (otherwise you will anger every one around you) but, in fact, how to limit it to a minimum!

IMPORTANT!

☞ Learn to say "NO" the decent way. Example: **"Thank you very much, but unfortunately I already have another appointment."** Remember now that your day has been planned, you have many appointments. Even your studies are an appointment!

☞ Watch the clock and limit your time. Explain the homework to your friend, but don't spend hours afterwards chatting about the cricket match when you are writing an important test.

☞ Determine how important the interruption is. Is your girlfriend's gossip really important enough to interrupt your studies?

☞ Ask Yourself: HOW IMPORTANT AND URGENT IS THIS INTERRUPTION?
　　　　　　　　IS IT GOOD?
　　　　　　　　IS IT NECESSARY?

j)　Priorities

If your day is too full to do everything you like, you have to set priorities. You don't have to take part in everything in life or to shine at everything. Neither do you have to do everything this year. Leave a bit of the fun and pleasure in life for the years to come …!

IMPORTANT!

☞ Set priorities for yourself and stick to them.

☞ Cut out some of your extra-mural activities if you're constantly tired and there is not enough time in your day to give attention to all the points in your Life Cycle.

☞ RETAIN BALANCE.

6. Plan your timetable

Use these guidelines to set up a TIMETABLE for yourself.

Activity	Hours spent
Sleep Determine what time you have to rise and then plan 8-9 hours for sleep. Block your sleeping time by filling in what time you go to bed and what time you're going to get up. *Try to go to bed at the same time every night and rise at the same time every morning.*	**8 hours 30 minutes**
Rising How long does it take you to get up, wash, dress, eat, brush your hair and teeth and quickly tidy your room? Mark the time on your timetable.	**30 minutes**
School Mark off the hours you spend at school. Include the time it takes you to get to school on time and get back home or to the hostel.	**6 hours** School **1 hour** Travel
Eating Determine at what times meals are served and mark off the times. Budget about 30 minutes to eat slowly. Use this time to relax and enjoy the company around you.	**30 minutes**
Extra-mural Look at your extra-mural timetable and mark off on which days and at what times your extra-mural activities are presented. Plan to get exercise at least 3–4 times per week.	**1 hour** Travel **1 hour** Sport
Practising Plan times in which you must practise your extra-mural activities such as music, drama, art etc.	**1 hour**
Hygiene Make time every day to see to your body, your skin, your teeth, hair, room, cupboards and clothes. Untidiness really creates a poor impression. Your family is not there to pick up behind you. Pick up and clean before you leave a room.	**30 minutes**

Activity	Hours spent
Studies Plan your study time in sessions of about 20 minutes each. Rest for 10 minutes and then study for 20 minutes again. Use this time for homework and leftover time to: * Read and summarise the day's work. * Read the next days work. * Learn for the coming tests. * Revise for the exams. * Prepare for tasks and projects. For every 1 minute you spend productively in class, you should study for 2 minutes.	**2 hours**
Rest Plan short rest periods between studies, by running around the house, stretching your legs or having a drink of water. (10 minutes after every 20 minutes)	10 minutes after every 20 minutes Altogether **1 hour**
Relaxation Make time for your friends, TV progarammes, computer and internet, as well as hobbies. Priorities are extremely important here. *You may not cut the previous times to fit in these times!* You also don't have to do everything every day. Choose amongst your relaxation activities if time catches up with you. Create a special time to spend with all members of your family. They are not going to be there forever. In particular, make time for special chats with your Mom and Dad so that the relationship between you remains spontaneous and honest.	**45 minutes**
Goal Create a special time to work on your goal, find out more about it or read up about it.	**15 minutes**
Weekends You don't have to go out every weekend. Neither do you have to go out and visit your friends every day. Use Fridays and Saturdays to visit your friends properly and be relaxed. Don't visit so much over the weekend that you start your week dead tired! Use one night to go out and one night to stay at home and "chill". Use weekends to get to know your town and environment really well. Everything in life is not to be found on the Internet, on a video or in the Mall! Remember: **"You have six days when you can do your work, but the seventh day of each week belongs to Me, your God. No one is to work on that day"** Exodus 20: 9-10.	**Weekends**
	TOTAL **24 HOURS**

7. *Hints that work!*

☞ Every day is not the same. Therefore, make a timetable for every day of the week and change your timetable if necessary.

☞ Do things that are IMPORTANT, BUT NOT URGENT, first and spend most of your time on that.

☞ Start in time to complete large tasks and to prepare for tests and exams.

☞ Do big difficult tasks first.

☞ See if you can save time be using odd times to complete small things. Pack right one drawer of your cupboards while waiting for your little sister to finish her bath. Read a book in the meantime while waiting in the surgery. Think about the suitcase with clothes. It's amazing how much you can eventually get done if you use add times to complete things.

☞ Be honest and stick to your timetable. Don't lose hope if you do deviate. Just start again with the next slot and follow the timetable from there onwards.

☞ Reward yourself every day that your timetable is successfully completed.

☞ The saying goes: "Time is Money." Picture every minute of the day as R1 in your pocket. If you spend it right, it stays in your pocket. If you spend it wrongly, you've lost it. Note at the end of the day, week and month how much money you've let slip through your fingers. It represents the opportunities you have lost.

☞ Work smarter, not harder.

☞ Learn to concentrate on one thing at a time and don't waste time by thinking of other things.

☞ Come to an agreement with your friends and family when you want to be left alone and when you want to study. Make a "DON'T DISTURB" sign and hang it from your doorknob.

☞ Don't look for excuses to drop the work you're busy with. You don't "Just quickly" have to go and do something every time.

☞ Take care of your health. Your health is your most precious gift and illness can destroy your goals. Stay away from substances that push your body beyond its limits. Avoid drugs, "regmakers" and overdoses of "Bioplus" or coffee. If you start to learn in time, you don't really need it. Exhaustion is a sign that you need rest.

☞ Think of a spring that is stretched out. If you continue to stretch it, it will eventually, be unable to recoil back to its original position.

☞ Don't Stress! Tension doesn't just shut down your brain, but also causes diseases.

☞ Guard against perfectionism. Love yourself. Be careful of burnout and of going overboard.

USE THE FOLLOWING TABLE TO SET UP A TIMETABLE FOR YOURSELF. STICK A COPY OF IT TO A PLACE WHERE YOU CAN SEE IT EVERY DAY!

"EVEN IF YOU WIN THE RAT RACE, WITHOUT JOY YOU WILL STILL BE A RAT!"

MY TIMETABLE

TIME	MONDAY	TIME	TUESDAY	TIME	WEDNESDAY	TIME	THURSDAY	TIME	FRIDAY
	RISE		RISE		RISE		RISE		RISE

Certificate

This is to confirm that

_____

worked through *Survive Your Life*

with concentraction

1.   I know why I am here on earth.
2.   I know who and what I am.
3.   I know how my brain functions.
4.   I realize that choices have certain consequences.
5.   I know how to set goals and what success really means.
6.   I know how to sustain good human relationships.
7   I realize that I am responsible for my own safety.
8.   I realize that my rights are linked to responsibilities.
9.   I know the implications of pre-marital sex.
1.0   I know what drugs do to my body and what addiction is.
1.1   I know how to spend my time correctly.
1.2   I strive towards balance in my life.
1.3   I live what I have learnt.

Signed on this _____ day of _____
at _____

_____
(My signature)

Resources

Literature

Barker, Allan (1997). *30 Minutes to Brainstorm Great Ideas;* Clays Ltd, England

Bosch, Candace C. & Vaughn, Sharon (1998). *Strategies for Teaching Students with Learning and Behaviour Problems;* Fourth Edition, Allyn & Bacon, Needham Heights, California

Buzan, Tony (1989). *Use Both Sides of Your Brain;* BBC Books, London

Buzan, Tony (1995). *Use Your Head;* BBC Books, London

Buzan, Tony (1996). *Use Your Memory;* BBC Books, London

Buzan, Tony & Gelb, Michael (1996). *Lessons from the Art of Juggling: How to Achieve Your Full Potential in Business, Learning and Life;* BBC Books, London

Canfield, Jack, Hanson Mark, Victor & Kirberger, Kimberly (1988). *Chicken Soup for the Teenage Soul II;* Health Communications Inc., Deerfield Beach, Florida

Cilliers, Charl, Coetzee, Japie & De Klerk, Jeanette (1991). *Ek en Ek;* Lux Verbi, South Africa

Covey, Sean (1998). *7 Habits of Highly Effective Teens;* Fireside Books, USA

Covey, Stephen R (1994). *The Seven Habits of Highly Effective People: Powerful Lessons in Personal Change;* Simon & Shuster Ltd, London

Ferner, D (1995). *Successful Time Management;* John Wiley & Sons Inc., CKanada

Fourie, Dawie (1998). *Ontgin jou Brein;* Human & Rousseau, Cape Town

Grové, S (1990). *Thank You Brain;* JL van Schaik Uitgewers, Pretoria

Grové, S (1996). *The Dance of the Brain;* Human & Rousseau, Cape Town

Holzhausen, Renier & Stander, Hennie (1997). *Vertel My Alles, Antwoorde op vrae wat jy te skaam is om te vra;* Colorgraphic, Durban

Johnson, Dawid W (1972). *Reaching Out – Interpersonal Effectiveness and Self-Actualization;* Fifth Edition, Allyn & Bacon, Needham Heights, California

Maarschalk, J (1997). *Breinboelies;* Sigma Press, Pretoria

Meyer, Johann (1988). *Lees beter, Leef beter;* Tafelberg Publishers, Cape Town

MacDonald, Gordon (1982). *Ordering your Private World;*

Rinder, Walter (1974). *The Humanness of You;* Celestial Arts, Milbrae, Kalifornië

Searll, Adéle (1995). *Get High on Life – beating drugs together: A guide for teenagers, parents and teachers;* Struik Book Distributors, Wynberg, Sandton

Van Niekerk, Lana (1998). *Gedagtes oor Sukses;* Christian Art, South Africa

Audio-Visual Material

Berg, Howard Stephen & Tradeu, Kevin. *Mega Speed Reading;* Tru Vantage Inc., USA

Lorayne, Harry. *Harry Lorayne's SUPER MIND POWER;* Harry Lorrayne Inc., New York, NY. Order programme from: http://www.sharewarejunkies.com

Meyer, J & Cillié, P. *Video Spoedleeskursus;* Oudiovista Production (Pty) Limited

Tradeu, Kevin. *Mega Memory;* Tru Vantage Inc., USA

Internet

General

Executive Summary: The World Health Report 1996 . . . . .http://www.who.int
Infoplease.com . . . . .http://www.infoplease.com
Constitution of the Republic of South Africa . . . . .http://www.polity.org.za
Crime Situation . . . . .http://www.saps.co.za

General protection

Kinds of abuse . . . . .http://www.saps.co.za
Concerned Counselling – Teen suicide .http://www.concernedcounseling.com
Discipline for Teenagers . . . . .http://www.family.go.com

HIV, Aids and sexually transmitted diseases

Facts about AIDS . . . . .http://www.aidministry.org
What you need to know about HIV/AIDS . . . . .http://www.glccftl.org
Stophiv.com . . . . .http://www.stophiv.com
Ask Noah About: AIDS . . . . .http://www.noah.cuny.edu
Talking to Kids about AIDS . . . . .http://www.qcfurball.com
Basic facts and statistics . . . . .http://www.aids.org.hk
PMC Recourse Centre . . . . .http://www.pmcguam.com
HIV & AIDS . . . . .http://www.lauralee.com
COHIS: AIDS/HIV information: Symptoms and Signs of HIV Infection . . . . .http://www.bu.edu
CDC: Facts about Adolescents and HIV/AIDS .http://www.the body.com

Teenage pregnancies

Parent talk newsletter: Adolescents: What teens really need to know about sex . . . . . . .http://www.tnpc.com
Ask Noah About: Pregnancy . . . . .http://www.noah.cuny.edu
Facts in brief: Teen sex and pregnancy, 1999 .http://www.agi-usa.org
Safe sex and the facts . . . . .http://www.probe.org
Tape #117: Myths about birth control . . . . .http://www.pixi.com

Drugs

Marijuana: Facts for teens . . . . .http://www.nida.nih.gov
NCADI – straight facts about drugs . . . . .http://www.health.org
Alcoholism: Facts, myths, signs . . . . .http://www.saps.co.za
Crime prevention: Drugs . . . . .http://www.saps.co.za

Studies

Access Eric: How important is homework?	http://ericps.uiuc.edu
BOLA – study skills	http://sol.brunel.ac.uk
Common grammar, usage & spelling problems	http://www.ntu.edu.sg
Engines for education	http://www.ils.nwu.edu
Education world, curriculum	http://www.education-world.com
Family involvement partnership of learning	http://www.ed.gov/family
Helping your child learn maths	http://www.ed.gov.pubs
Kids source online: Helping your child with homework	http://www.kidsource.com
Learning Centre, School of Liberal Arts, Purdue	http://www.sla.purdue.edu
Mind maps	http://www.ozemail.com
Mind tools	http://www.mindtools.com
Pathways: Learning skills and Graphic Organisers	http://www.ncrel.org
Student Learning Centre	http://128.32.89.153
Study guides	http://www.iss.stthomas.edu
University of Waterloo, The study skills package	http://www.adm.uwaterloo.ca
USCA Continuing Education, Kids in College	http://www.usca.sc.edu
Wozniak, Poitr, Dr. Super Memo	http://www.supermemo.com

Reading

Measuring reading speed	http://vision,psych.umn.edu
Learning skills program – tips for increasing reading speed	http://www.coun.uvic.ca
Virginia Tech Division of Student Affairs – suggestions for improving reading speed	http://www.ucc.vt.edu
The speed reading course	http://www.trans4mind.com

Creativity

Innovation Network: Articles & reports, broken crayons & creativity	http://www.thinksmart.com
Creativity basics	http://www.ozemail.com
KidSource: Fostering creativity in gifted students	http://www.kidsource.com
KidSource: Creativity for emotional intelligence: Ideas and activities	http://www.kidsource.com

Time management

Techniques for time procrastination	http://128.32.89.153
Mind tools – time management skills	http://www.psychwww.com
Brighten up your quality of life	http://www.abanet.org
Academic Skills Center – time management	http://www.sas.calpoly.edu
Study and time management tips	http://www.smhs.org

Encyclopaedias

Grolier Multimedia Encyclopaedia 1998
Encarta 97 Encyclopaedia

Course material

ARISE. *Learn2Learn*
Meyer, Paul. *The dynamics of personal motivation*
McCarthy. *The 4Mat System: Teaching to learning styles with right/left mode techniques*
Nortjé, A. *Leierskap*
Pacific Institute. *Investment in excellence, steps to success*
Patient, David R & Orr, Neil. *Knowledge in action – empowerment concepts*
Viviers, S. *Die bestuur van mense*
Viviers, S. *Effektiewe menseverhoudinge*
Viviers, S. *Eendag my eie besigheid*

Graphic programmes

Masterclips
Corel Gallery